R. Gupta's®

AF668474

UGC-NET

Junior Research Fellowship and Assistant Professor Exam

Teaching & Research Aptitude

Paper–I

Previous Years' Papers & Test Papers

(Solved with Explanations)

RAMESH PUBLISHING HOUSE, New Delhi

Published by
O.P. Gupta *for* Ramesh Publishing House

Admin. Office
12-H, New Daryaganj Road, Opp. Officers' Mess,
New Delhi-110002 ✆ 23261567, 23275224, 23275124

E-mail: info@rameshpublishinghouse.com
Website: www.rameshpublishinghouse.com

Showroom
- Balaji Market, Nai Sarak, Delhi-6 ✆ 23253720, 23282525
- 4457, Nai Sarak, Delhi-6, ✆ 23918938

Book Code: R-790

ISBN: 978-93-5012-100-9

Price: ₹ 170

Printed at: Deepak Offset, Delhi

CONTENTS

PREVIOUS PAPERS (SOLVED)

TEST PAPERS (SOLVED)

Previous Years' Paper (Solved)

UGC-NET (JRF) EXAM JULY, 2016*

PAPER–I

Note :
- This paper contains **Sixty (60)** multiple choice questions, each question carrying **two (2)** marks.
- Candidate is expected to answer any **Fifty (50)** questions.
- In case more than **Fifty (50)** questions are attempted, only the first **Fifty (50)** questions will be evaluated.

1. Select the alternative which consists of positive factors contributing to effectiveness of teaching :

List of factors :

(*a*) Teacher's knowledge of the subject.

(*b*) Teacher's socio-economic background.

(*c*) Communication skill of the teacher.

(*d*) Teacher's ability to please the students.

(*e*) Teacher's personal contact with students.

(*f*) Teacher's competence in managing and monitoring the classroom transactions.

Codes :

A. (*b*), (*c*) and (*d*) B. (*c*), (*d*) and (*f*)
C. (*b*), (*d*) and (*e*) D. (*a*), (*c*) and (*f*)

2. The use of teaching aids is justified on the grounds of :

A. attracting students' attention in the classroom.
B. minimising indiscipline problems in the classroom.
C. optimising learning outcomes of students.
D. effective engagement of students in learning tasks.

3. Assertion (A) : The purpose of higher education is to promote critical and creative thinking abilities among students.

Reason (R) : These abilities ensure job placements.

Choose the correct answer from the following code :

A. Both (A) and (R) are true and (R) is the correct explanation of (A).
B. Both (A) and (R) are true, but (R) is not the correct explanation of (A).
C. (A) is true, but (R) is false.
D. (A) is false, but (R) is true.

4. Match the items of the first set with that of the second set in respect of evaluation system. Choose the correct code :

Set–I	Set–II
(*a*) Formative evaluation	1. Evaluating cognitive and co-cognitive aspects with regularity
(*b*) Summative evaluation	2. Tests and their interpretations based on a group and certain yardsticks
(*c*) Continuous and comprehensive evaluation	3. Grading the final learning outcomes
(*d*) Norm and criterion referenced tests	4. Quizzes and discussions

Codes :

	(*a*)	(*b*)	(*c*)	(*d*)
A.	4	3	1	2
B.	1	2	3	4
C.	3	4	2	1
D.	1	3	4	2

* *Exam held on 10 July, 2016.*

5. A researcher intends to explore the effect of possible factors for the organization of effective mid-day meal interventions. Which research method will be most appropriate for this study?
A. Historical method
B. Descriptive survey method
C. Experimental method
D. Ex-post-facto method

6. Which of the following is an initial mandatory requirement for pursuing research?
A. Developing a research design
B. Formulating a research question
C. Deciding about the data analysis procedure
D. Formulating a research hypothesis

7. The format of thesis writing is the same as in :
A. preparation of a research paper/article
B. writing of seminar presentation
C. a research dissertation
D. presenting a workshop / conference paper

8. In qualitative research paradigm, which of the following features may be considered critical?
A. Data collection with standardised research tools.
B. Sampling design with probability sample techniques.
C. Data collection with bottom-up empirical evidences.
D. Data gathering to take place with top-down systematic evidences.

9. From the following list of statements identify the set which has negative implications for 'research ethics' :
(*i*) A researcher critically looks at the findings of another research.
(*ii*) Related studies are cited without proper references.
(*iii*) Research findings are made the basis for policy making.
(*iv*) Conduct of practitioner is screened in terms of reported research evidences.
(*v*) A research study is replicated with a view to verify the evidences from other researches.
(*vi*) Both policy making and policy implementing processes are regulated in terms of preliminary studies.

Codes :
A. (*i*), (*ii*) and (*iii*)
B. (*ii*), (*iii*) and (*iv*)
C. (*ii*), (*iv*) and (*vi*)
D. (*i*), (*iii*) and (*v*)

10. In a research on the effect of child-rearing practices on stress-proneness of children in completing school projects, the hypothesis formulated is that 'child rearing practices do influence stress-proneness'. At the data-analysis stage a null hypothesis is advanced to find out the tenability of research hypothesis. On the basis of the evidence available, the null hypothesis is rejected at 0.01 level of significance. What decision may be warranted in respect of the research hypothesis?
A. The research hypothesis will also be rejected.
B. The research hypothesis will be accepted.
C. Both the research hypothesis and the null hypothesis will be rejected.
D. No decision can be taken in respect of the research hypothesis.

Directions (Qs. Nos. 11-16) : *Read the following passage carefully and answer the questions.*

In terms of labour, for decades the relatively low cost and high quality of Japanese workers conferred considerable competitive advantage across numerous durable goods and consumer-electronics industries (*e.g.,* Machinery, automobiles, televisions, radios). Then labour-based advantages shifted to South Korea, then to Malaysia, Mexico and other nations. Today, China appears to be capitalizing best on the basis of labour. Japanese firms still remain competitive in markets for such durable goods, electronics and other products, but the labour force is no longer sufficient for competitive advantage over manufacturers in other industrializing nations. Such shifting of labour-based advantage is clearly not limited to manufacturing industries. Today, a huge number of IT and service jobs are moving from Europe and North America to India, Singapore, and like countries with relatively well-educated, low-cost workforces possessing technical skills. However, as educational levels and technical skills continue to rise in other countries, India, Singapore, and like nations enjoying labour-based competitive advantage today are likely to find such advantage cannot be sustained through emergence of new competitors.

In terms of capital, for centuries the days of gold coins and later even paper money restricted financial flows. Subsequently regional concentrations were formed where large banks, industries and markets coalesced. But today capital flows internationally at rapid speed. Global commerce no longer requires regional interactions among business players. Regional capital concentrations in places such as New York, London and Tokyo still persist, of course, but the capital concentrated there is no longer sufficient for competitive advantage over other capitalists distributed worldwide. Only if an organization is able to combine, integrate and apply its resources (*e.g.* Land, labour, capital, IT) in an effective manner that is not readily imitable by competitors can such an organization enjoy competitive advantage sustainable overtime.

In a knowledge-based theory of the firm, this idea is extended to view organizational knowledge as a resource with atleast the same level of power and importance as the traditional economic inputs. An organization with superior knowledge can achieve competitive advantage in markets that appreciate the application of such knowledge. Semiconductors, genetic engineering, pharmaceuticals, software, military warfare, and like knowledge-intensive competitive arenas provide both time-proven and current examples. Consider semiconductors (*e.g.* computer chips), which are made principally of sand and common metals. These ubiquitous and powerful electronic devices are designed within common office buildings, using commercially available tools, and fabricated within factories in many industrialized nations. Hence, land is not the key competitive resource in the semiconductor industry.

Based on the passage answer the following questions :

11. Which country enjoyed competitive advantages in automobile industry for decades?
A. South Korea B. Japan
C. Mexico D. Malaysia

12. Why labour-based competitive advantages of India and Singapore cannot be sustained in IT and service sectors?
A. Due to diminishing levels of skill.
B. Due to capital-intensive technology making inroads.
C. Because of new competitors.
D. Because of shifting of labour-based advantage in manufacturing industries.

13. How can an organisation enjoy competitive advantage sustainable overtime?
A. Through regional capital flows.
B. Through regional interactions among business players.
C. By making large banks, industries and markets coalesced.
D. By effective use of various instrumentalities.

14. What is required to ensure competitive advantages in specific markets?
A. Access to capital
B. Common office buildings
C. Superior knowledge
D. Common metals

15. The passage also mentions about the trend of :
A. Global financial flow
B. Absence of competition in manufacturing industry
C. Regionalisation of capitalists
D. Organizational incompatibility

16. What does the author lay stress on in the passage?
A. International commerce
B. Labour-intensive industries
C. Capital resource management
D. Knowledge-driven competitive advantage

17. Imagine you are working in an educational institution where people are of equal status. Which method of communication is best suited and normally employed in such a context?
A. Horizontal communication
B. Vertical communication
C. Corporate communication
D. Cross communication

18. Identify the important element a teacher has to take cognizance of while addressing students in a classroom.
A. Avoidance of proximity
B. Voice modulation
C. Repetitive pause
D. Fixed posture

19. What are the barriers to effective communication?
A. Moralising, being judgemental and comments of consolation.
B. Dialogue, summary and self-review.
C. Use of simple words, cool reaction and defensive attitude.
D. Personal statements, eye contact and simple narration.

20. The choice of communication partners is influenced by factors of :
A. Proximity, utility, loneliness
B. Utility, secrecy, dissonance
C. Secrecy, dissonance, deception
D. Dissimilarity, dissonance, deviance

21. As a teacher, select the best option to ensure your effective presence in the classroom.
A. Use of peer command
B. Making aggressive statements
C. Adoption of well-established posture
D. Being authoritarian

22. Every communicator has to experience :
A. Manipulated emotions
B. Anticipatory excitement
C. The issue of homophiles
D. Status dislocation

23. In certain code, SELECTION is coded as QCJCARGML. The code of AMERICANS will be :
A. YKCPGAYLQ B. BNFSJDBMR
C. QLYAGPCKY D. YQKLCYPAG

24. In the series
3, 11, 23, 39, 59, ...
The next term will be :
A. 63 B. 73
C. 83 D. 93

25. Two railway tickets from city A to B and three tickets from city A to C cost ₹ 177. Three tickets from city A to B and two tickets from city A to C cost ₹ 173. The fare for city B from city A will be ₹ :
A. 25 B. 27
C. 30 D. 33

26. A person walks 10 m infront and 10 m to the right. Then every time turning to his left, he walks 5, 15 and 15 m respectively. How far is he now from his starting point?
A. 20 m B. 15 m
C. 10 m D. 5 m

27. A is sister of B. F is daughter of G. C is mother of B. D is father of C. E is mother of D. A is related to D as :
A. Grand daughter B. Daughter
C. Daughter-in-law D. Sister

28. In the series
AB, EDC, FGHI, ...?...., OPQRST, the missing term is :
A. JKLMN B. JMKNL
C. NMLKJ D. NMKLJ

29. Among the following propositions two are related in such a way that one is the denial of the other. Which are those propositions? Select the correct code :
Propositions :
(*a*) All women are equal to men
(*b*) Some women are equal to men
(*c*) Some women are not equal to men
(*d*) No women are equal to men
Codes :
A. (*a*) and (*b*)
B. (*a*) and (*d*)
C. (*c*) and (*d*)
D. (*a*) and (*c*)

30. If the proposition 'All thieves are poor' is false, which of the following propositions can be claimed certainly to be true?

Propositions :

A. Some thieves are poor.
B. Some thieves are not poor.
C. No thief is poor.
D. No poor person is a thief.

31. Consider the following statement and select the correct code stating the nature of the argument involved in it :

To suppose that the earth is the only populated world in the infinite space is as absurd as to assert that in an entire field of millet only one grain will grow.

A. Astronomical
B. Anthropological
C. Deductive
D. Analogical

32. Select the code which is not correct about Venn diagram :

A. Venn diagram represents propositions as well as classes.
B. It can provide clear method of notation.
C. It can be either valid or invalid.
D. It can provide the direct method of testing the validity.

33. Select the code which is not correct in the context of deductive argument with two premises :

A. An argument with one true premise, one false premise and a false conclusion may be valid.
B. An argument with two true premises and a false conclusion may be valid.
C. An argument with one true premise, one false premise and a true conclusion may be valid.
D. An argument with two false premises and a false conclusion may be valid.

34. Given below are two premises and four conclusions are drawn from them (taking singly or together). Select the code that states the conclusions validly drawn.

Premises :

(*i*) All religious persons are emotional.
(*ii*) Ram is a religious person.

Conclusions :

(*a*) Ram is emotional.
(*b*) All emotional persons are religious.
(*c*) Ram is not a non-religious person.
(*d*) Some religious persons are not emotional.

Codes :

A. (*a*), (*b*), (*c*) and (*d*)
B. (*a*) only
C. (*a*) and (*c*) only
D. (*b*) and (*c*) only

Directions (Qs. Nos. 35-37) : *The following table shows the percentage profit (%) earned by two companies A and B during the years 2011-15. Answer these questions based on the data contained in the table :*

Profit earned by two companies

Year	Percentage Profit (%)	
	A	B
2011	20	30
2012	35	40
2013	45	35
2014	40	50
2015	25	35

Where, per cent (%) Profit

$$= \frac{\text{Income} - \text{Expenditure}}{\text{Expenditure}} \times 100$$

35. If the total expenditure of the two companies was ₹ 9 lakh in the year 2012 and the expenditure of A and B were in the ratio 2 : 1, then what was the income of the company A in that year?

A. ₹ 9.2 lakh
B. ₹ 8.1 lakh
C. ₹ 7.2 lakh
D. ₹ 6.0 lakh

36. What is the average percentage profit earned by the company B?

A. 35%
B. 42%
C. 38%
D. 40%

37. In which year, the percentage profit earned by the company B is less than that of company A?

A. 2012
B. 2013
C. 2014
D. 2015

Directions (Qs. Nos. 38-40) : *The following table shows the number of people in different age groups who responded to a survey about their favourite style of music. Use this information to answer the questions that follow, to the nearest whole percentage :*

Style of Music ↓ / Age →	Number of people (Years) 15-20	(Years) 21-30	(Years) 31+
Classical	6	4	17
Pop	7	5	5
Rock	6	12	14
Jazz	1	4	11
Blues	2	3	15
Hip-Hop	9	3	4
Ambient	2	2	2

38. Approximately what percentage of the total sample were aged 21-30?

A. 31% B. 23%
C. 25% D. 14%

39. Approximately what percentage of the total sample indicates that Hip-Hop is their favourite style of music?

A. 6% B. 8%
C. 14% D. 12%

40. What percentage of respondents aged 31+ indicated a favourite style other than classical music?

A. 64% B. 60%
C. 75% D. 50%

41. The statement "the study, design, development, implementation, support or management of computer-based information systems, particularly software applications and computer Hardware" refers to :

A. Information Technology (IT)
B. Information and Collaborative Technology (ICT)
C. Information and Data Technology (IDT)
D. Artificial Intelligence (AI)

42. If the binary equivalent of the decimal number 48 is 110000, then the binary equivalent of the decimal number 51 is given by :

A. 110011 B. 110010
C. 110001 D. 110100

43. The process of copying files to a CD-ROM is known as :

A. Burning B. Zipping
C. Digitizing D. Ripping

44. An unsolicited e-mail message sent to many recipients at once is a :

A. Worm B. Virus
C. Threat D. Spam

45. ________ is a type of memory circuitry that holds the computer's start-up routine.

A. RIM (Read Initial Memory)
B. RAM (Random Access Memory)
C. ROM (Read Only Memory)
D. Cache Memory

46. An ASCII is a character-encoding scheme that is employed by personal computers in order to represent various characters, numbers and control keys that the computer user selects on the keyboard. ASCII is an acronym for :

A. American Standard Code for Information Interchange
B. American Standard Code for Intelligent Information
C. American Standard Code for Information Integrity
D. American Standard Code for Isolated Information

47. Identify the air pollutant in urban areas which irritates eyes and also respiratory tract of human beings.

A. Particulate matter B. Oxides of nitrogen
C. Surface ozone D. Carbon monoxide

48. Which of the following is the largest source of water pollution in major rivers of India?

A. Untreated sewage
B. Agriculture run-off
C. Unregulated small scale industries
D. Religious practices

49. Sustainable development goals have specific targets to be achieved by : ...30

A. 2022 B. 2050

C. 2040

50. Indian government' ... ear 2022, is : ...t of producing power from biomass b...

A. 50 MW B. 25 MW

C. 15 M... D. 10 MW

51. Ass... : Conserving our soil resources ... human survival.

...: Soil is home to many micro-...s and contains minerals.

... the correct code :

...Both (A) and (R) are correct and (R) is the correct explanation of (A).

B. Both (A) and (R) are correct, but (R) is not the correct explanation of (A).

C. (A) is true and (R) is false.

D. (A) is false and (R) is true.

52. World Meteorological Organisation's (WMO) objective has been to reduce the number of deaths due to hydrometeorological disasters over the decade 2010-2019 by (with reference to the decade 1994-2003) :

A. 25% B. 50%

C. 75% D. 80%

53. Which of the following core values among the institutions of higher education are promoted by the NAAC (National Assessment and Accreditation Council)?

(*a*) Contributing to national development.

(*b*) Fostering global competencies among the students.

(*c*) Inculcating a value system among students and teachers.

(*d*) Promoting the optimum utilization of the infrastructure.

Select the correct answer from the codes given below :

Codes :

A. (*b*), (*c*) and (*d*)

B. (*a*), (*b*) and (*c*)

C. (*a*), (*c*) and (*d*)

D. (*a*), (*b*), (*c*) and (*d*)

54. The best way for providing value education is through :

A. discussions on scriptural texts.

B. lectures / discourses on values

C. seminars / symposia on values

D. mentoring / reflective sessions on values

55. The National Judicial Appointments Commission (NJAC) has been declared unconstitutional by :

A. The Supreme Court of India

B. The High Court

C. The High Court and the Supreme Court both

D. The President of India

56. Which of the following statements about the Indian political system is/are correct?

(*a*) The President is both Head of the State and Head of the Government.

(*b*) Parliament is Supreme.

(*c*) The Supreme Court is the guardian of the Constitution.

(*d*) The Directive Principles of State Policy are justiciable.

Select the correct answer from the codes given below :

A. (*a*), (*b*), (*c*) and (*d*) B. (*b*), (*c*) and (*d*)

C. (*b*) and (*c*) D. (*c*) only

57. Which of the following are the fundamental duties?

(*a*) To respect the National Flag.

(*b*) To protect and improve the natural environment.

(*c*) For a parent to provide opportunities for education to his/her child.

(*d*) To protect monuments and places of national importance.

Select the correct answer from the codes given:

Codes :

A. (*a*), (*b*) and (*c*) B. (*a*), (*b*) and (*d*)

C. (*a*), (*c*) and (*d*) D. (*a*), (*b*), (*c*) and (*d*)

58. Which of the following statements are correct in respect of NITI Aayog?

(*a*) It is a constitutional body.

(*b*) It is a statutory body.

(c) It is neither a constitutional body nor a statutory body.

(d) It is a think-tank.

Select the correct answer from the codes given below :

A. (a) and (d) B. (b) and (d)

C. (c) and (d) D. (b), (c) and (d)

59. A college level assistant professor has planned his/her lectures with an intent to develop cognitive dimensions of students centered on skills of analysis and synthesis. Below, given are two sets of items Set–I consisting of levels of cognitive interchange and Set–II comprising basic requirements for promoting them. Match the two sets and indicate your answer by choosing the correct alternative from the code:

Set–I (Levels of Cognitive Interchange)	***Set–II (Basic requirements for promoting cognitive interchange)***
(a) Memory level	1. Giving opportunity for discriminating examples and non-examples of a point.
(b) Understanding level	2. Recording the important points made during the presentations.
(c) Reflective level	3. Asking the students to discuss various items of information.
	4. Critically analyzing the points to be made nd discussed.

Codes :

	(a)	(b)	(c)
A.	2	4	1
B.	3	4	2
C.	2	1	4
D.	1	2	3

60. Which set of learner characteristics considered helpful in designing ef teaching-learning systems? Select the co alternative from the codes given below :

(i) Prior experience of learners in respect of the subject.

(ii) Interpersonal relationships of learner's family friends.

(iii) Ability of the learners in respect of the subject.

(iv) Student's language background.

(v) Interest of students in following the prescribed dress code.

(vi) Motivational-orientation of the students.

Codes :

A. (i), (ii), (iii) and (iv)

B. (i), (iii), (iv) and (vi)

C. (ii), (iii), (iv) and (v)

D. (iii), (iv), (v) and (vi)

ANSWERS

1	2	3	4	5	6	7	8	9	10
D	C	B	A	D	B	C	C	C	B
11	**12**	**13**	**14**	**15**	**16**	**17**	**18**	**19**	**20**
B	C	D	C	A	D	A	B	A	A
21	**22**	**23**	**24**	**25**	**26**	**27**	**28**	**29**	**30**
C	B	A	C	D	D	A	C	D	B
31	**32**	**33**	**34**	**35**	**36**	**37**	**38**	**39**	**40**
D	C	B	C	B	C	B	C	D	C
41	**42**	**43**	**44**	**45**	**46**	**47**	**48**	**49**	**50**
A	A	A	D	C	A	C	A	B	D
51	**52**	**53**	**54**	**55**	**56**	**57**	**58**	**59**	**60**
B	B	B	D	A	D	A	C	C	B

EXPLANATORY ANSWERS

7. Documentation is important in writing a research paper, thesis and dissertation to determine if a researcher has read and used several research works and other materials as reference. A research paper, thesis and dissertation is worthless without documentation to serve as proof of the research.

Generally speaking, a research paper, thesis or dissertation is *scientific* if it has several documented materials. But it is *unscientific* if the writer does not explain the relationships of the documented materials to his study and most of the writings of his research paper, thesis or dissertation are documented materials where he has no ideas of his own.

17. Horizontal communication is the transmission of information between people, divisions, departments or units within the same level of organizational hierarchy. You can distinguish it from vertical communication, which is the transmission of information between different levels of the organizational hierarchy. Horizontal communication is often referred to as 'lateral communication'.

Horizontal communication presents some distinct advantages. It decreases misunderstanding between departments working on the same project, thereby increasing efficiency and productivity. It may result in better implementation of top-level decisions because employees on lower levels are permitted to coordinate directly with each other in the implementation of the decision made at the top.

23. SELECTION is coded as

S	E	L	E	C	T	I	O	N
–2	–2	–2	–2	–2	–2	–2	–2	–2
Q	C	J	C	A	R	G	M	L

∴ AMERICANS will be coded as

A	M	E	R	I	C	A	N	S
–2	–2	–2	–2	–2	–2	–2	–2	–2
Y	K	C	P	G	A	Y	L	Q

24. In the series

3   11   23   39   59   [83]

+8   +12   +16   +20   +24

Hence, the next term will be 83.

25. Let fare of A to B = ₹ x

and fare of A to C = ₹ y

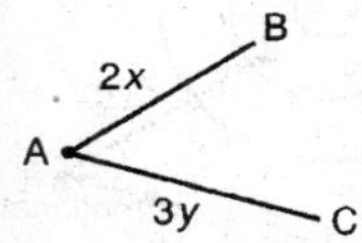

According to the question,

$$2x + 3y = ₹\ 177 \quad ...(i)\ ] \times 3$$
$$3x + 2y = ₹\ 173 \quad ...(ii)\ ] \times 2$$
$$6x + 9y = 531$$
$$6x + 4y = 346$$
$$- \quad - \quad -$$
$$5y = 185 \Rightarrow y = 37$$

Putting the value of y in (i)

$$2x + 3 \times 37 = 177$$
$$\Rightarrow \quad 2x = 177 - 111$$
$$\Rightarrow \quad 2x = 66$$
$$\Rightarrow \quad x = 33$$
$$\therefore \quad \text{Fare of A to B} = ₹\ 33$$

Hence, the fare for city B from A will be ₹ 33.

27.

(–) E
|
D (+)
|
(–) C   और   G (?)
| |
(–) A — B (?)   P (–)

Relation between A to D is Grand daughter.

28. AB, EDC, FGHI, <u>NMLKJ</u>, OPQRST

Hence, the missing term is NMLKJ.

32. The Venn diagrams constitute an *iconic* representation of the standard form categorical propositions, in which spatial inclusions and exclusions correspond to the nonspatial inclusions and exclusions of classes. They provide an exceptionally clear method of notation. They also provide the basis for the simplest and most direct method of testing the validity of categorical syllogisms.

34.

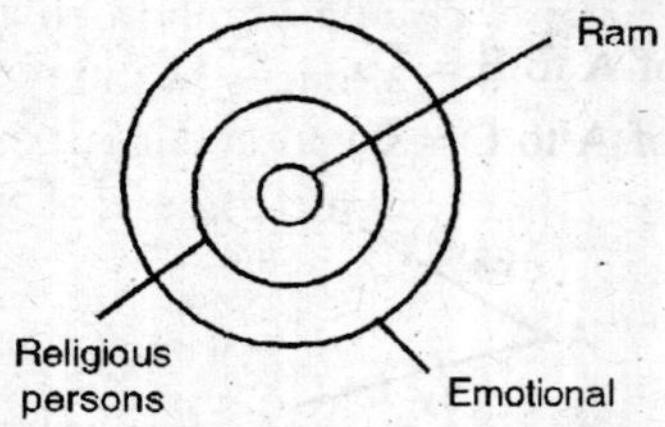

Hence, Ram is emotional and also Ram is not a non-religious person.

35. In 2012, Total expenditure = ₹ 9 lakh

$\therefore$ Expenditure of A = $\frac{2}{3}\times 9 = 6$ lakh

Expenditure of B = $\frac{1}{3}\times 9 = 3$ lakh

Let income of Company A = ₹ x

$$35\% = \left(\frac{x-6 \text{ lakh}}{6}\right)\times 100$$

$$\frac{35}{100} = \frac{(x-6)}{6}$$

$$\Rightarrow \quad \frac{35\times 6}{100} = (x-6)$$

$$\Rightarrow \quad \frac{21}{10} = (x-6)$$

$$\Rightarrow \quad 10x - 60 = 21$$

$$\Rightarrow \quad 10x = 81$$

$$\Rightarrow \quad x = \frac{81}{10} \text{ lakh} = 8.1 \text{ lakh}$$

$\therefore$ Income of company A = 8.1 lakh.

36. Total % profit of Company B
= (30 + 40 + 35 + 50 + 35) = 190

Required average = $\frac{190}{5} = 38\%$.

37. Required year is 2013, the percentage profit earned by the company B is less than that of company A.

38. Total no. of people = 134

No. of people (21 – 30) years = 33

$$\text{Required } \% = \frac{33}{134}\times 100$$
$$= 25\% \text{ (Approx.).}$$

39. $$\text{Required } \% = \frac{16}{134}\times 100$$
$$= \frac{800}{67} = 12\% \text{ (Approx.).}$$

40. $$\text{Required } \% = \frac{68}{134}\times 100$$
$$= 50\% \text{ (Approx.).}$$

41. Information Technology (IT), as defined by the Information Technology Association of America (ITAA), is "the study, design, development, implementation, support or management of computer-based information systems, particularly software applications and computer hardware". IT deals with the use of electronic computers and computer software to convert, store, protect, process, transmit, and securely retrieve information. Information Technology (IT) is a general term that describes any technology that helps to produce, manipulate, store, communicate, and/or disseminate information.

42. Decimal to Binary Conversion

2	51	1
2	25	1
2	12	0
2	6	0
2	3	1
	1	

$\therefore \quad (51)_{10} = (110011)_2.$

43. Copying files to a CD or DVD is often called "burning". To burn to one of these optical disc drives you need a disc of the appropriate type. Disc types you're likely to encounter include:

- CD-R (a recordable disc that you can only write data to once)
- CD-RW (a rewritable disc that you can erase and burn again)
- DVD-R and DVD+R
- DVD-RW and DVD+RW.

44. Spam, an unsolicited e-mail message sent to many recipients at once, is commonly known as Internet junk mail. The content of spam ranges from selling a product or service, to promoting a business opportunity, to advertising offensive material. It is strongly advised not to reply to spam messages for any reason if you want to keep your personal data private.

45. ROM (read-only memory) is a type of memory circuitry that holds the computer's startup routine. ROM is housed in a single integrated circuitusually a fairly large, caterpillar-like DIP package—which is plugged into the system board.

46. ASCII is an acronym of "American Standard Code for Information Interchange". The ASCII coding system is an agreement made by organizations working in the computing business. As its name implies, the coding system was developed in the United States where the commercial use of computers began.

47. Ozone, nitrogen oxide and organic compounds (PAN, $CH_2 = O$, $CH_2 = CHCHO$) are main constituents of photochemical smog each of which produce hazardous effects.

- Aldehydes and PAN components of smog cause irritation to eyes and affect the respiratory tract of human beings.
- Ozone causes cracks in rubber materials and is also harmful to fabric, crops and ornamental plants.
- The toxic nature of photochemical smog cause coughing, wheezing, bronchial constrictions and irritation to respiratory mucous system.
- The highly toxic PAN attacks newly grown leaves and causes bronzing and glazing of their surfaces.
- The brownish colour of photochemical smog due to NO_2 reduces visibility. NO_2 also produces throat and eye irritation and leads to several chronic disease of throat, eyes, lungs and heart.

48. Water pollution is a major environmental issue in India. The largest source of water pollution in India is untreated sewage. Other sources of pollution include agricultural runoff and unregulated small scale industry. Most rivers, lakes and surface water in India are polluted. A 2007 study found that discharge of untreated sewage is the single most important source of pollution of surface and groundwater in India. There is a large gap between generation and treatment of domestic waste water in India. The problem is not only that India lacks sufficient treatment capacity but also that the sewage treatment plants that exist do not operate and are not maintained.

49. In September, 2015 the UN General Assembly adopted the 17 Sustainable Development Goals (the SDGs), with 169 specific targets, to guide the world's development agenda through 2030. One of the goals is to "Ensure availability and sustainable management of water and sanitation for all", and one of the six targets to be achieved under this is "By 2030, implement integrated water resources management at all levels, including through transboundary cooperation as appropriate".

55. The National Judicial Appointments Commission (NJAC) is unconstitutional, ruled the Supreme Court of India. The verdict effectively rejects a major law passed by Parliament last year, which was subsequently ratified by 20 state Assemblies, and restores the collegium system of appointing judges.

56. The Supreme Court of India is the guardian of the Constitution. There are two points of significance of the Supreme Court's rule as the protector and guardian of the Constitution.

- First, as the highest Federal Court, it is within the power and authority of the Supreme Court to settle any dispute regarding division of powers between the Union and the States.
- Secondly, it is in the Supreme Court's authority to safeguard the fundamental rights of the citizens.

In order to discharge these two functions it is sometimes necessary for the Supreme Court to examine or review the legality of the laws enacted by both the Union and the State Governments. This is known as the power of Judicial Review. Indian Supreme Court enjoys limited power of Judicial Review.

57. Fundamental Duties

The Forty-second Constitution Amendment Act has inserted Part IVA with Art. 51A having a set of Fundamental Duties. It says that it shall be the duty of every citizen of India:

(*a*) to abide by the Constitution and respect its ideals and institutions, the National Flag and the National Anthem;

(*b*) to cherish and follow the noble ideals which inspired our national struggle for freedom;

(*c*) to uphold and protect the sovereignty, unity and integrity of India;

(*d*) to defend the country and render national service when called upon to do so;

(*e*) to promote harmony and the spirit of common brotherhood amongst all the people of India transcending religious, linguistic and regional or sectional diversities; to renounce practices derogatory to the dignity of women;

(*f*) to value and preserve the rich heritage of our composite culture;

(*g*) to protect and improve the natural environment including forests, lakes, rivers and wildlife and to have compassion for living creatures;

(*h*) to develop the scientific temper, humanism and the spirit of inquiry and reform;

(*i*) to safeguard public property and to abjure violence;

(*j*) to strive for excellence in all spheres of individual and collective activity so that the nation constantly rises to higher levels of endeavour and achievement.

(*k*) to provide as a parent or a guardian opportunities for education to his/her child or ward between the age of 6 to 14 years.

58. NITI Aayog is a Think tank for Government policy formulation. NITI Aayog too is a non-Constitutional, non-statutory body formed by a cabinet resolution. It is not accountable to parliament, and if line-ministries fail to achieve targets, NITI Aayog cannot punish them.

Previous Years' Paper (Solved)

UGC-NET (JRF) EXAM DECEMBER, 2015

PAPER–I

Note : This paper consists **Sixty (60)** multiple-choice type of questions, out of which the candidate would be required to answer **any Fifty (50)** questions. In the event of candidate attempting more than **Fifty (50)** questions, the **first Fifty (50)** questions attempted by the Candidate would be evaluated.

1. Greater the handicap of the students coming to the educational institutions, greater the demand on the:

A. Family B. Society
C. Teacher D. State

2. What are the characteristics of Continuous and Comprehensive Evaluation?

(*a*) It increases the workload on students by taking multiple tests.
(*b*) It replaces marks with grades.
(*c*) It evaluates every aspect of the student.
(*d*) It helps in reducing examination phobia.

Select the **correct** answer from the codes given below:

A. (*a*), (*b*), (*c*) and (*d*) B. (*b*) and (*d*)
C. (*a*), (*b*) and (*c*) D. (*b*), (*c*) and (*d*)

3. Which of the following attributes denote great strengths of a teacher?

(*a*) Full-time active involvement in the institutional management
(*b*) Setting examples
(*c*) Willingness to put assumptions to the test
(*d*) Acknowledging mistakes

Select the **correct** answer from the codes given below:

A. (*a*), (*b*) and (*d*) B. (*b*), (*c*) and (*d*)
C. (*a*), (*c*) and (*d*) D. (*a*), (*b*), (*c*) and (*d*)

4. Which one of the following statements is **correct** in the context of multiple - choice type questions?

A. They are more objective than true-false type questions.
B. They are less objective than essay type questions.
C. They are more subjective than short-answer type questions.
D. They are more subjective than true-false type questions.

5. As Chairman of an independent commission on education, Jacques Delors report to UNESCO was titled:

A. International Commission on Education Report
B. Millennium Development Report
C. Learning : The Treasure Within
D. World Declaration on Education for All

6. What are required for good teaching?

(*a*) Diagnosis (*b*) Remedy
(*c*) Direction (*d*) Feedback

Select the **correct** answer from the codes given below:

A. (*a*), (*b*), (*c*) and (*d*)
B. (*a*) and (*b*)
C. (*b*), (*c*) and (*d*)
D. (*c*) and (*d*)

7. Which of the following statements is **not** true in the context of participatory research?

A. It recognizes knowledge as power.
B. It emphasises on people as experts.
C. It is a collective process of enquiry.
D. Its sole purpose is production of knowledge.

8. Which of the following statements is **true** in the context of the testing of a hypothesis?
A. It is only the alternative hypothesis, that can be tested
B. It is only the null hypothesis, that can be tested
C. Both, the alternative and the null hypotheses can be tested
D. Both, the alternative and the null hypotheses cannot be tested

9. Which of the following are the basic rules of APA style of referencing format?
(*a*) Italicize titles of shorter works such as journal articles or essays
(*b*) Invert authors' names (last name first)
(*c*) Italicize titles of longer works such as books and journals
(*d*) Alphabetically index reference list
Select the **correct** answer from the codes given below:
A. (*a*) and (*b*) B. (*b*), (*c*) and (*d*)
C. (*c*) and (*d*) D. (*a*), (*b*), (*c*) and (*d*)

10. Which of the following are the characteristics of a seminar?
(*a*) It is a form of academic instruction
(*b*) It involves questioning, discussion and debates
(*c*) It involves large groups of individuals
(*d*) It needs involvement of skilled persons
Select the **correct** answer from the codes given below:
A. (*b*) and (*c*) B. (*b*) and (*d*)
C. (*b*), (*c*) and (*d*) D. (*a*), (*b*) and (*d*)

11. A researcher is interested in studying the prospects of a particular political party in an urban area. What tool should he prefer for the study?
A. Rating scale B. Interview
C. Questionnaire D. Schedule

12. Ethical norms in research do **not** involve guidelines for:
A. Thesis format
B. Copyright
C. Patenting policy
D. Data sharing policies

Direction (Qs. 13 to 17): *Read the following passage carefully and answer the question.*

I did that thing recently where you have to sign a big card - which is a horror unto itself, especially as the keeper of the Big Card was leaning over me at the time. Suddenly I was on the spot, a rabbit in the headlights, torn between doing a fun message or some sort of in-joke or a drawing. Instead overwhelmed by the myriad options available to me, I decided to just write : "Good luck, best, Joel".

It was then that I realised, to my horror, that I had forgotten how to write. My entire existence is "tap letters into computer". My shopping lists are hidden in the notes function of my phone. If I need to remember something I send an e-mail to myself. A pen is something I chew when I'm struggling to think. Paper is something I pile beneath my laptop to make it a more comfortable height for me to type on.

A poll of 1,000 teens by the stationers, Bic found that one in 10 don't own a pen, a third have never written a letter, and half of 13 to 19 years - old have never been forced to sit down and write a thank you letter. More than 80% have never written a love letter, 56% don't have letter paper at home. And a quarter have never known the unique torture of writing a birthday card. The most a teen ever has to use a pen is on an exam paper.

Bic, have you heard of mobile phones? Have you heard of e-mail, facebook and snap chatting? This is the future. Pens are dead. Paper is dead. Handwriting is a relic.

"Handwriting is one of the most creative outlets we have and should be given the same importance as other art forms such as sketching, painting or photography."

Answer the following questions:

13. When confronted with signing a big card, the author felt like "a rabbit in the headlight". What does this phrase mean?
A. A state of confusion
B. A state of pleasure
C. A state of anxiety
D. A state of pain

14. According to the author, which one is **not** the most creative outlet of pursuit?
A. Handwriting B. Photography
C. Sketching D. Reading

15. The entire existence of the author revolves round:
(*a*) Computer
(*b*) Mobile phone
(*c*) Typewriter
Identify the **correct** answer from the codes given below:
A. (*b*) only B. (*a*) and (*b*) only
C. (*a*), (*b*) and (*c*) D. (*b*) and (*c*) only

16. How many teens, as per the Bic survey, do **not** own a pen?
A. 800 B. 560
C. 500 D. 100

17. What is the main concern of the author?
A. That the teens use social networks for communication
B. That the teens use mobile phones
C. That the teens use computer
D. That the teens have forgotten the art of handwriting

18. The main objectives of student evaluation of teachers are:
(*a*) To gather information about student weaknesses.
(*b*) To make teachers take teaching seriously.
(*c*) To help teachers adopt innovative methods of teaching.
(*d*) To identify the areas of further improvement in teacher traits.
Identify the **correct** answer from the codes given below:
A. (*a*) and (*b*) only B. (*b*), (*c*) and (*d*) only
C. (*a*), (*b*) and (*c*) only D. (*a*) only

19. Using the central point of the classroom communication as the beginning of a dynamic pattern of ideas is referred to as:
A. Systemisation
B. Problem - orientation
C. Idea protocol
D. Mind mapping

20. Aspects of the voice, other than the speech are known as:
A. Physical language B. Personal language
C. Para language D. Delivery language

21. Every type of communication is affected by its:
A. Reception B. Transmission
C. Non-regulation D. Context

22. Attitudes, actions and appearances in the context of classroom communication are considered as:
A. Verbal B. Non-verbal
C. Impersonal D. Irrational

23. Most often, the teacher - student communication is:
A. Spurious B. Critical
C. Utilitarian D. Confrontational

24. In a classroom, a communicator's trust level is determined by:
A. the use of hyperbole
B. the change of voice level
C. the use of abstract concepts
D. eye contact

25. The next term in the series
2, 5, 10, 17, 26, 37, ___?___ is :
A. 50 B. 57
C. 62 D. 72

26. A group of 210 students appeared in some test. The mean of $\frac{1}{3}$rd of students is found to be 60. The mean of the remaining students is found to be 78. The mean of the whole group will be :
A. 80 B. 76
C. 74 D. 72

27. Anil after travelling 6 km towards East from his house realized that he has travelled in a wrong direction. He turned and travelled 12 km towards West, turned right and travelled 8 km to reach his office. The straight distance of the office from his house is:
A. 20 km B. 14 km
C. 12 km D. 10 km

28. The next term in the series:
B2E, D5H, F12K, H27N, ___?___ is:
A. J56I B. I62Q
C. Q62J D. J58Q

29. A party was held in which a grandmother, father, mother, four sons, their wives and one son and two daughters to each of the sons were present. The number of females present in the party is:
A. 12 B. 14
C. 18 D. 24

30. P and Q are brothers. R and S are sisters. The son of P is brother of S. Q is related to R as:
A. Son B. Brother
C. Uncle D. Father

31. Consider the argument given below:

'Pre - employment testing of teachers is quite fair because doctors, architects and engineers who are now employed had to face such a testing.'

What type of argument it is ?
A. Deductive B. Analogical
C. Psychological D. Biological

32. Among the following propositions two are related in such a way that they can both be true although they cannot both be false. Which are those propositions? Select the **correct** code.

Propositions:
(*a*) Some priests are cunning.
(*b*) No priest is cunning.
(*c*) All priests are cunning.
(*d*) Some priests are not cunning.

Codes:
A. (*a*) and (*b*) B. (*c*) and (*d*)
C. (*a*) and (*c*) D. (*a*) and (*d*)

33. A Cluster of propositions with a structure that exhibits some inference is called:
A. An inference B. An argument
C. An explanation D. A valid argument

34. Consider the following **assertion (A)** and **reason (R)** and select the **correct** code given below :

Assertion (A): No man is perfect.

Reason (R): Some men are not perfect.
A. Both (A) and (R) are true but (R) does not provide sufficient reason for (A)
B. Both (A) and (R) are true and (R) provides sufficient reason for (A)
C. (A) is true but (R) is false
D. (A) is false but (R) is true

35. A definition that has a meaning that is deliberately assigned to some symbol is called:
A. Lexical B. Precising
C. Stipulative D. Persuasive

36. If the proposition 'No men are honest' is taken to be false which of the following proposition/propositions can be claimed certainly to be true?

Propositions:
A. All men are honest
B. Some men are honest
C. Some men are not honest
D. No honest person is man

Given below in the table is the decadal data of Population and Electrical Power Production of a country.

Year	*Population (million)*	*Electrical Power Production (GW)**
1951	20	10
1961	21	20
1971	24	25
1981	27	40
1991	30	50
2001	32	80
2011	35	100
	* 1 GW = 1000 million watt	

Directions (Qs. 37 to 42): *Based on the above table answer the questions.*

37. Which decade registered the maximum growth rate (%) of population?
A. 1961-71 B. 1971-81
C. 1991-2001 D. 2001-2011

38. Average decadal growth rate (%) of population is:
A. ~ 12.21% B. ~ 9.82%
C. ~ 6.73% D. ~ 5%

39. Based on the average decadal growth rate, what will be the population in the year 2021?
A. 40.34 million B. 38.49 million
C. 37.28 million D. 36.62 million

40. In the year 1951, what was the power availability per person?
A. 100 W B. 200 W
C. 400 W D. 500 W

41. In which decade, the average power availability per person was maximum?
A. 1981-1991 B. 1991-2001
C. 2001-2011 D. 1971-1981

42. By what percentage (%) the power production increased from 1951 to 2011?
A. 100% B. 300%
C. 600% D. 900%

43. NMEICT stands for:
A. National Mission on Education through ICT
B. National Mission on E-governance through ICT
C. National Mission on E-commerce through ICT
D. National Mission on E-learning through ICT

44. Which of the following is an instant messaging application?
(*a*) WhatsApp (*b*) Google Talk
(*c*) Viber
Select the **correct** answer from the codes given below:
A. (*a*) and (*b*) only B. (*b*) and (*c*) only
C. (*a*) only D. (*a*), (*b*) and (*c*)

45. In a Computer a byte generally consists of:
A. 4 bits B. 8 bits
C. 16 bits D. 10 bits

46. Which of the following is **not** an input device?
A. Microphone B. Keyboard
C. Joystick D. Monitor

47. Which of the following is an open source software?
A. MS Word B. Windows
C. Mozilla Firefox D. Acrobat Reader

48. Which of the following enables us to send the same letter to different persons in MS Word?
A. Mail join B. Mail copy
C. Mail insert D. Mail merge

49. Inside rural homes, the source/sources of Nitrogen Oxide Pollution may be:
(*a*) Unvented gas stoves
(*b*) Wood stoves
(*c*) Kerosene heaters
Choose the **correct** code:
A. (*a*) and (*b*) only
B. (*b*) and (*c*) only
C. (*b*) only
D. (*a*), (*b*) and (*c*)

50. Which of the following pollutants can cause cancer in humans?
A. Pesticides B. Mercury
C. Lead D. Ozone

51. **Assertion (A):** People population control measures do not necessarily help in checking environmental degradation.
Reason (R): The relationship between population growth and environmental degradation is rather complex.
Choose the **correct** answer from the following:
A. Both (A) and (R) are true and (R) is the correct explanation of (A)
B. Both (A) and (R) are true but (R) is not the correct explanation of (A)
C. (A) is true but (R) is false
D. (A) is false but (R) is true

52. Which of the following phenomena is **not** a natural hazard?
A. Wildfire
B. Lightning
C. Landslide
D. Chemical contamination

53. As part of National Climate Change Policy, Indian government is planning to raise the installed capacity of renewable energy by the year 2030 to:
A. 175 GW B. 200 GW
C. 250 GW D. 350 GW

54. At present, in terms of per capita energy consumption (kWh/year), identify the **correct** sequence.

A. Brazil > Russia > China > India
B. Russia > China > India > Brazil
C. Russia > China > Brazil > India
D. China > Russia > Brazil > India

55. Which of the following are the objectives of Rashtriya Uchchatar Shiksha Abhiyan (RUSA)?

(*a*) To improve the overall quality of state institutions.
(*b*) To ensure adequate availability of quality faculty.
(*c*) To create new institutions through upgradation of existing autonomous colleges.
(*d*) To downgrade universities with poor infrastructure into autonomous colleges.

Select the **correct** answer from the codes given below:

A. (*a*), (*b*), (*c*) and (*d*) B. (*a*), (*b*) and (*c*)
C. (*a*), (*c*) and (*d*) D. (*a*), (*b*) and (*d*)

56. The grounds on which discrimination in admission to educational institutions is constitutionally prohibited are:

(*a*) Religion
(*b*) Sex
(*c*) Place of birth
(*d*) Nationality

Select the **correct** answer from the codes given below:

A. (*b*), (*c*) and (*d*) B. (*a*), (*b*) and (*c*)
C. (*a*), (*b*) and (*d*) D. (*a*), (*b*), (*c*) and (*d*)

57. Which of the following statements are **correct** about Lok Sabha?

(*a*) The Constitution puts a limit on the size of the Lok Sabha.
(*b*) The size and shape of the Parliamentary Constituencies is determined by the Election Commission.
(*c*) First - past - the Post electoral system is followed.
(*d*) The Speaker of Lok Sabha does not have a casting vote in case of an equality of votes.

Select the **correct** answer from the codes given below:

A. (*a*) and (*c*)
B. (*a*), (*b*) and (*c*)
C. (*a*), (*c*) and (*d*)
D. (*a*), (*b*), (*c*) and (*d*)

58. Public Order as an item in the Constitution figures in:

A. the Union List
B. the State List
C. the Concurrent List
D. the Residuary Powers

59. The term of office of the Advocate General of a State is:

A. 4 years
B. 5 years
C. 6 years or 65 years of age whichever is earlier
D. not fixed

60. Which among the following States has the highest number of seats in the Lok Sabha?

A. Maharashtra B. Rajasthan
C. Tamil Nadu D. West Bengal

ANSWERS

1	2	3	4	5	6	7	8	9	10
C	D	B	A	C	A	D	B	B	D
11	**12**	**13**	**14**	**15**	**16**	**17**	**18**	**19**	**20**
C	A	A	D	B	D	D	B	D	C
21	**22**	**23**	**24**	**25**	**26**	**27**	**28**	**29**	**30**
D	B	C	D	A	D	D	D	B	C

31	32	33	34	35	36	37	38	39	40
B	D	B	A	C	B	A	B	B	D
41	**42**	**43**	**44**	**45**	**46**	**47**	**48**	**49**	**50**
C	D	A	D	B	D	C	D	D	A
51	**52**	**53**	**54**	**55**	**56**	**57**	**58**	**59**	**60**
A	D	D	C	B	B	A	B	D	A

SOME SELECTED EXPLANATORY ANSWERS

5. Jacques Delors is the chairman of the International Commission on Education for the Twenty-first Century. The result of three years of research and debate by an international panel of 14 specialists on how education should confront the complex challenges of the next century, the 266-page report is being published simultaneously in English and French.

Entitled "Learning: the Treasure Within," the report revolves around six main lines of enquiry which will guide UNESCO's future education policies and those of its 184 Member States. The lines focus on the relationship between education and the six subject areas of development, science, citizenship, culture, social cohesion, and work.

20. **Paralanguage** is a component of meta-communication that may modify or nuance meaning, or convey emotion, such as prosody, pitch, volume, intonation etc. It is sometimes defined as relating to nonphonemic properties only.

The paralinguistic properties of speech play an important role in human communication. There are no utterances or speech signals that lack paralinguistic properties, since speech requires the presence of a voice that can be modulated. This voice must have some properties, and all the properties of a voice as such are paralinguistic.

21. Each context has an influence on the communication process. Contexts can overlap, creating an even more dynamic process. You have been communicating in many of these contexts across your lifetime, and you'll be able to apply what you've learned through experience in each context to business communication.

25.

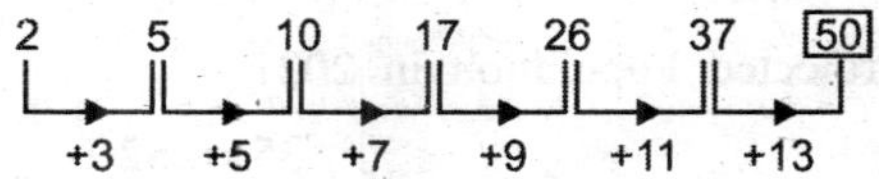

28.

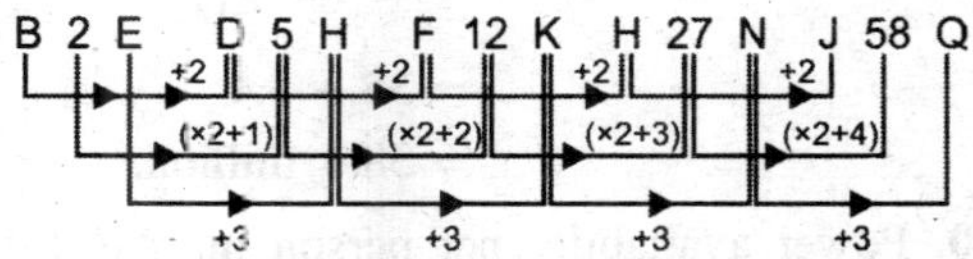

33. **Argument:** An argument is any group of propositions of which one is claimed to follow from the others, which are regarded as providing support or grounds for the truth of that one.

35. A definition that has a meaning which is deliberately assigned to some symbol is called stipulative. One who introduces a new symbol is free to assign, or stipulate, whatever meaning he cares to. Even an old term in a new context may also have its present meaning stipulated. What are here called *stipulative* definitions are sometimes referred to as *nominal* or *verbal* definitions.

37. Growth rate (%) of population in decade

1961-71 :

$$\left(\frac{24-21}{21}\right)\times 100 = \frac{100}{7} = 14.285\%$$

1971-81 :

$$\left(\frac{27-24}{24}\right)\times 100 = \frac{3}{24}\times 100 = 12.5\%$$

1991-2001 :

$$\left(\frac{32-30}{30}\right)\times 100 = \frac{2}{30}\times 100 = 6.67\%$$

2001-2011 :

$$\left(\frac{35-32}{32}\right)\times 100 = \frac{2}{32}\times 100 = 9.375\%$$

∴ Maximum growth rate (%) of population registered on 1961-71.

38. Average decadal growth rate (%) of population

$$= \frac{5+14.28+12.5+11.11+6.67+9.38}{6}$$

= 9.82%.

39. Projected Population in 2021

$$= 35 + \frac{35\times 9.82}{100}$$

= 35 + 3.4

= 38.4 million.

40. Power availabilty per person in year 1951

$$= \frac{10\times 1000}{20} = 500 \text{ W.}$$

41. Average Power availability per person in decade

1981-91 : $\frac{(40+50)\times 1000}{(27+30)} \cong 1579$ W

1991-2001 : $\frac{(50+80)\times 1000}{(30+32)} \cong 2097$ W

2001-2011 : $\frac{(80+100)\times 1000}{(32+35)} \cong 2686.5$ W

1971-1981 : $\frac{(25+40)\times 1000}{(24+27)} \cong 1274.5$ W

So, Average Power availability per person was maximum in 2001-2011.

42. Percentage (%) increase in power production from 1951 to 2011

$$= \left(\frac{100-10}{10}\right)\times 100$$

= 900%.

43. National Mission on Education through Information and Communication Technology is abbreviated as NMEICT .

45. The byte is a unit of digital information that most commonly consists of eight bits. Historically, the byte was the number of bits used to encode a single character of text in a computer and for this reason it is the smallest addressable unit of memory in many computer architectures.

50. Pesticides are the only toxic substances released intentionally into our environment to kill living things. Pesticides are used in our schools, parks, and public lands. Pesticides are sprayed on agricultural fields and wood lots. Pesticides can be found in our air, our food, our soil, our water and even in our breast milk.

Pesticides can cause many types of cancer in humans. Some of the most prevalent forms include leukemia, non-Hodgkins lymphoma, brain, bone, breast, ovarian, prostate, testicular and liver cancers.

Previous Years' Paper (Solved)

UGC-NET (JRF) EXAM JUNE, 2015*

PAPER–I

Note : This paper contains **Sixty (60)** multiple choice questions, each question carrying **two (2)** marks. Candidate is expected to answer any **Fifty (50)** questions. In case more than **Fifty (50)** questions are attempted, only the first **Fifty (50)** questions will be evaluated.

1. Which of the following is the highest level of cognitive ability?

A. Knowing B. Understanding
C. Analysing D. Evaluating

2. Which of the following factors does **not** impact teaching?

A. Teacher's knowledge
B. Class-room activities that encourage learning
C. Socio-economic background of teachers and students
D. Learning through experience

3. Which of the following statements about teaching aids are correct?

(*a*) They help in retaining concepts for longer duration.
(*b*) They help students learn better.
(*c*) They make teaching learning process interesting.
(*d*) They enhance rote learning.

Select the correct answer from the codes given below:

A. (*a*), (*b*), (*c*) and (*d*) B. (*a*), (*b*) and (*c*)
C. (*b*), (*c*) and (*d*) D. (*a*), (*b*) and (*d*)

4. Techniques used by a teacher to teach include:

(*a*) Lecture
(*b*) Interactive lecture
(*c*) Group work
(*d*) Self study

Select the correct answer from the codes given below :

A. (*a*), (*b*) and (*c*) B. (*a*), (*b*), (*c*) and (*d*)
C. (*b*), (*c*) and (*d*) D. (*a*), (*b*) and (*d*)

5. Achievement tests are commonly used for the purpose of :

A. Making selections for a specific job
B. Selecting candidates for a course
C. Identifying strengths and weaknesses of learners
D. Assessing the amount of learning after teaching

6. A good teacher is one who:

A. gives useful information
B. explains concepts and principles
C. gives printed notes to students
D. inspires students to learn

7. Which of the following statements regarding the meaning of research are correct?

(*a*) Research refers to a series of systematic activity or activities undertaken to find out the solution of a problem.
(*b*) It is a systematic, logical and an unbiased process wherein verification of hypothesis, data analysis, interpretation and formation of principles can be done.
(*c*) It is an intellectual enquiry or quest towards truth.
(*d*) It leads to enhancement of knowledge.

Select the correct answer from the codes given below :

A. (*a*), (*b*) and (*c*) B. (*b*), (*c*) and (*d*)
C. (*a*), (*c*) and (*d*) D. (*a*), (*b*), (*c*) and (*d*)

* Held on 28/06/2005

8. A good thesis writing should involve:
(*a*) reduction of punctuation and grammatical errors to a minimum.
(*b*) careful checking of references.
(*c*) consistency in the way the thesis is written.
(*d*) a clear and well written abstract.
Select the correct answer from the codes given below:
A. (*a*), (*b*), (*c*) and (*d*) B. (*a*), (*b*) and (*c*)
C. (*a*), (*b*) and (*d*) D. (*b*), (*c*) and (*d*)

9. Jean Piaget gave a theory of cognitive development of humans on the basis of his:
A. Fundamental Research
B. Applied Research
C. Action Research
D. Evaluation Research

10. "Male and female students perform equally well in a numerical aptitude test." This statement indicates a :
A. research hypothesis
B. null hypothesis
C. directional hypothesis
D. statistical hypothesis

11. The conclusions/findings of which type of research cannot be generalized to other situations?
A. Historical Research
B. Descriptive Research
C. Experimental Research
D. Causal Comparative Research

12. Which of the following steps are required to design a questionnaire?
(*a*) Writing primary and secondary aims of the study.
(*b*) Review of the current literature.
(*c*) Prepare a draft of questionnaire.
(*d*) Revision of the draft.
Select the correct answer from the codes given below:
A. (*a*), (*b*) and (*c*) B. (*a*), (*c*) and (*d*)
C. (*b*), (*c*) and (*d*) D. (*a*), (*b*), (*c*) and (*d*)

Directions (Qs. 13-18): *Read the following passage carefully and answer the questions given below:*

Story telling is not in our genes. Neither it is an evolutionary history. It is the essence of what makes us Human.

Human beings progress by telling stories. One event can result in a great variety of stories being told about it. Sometimes those stories differ greatly. Which stories are picked up and repeated and which ones are dropped and forgotten often determines how we progress. Our history, knowledge and understanding are all the collections of the few stories that survive. This includes the stories that we tell each other about the future. And how the future will turn out depends partly, possibly largely, on which stories we collectively choose to believe.

Some stories are designed to spread fear and concern. This is because some story-tellers feel that there is a need to raise some tensions. Some stories are frightening, they are like totemic warnings: "Fail to act now and we are all doomed." Then there are stories that indicate that all will be fine so long as we leave everything upto a few especially able adults. Currently, this trend is being led by those who call themselves "rational optimists". They tend to claim that it is human nature to compete and to succeed and also to profit at the expense of others. The rational optimists however, do not realize how humanity has progressed overtime through amiable social networks and how large groups work in less selfishness and in the process accommodate rich and poor, high and low alike. This aspect in story-telling is considered by the 'Practical Possibles', who sit between those who say all is fine and cheerful and be individualistic in your approach to a successful future, and those who ordain pessimism and fear that we are doomed.

What the future holds for us is which stories we hold on to and how we act on them.

13. Our knowledge is a collection of:
A. all stories that we have heard during our life-time

B. some stories that we remember
C. a few stories that survive
D. some important stories

14. Story telling is:
A. an art
B. a science
C. in our genes
D. the essence of what makes us human

15. How the future will turn out to be, depends upon the stories?
A. We collectively choose to believe in
B. Which are repeatedly narrated
C. Designed to spread fear and tension
D. Designed to make prophecy

16. Rational optimists:
(*a*) Look for opportunities
(*b*) Are sensible and cheerful
(*c*) Are selfishly driven
Identify the correct answer from the codes given below:
A. (*a*), (*b*) and (*c*) B. (*a*) only
C. (*a*) and (*b*) only D. (*b*) and (*c*) only

17. Humans become less selfish when:
A. they work in large groups
B. they listen to frightening stories
C. they listen to cheerful stories
D. they work in solitude

18. 'Practical Possibles' are the ones who:
A. follow Midway Path
B. are doom-mongers
C. are self-centred
D. are cheerful and carefree

19. Effectiveness of communication can be traced from which of the following?
(*a*) Attitude surveys
(*b*) Performance records
(*c*) Students attendance
(*d*) Selection of communication channel
Select the correct answer from the codes given below:
A. (*a*), (*b*), (*c*) and (*d*) B. (*a*), (*b*) and (*c*)
C. (*b*), (*c*) and (*d*) D. (*a*), (*b*) and (*d*)

20. Assertion (A): Formal communication tends to be fast and flexible.
Reason (R): Formal communication is a systematic and orderly flow of information.
A. Both **(A)** and **(R)** are correct and **(R)** is correct explanation of **(A)**
B. Both **(A)** and **(R)** are correct, but **(R)** is not correct explanation of **(A)**
C. **(A)** is correct, but **(R)** is false
D. **(A)** is false, but **(R)** is correct

21. Which of the following are the characteristic features of communication?
(*a*) Communication involves exchange of ideas, facts and opinions.
(*b*) Communication involves both information and understanding.
(*c*) Communication is a continuous process.
(*d*) Communication is a circular process.
Select the correct answer from the codes given below:
A. (*a*), (*b*) and (*c*) B. (*a*), (*b*) and (*d*)
C. (*b*), (*c*) and (*d*) D. (*a*), (*b*), (*c*) and (*d*)

22. The term 'grapevine' is also known as :
A. Downward communication
B. Informal communication
C. Upward communication
D. Horizontal communication

23. Which of the following is **not** a principle of effective communication?
A. Persuasive and convincing dialogue
B. Participation of the audience
C. One-way transfer of information
D. Strategic use of grapevine

24. In communication, the language is:
A. The verbal code
B. Intrapersonal
C. The symbolic code
D. The non-verbal code

25. The next term in the series is:
2, 5, 9, 19, 37, ?
A. 73 B. 75
C. 78 D. 80

26. In certain code MATHURA is coded as JXQEROX. The code of HOTELS will be :

A. LEQIBP B. ELQBIP
C. LEBIQP D. ELIPQB

27. One day Prakash left home and walked 10 km towards south, turned right and walked 5 km, turned right and walked 10 km and turned left and walked 10 km. How many km will he have to walk to reach his home straight?

A. 10 B. 20
C. 15 D. 30

28. A girl introduced a boy as the son of the daughter of the father of her uncle. The boy is related to the girl as :

A. Brother B. Uncle
C. Nephew D. Son

29. In an examination 10,000 students appeared. The result revealed the number of students who have:

passed in all five subjects	=	5583
passed in three subjects only	=	1400
passed in two subjects only	=	1200
passed in one subject only	=	735
failed in English only	=	75
failed in Physics only	=	145
failed in Chemistry only	=	140
failed in Mathematics only	=	200
failed in Bio-science only	=	157

The number of students passed in at least four subjects is:

A. 6300 B. 6900
C. 7300 D. 7900

30. At present a person is 4 times older than his son and is 3 years older than his wife. After 3 years the age of the son will be 15 years. The age of the person's wife after 5 years will be:

A. 42 B. 48
C. 45 D. 50

31. If we want to seek new knowledge of facts about the world, we must rely on reason of the type:

A. Inductive B. Deductive
C. Demonstrative D. Physiological

32. A deductive argument is invalid if :

A. Its premises and conclusions are all false
B. Its premises are true but its conclusion is false
C. Its premises are false but its conclusion is true
D. Its premises and conclusions are all true

33. Inductive reasoning is grounded on:

A. Integrity of nature
B. Unity of nature
C. Uniformity of nature
D. Harmony of nature

34. Among the following statements **two** are contradictory to each other. Select the correct code that represents them:

Statements:

(*a*) All poets are philosophers.
(*b*) Some poets are philosophers.
(*c*) Some poets are not philosophers.
(*d*) No philosopher is a poet.

Codes:

A. (*a*) and (*b*) B. (*a*) and (*d*)
C. (*a*) and (*c*) D. (*b*) and (*c*)

35. Which of the codes given below contains only the **correct** statements? Select the code:

Statements:

(*a*) Venn diagram represents the arguments graphically.
(*b*) Venn diagram can enhance our understanding.
(*c*) Venn diagram may be called valid or invalid.
(*d*) Venn diagram is clear method of notation.

Codes:

A. (*a*), (*b*) and (*c*)
B. (*a*), (*b*) and (*d*)
C. (*b*), (*c*) and (*d*)
D. (*a*), (*c*) and (*d*)

36. When the purpose of a definition is to explain the use or to eliminate ambiguity the definition is called:

A. Stipulative B. Theoretical
C. Lexical D. Persuasive

Direction (Qs. 37-42): *Answer the question based on the tabulated data given below:*

A company has 20 employees with their age (in years) and salary (in thousand rupees per month) mentioned against each of them:

S.No.	Age (in years)	Salary (in thousand rupees per month)
1.	44	35
2.	32	20
3.	54	45
4.	42	35
5.	31	20
6.	53	60
7.	42	50
8.	51	55
9.	34	25
10.	41	30
11.	33	30
12.	31	35
13.	30	35
14.	37	40
15.	44	45
16.	36	35
17.	34	35
18.	49	50
19.	43	45
20.	45	50

37. Classify the data of age of each employee in class interval of 5 years. Which class interval of 5 years has the maximum average salary?
A. 35-40 years B. 40-45 years
C. 45-50 years D. 50-55 years

38. What is the frequency (%) in the class interval of 30-35 years?
A. 20% B. 25%
C. 30% D. 35%

39. What is the average age of the employees?
A. 40.3 years B. 38.6 years
C. 47.2 years D. 45.3 years

40. What is the fraction (%) of employees getting salary ≥ 40,000 per month?
A. 45% B. 50%
C. 35% D. 32%

41. What is the average salary (in thousand per month) in the age group 40-50 years?
A. 35 B. 42.5
C. 40.5 D. 36.5

42. What is the fraction of employees getting salary less than the average salary of all the employees?
A. 45% B. 50%
C. 55% D. 47%

43. Encoding or scrambling data for transmission across a network is known as :
A. Protection B. Detection
C. Encryption D. Decryption

44. Which of the following is **not** an output device?
A. Printer B. Speaker
C. Monitor D. Keyboard

45. Which of the following represents one billion characters ?
A. Kilobyte B. Megabyte
C. Gigabyte D. Terabyte

46. Which of the following is **not** open source software?
A. Internet explorer
B. Fedora Linux
C. Open office
D. Apache HTTP server

47. Which one of the following represents the binary equivalent of the decimal number 25?
A. 10101 B. 01101
C. 11001 D. 11011

48. Which is an instant messenger that is used for chatting?
A. Altavista B. MAC
C. Microsoft Office D. Google Talk

49. In which of the countries per capita use of water is maximum?
A. USA B. European Union
C. China D. India

50. India's contribution to total global carbon dioxide emissions is about:
A. ~ 3% B. ~ 6%
C. ~ 10% D. ~ 15%

51. Two earthquakes A and B happen to be of magnitude 5 and 6 respectively on Richter Scale. The ratio of the energies released E_B/E_A will be approximately:

A. ~8 B. ~16
C. ~32 D. ~64

52. Which of the following combinations represent renewable natural resources?

A. Fertile soil, fresh water and natural gas
B. Clean air, phosphates and biological diversity
C. Fishes, fertile soil and fresh water
D. Oil, forests and tides

53. In the recently launched Air Quality Index in India, which of the following pollutants is **not** included?

A. Carbon monoxide
B. Fine particulate matter
C. Ozone
D. Chlorofluorocarbons

54. The factors which are most important in determining the impact of anthropogenic activities on environment are :

A. Population, affluence per person, land available per person
B. Population, affluence per person and the technology used for exploiting resources
C. Atmospheric conditions, population and forest cover
D. Population, forest cover and land available per person

55. The session of the Parliament is summoned by:

A. The President
B. The Prime Minister
C. The Speaker of the Lok Sabha
D. The Speaker of the Lok Sabha and the Chairman of the Rajya Sabha

56. Civil Service Day is celebrated in India on:

A. 21st April B. 24th April
C. 21st June D. 7th July

57. The South Asia University is situated in the city of :

A. Colombo B. Dhaka
C. New Delhi D. Kathmandu

58. The University Grants Commission was established with which of the following aims?

(*a*) Promotion of research and development in higher education
(*b*) Identifying and sustaining institutions of potential learning
(*c*) Capacity building of teachers
(*d*) Providing autonomy to each and every higher educational institution in India.

Select the correct answer from the codes given below :

A. (*a*), (*b*), (*c*) and (*d*) B. (*a*), (*b*) and (*c*)
C. (*b*), (*c*) and (*d*) D. (*a*), (*b*) and (*d*)

59. The Gross Enrolment Ratio (GER) in institutions of higher education in India at present (2015) is about:

A. 8 per cent B. 12 per cent
C. 19 per cent D. 23 per cent

60. The total number of central universities in India in April 2015 was:

A. 08 B. 14
C. 27 D. 43

ANSWERS

1	2	3	4	5	6	7	8	9	10
D	C	B	A	D	D	D	A	A	B
11	**12**	**13**	**14**	**15**	**16**	**17**	**18**	**19**	**20**
A	D	C	D	A	A	A	A	B	D
21	**22**	**23**	**24**	**25**	**26**	**27**	**28**	**29**	**30**
D	B	C	A	B	B	C	A	A	D

31	32	33	34	35	36	37	38	39	40
A	B	C	C	B	C	D	D	A	A
41	**42**	**43**	**44**	**45**	**46**	**47**	**48**	**49**	**50**
B	C	C	D	C	A	C	D	B	B
51	**52**	**53**	**54**	**55**	**56**	**57**	**58**	**59**	**60**
C	C	D	B	A	A	C	B	C	D

SOME SELECTED EXPLANATORY ANSWERS

1. Bloom identified six levels within the cognitive domain, from the simple recall or recognition of facts, as the lowest level, through increasingly more complex and abstract mental levels, to the highest order which is classified as evaluation.

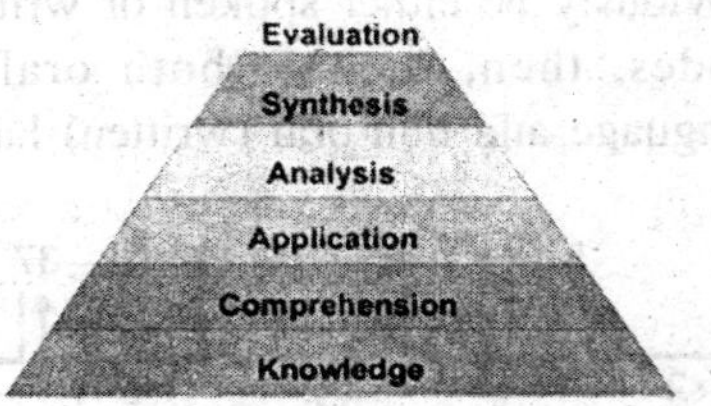

Evaluation is concerned with the ability to judge the value of material (statement, novel, poem, research report) for a given purpose. The judgements are to be based on definite criteria. These may be internal criteria (organization) or external criteria (relevance to the purpose) and the student may determine the criteria or be given them. Learning outcomes in this area are highest in the cognitive hierarchy because they contain elements of all the other categories, plus conscious value judgements based on clearly defined criteria.

5. An **achievement test** is a test of developed skill or knowledge. It is the assessment of the amount of the learning after teaching. The most common type of achievement test is a standardized test developed to measure skills and knowledge learned in a given grade level, usually through planned instruction, such as training or classroom instruction. Achievement tests are often contrasted with tests that measure aptitude, a more general and stable cognitive trait.

6. It is not an exaggeration to say that a great teacher can change a student's life. As some of the most influential role models for developing students, teachers are responsible for more than just academic enrichment. If you want to be a great educator, you must connect with your pupils and reach them on multiple levels, because the best teachers are committed to their students' well-being both inside and outside the classroom.

Inspiring students is integral to ensuring their success and encouraging them to fulfil their potential. Students who are inspired by their teachers can accomplish amazing things, and that motivation almost always stays with them. Inspiration can also take many forms, from helping a pupil through the academic year and their short-term goals, to guiding them towards their future career. Years after graduation, many working professionals will still cite a particular teacher as the one who fostered their love of what they currently do and attribute their accomplishments to that educator.

9. Piaget's theory of cognitive development is a comprehensive theory about the nature and development of human intelligence. Piaget believed that one's childhood plays a vital and active role in a person's development. Piaget's idea is primarily known as a developmental stage theory. It is based on his fundamental research.

To Piaget, cognitive development was a progressive reorganization of mental processes resulting from biological maturation and environmental experience.

10. In inferential statistics the **null hypothesis** usually refers to a general statement or default position that there is no relationship between two measured phenomena, or no difference among groups.

For example "Male and female students perform equally well in a numerical aptitude test".

19. Communication is an exchange of feelings, ideas, and information, whether by speaking, writing, signals, or behaviours. Effective communication is an essential component of organizational success at all levels.

It can be traced out by following points:

(a) Attitude surveys

(b) Performance records

(c) Students attendance

20. Formal communication refers to the communication transmitted through the officially established chain of command in the organisation structure. The organisation structure reflecting superior subordinate relationships determines the flow of formal communication. Formal communication, **according to the direction or flow may be of three types-(a) upward, (b) downward, and (c) horizontal. Formal communication is generally in writing and includes transmission of orders,** instructions and decisions. Speed of communication is abit slow and time consuming. By Nature, it is systematic and orderly flow of information.

22. Informal communication is also known as grapevine communication because there is no definite route of communication for sharing information.

In this form of communication, information converges a long way by passing from one person to another person leaving no indication from which point it started. This is quite similar to the vine of grapes. It is also difficult to find out the beginning and the end of the grapevine.

23. One-way communication is a misnomer. The one-way process is not communication; it is simply the dispensing of information to another person, incormation that may or may not be received in the form intended. It is not a way of effective communication because the one-way posture inhibits interchange, and limits feedback.

24. Verbal means "consisting of words". Therefore, a verbal code is a set of rules about the use of words in the creation of messages. It is language we use for communication. Words can obviously be either spoken or written. Verbal codes, then, include both oral (spoken) language and non-oral (written) language.

25. 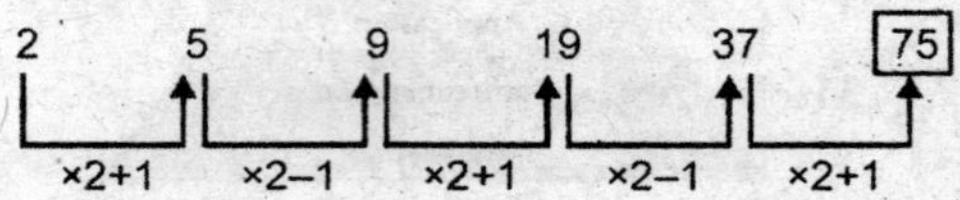

Hence, the next term in the series is 75.

26. M A T H U R A

–3↓ –3↓ –3↓ –3↓ –3↓ –3↓ –3↓

J X Q E R O X

Similarly,

H O T E L S

–3↓ –3↓ –3↓ –3↓ –3↓ –3↓

E L Q B I P

27. 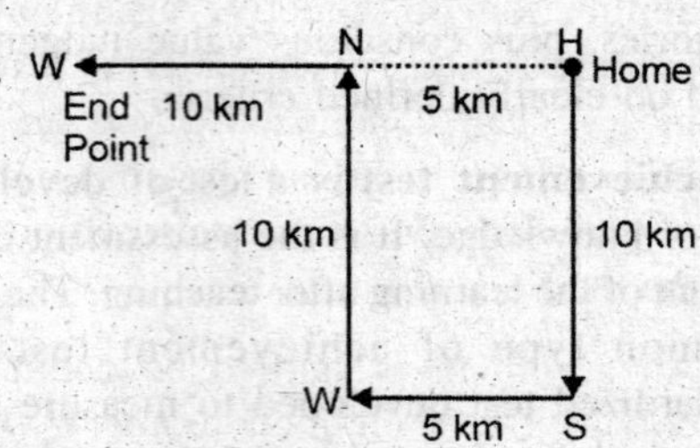

He has to walk 15 km to reach his home straight.

28.

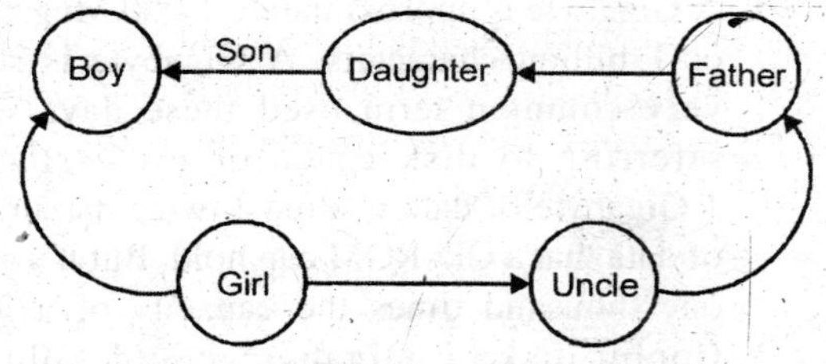

Hence the relation between boy and girl is brother and sister.

∴ The boy is related to the girl as brother.

29. Required no. of Students passed in at least four subjects is 5583 + 717 = 6300.

30. Let present age of son = x years

Present age of father = $4x$ years

Wife's present age = $4x - 3$ years

According to the question,

$$x + 3 = 15 \Rightarrow x = 12$$

Wife's present age = 4 × 12 – 3 = 45 years

After 5 years wife's age = 45 + 5 = 50 years.

31. Inductive reasoning is one in which the premises seek to supply strong evidence for the truth of the conclusion. While the conclusion of a deductive argument is certain, the truth of the conclusion of an inductive argument is *probable*, based upon the evidence given.

Inductive reasoning is also known as hypothesis construction because any conclusions made are based on current knowledge and predictions. As with deductive arguments, biases can distort the proper application of inductive argument, thereby preventing the reasoner from forming the most logical conclusion based on the clues. Examples of these biases include the availability heuristic, confirmation bias, and the predictable-world bias.

32. An argument is said to be deductive if its conclusion is claimed to *necessarily* follow from its premises. That is, if it is claimed that since the premises are true or acceptable, the conclusion must also be true or acceptable, then the argument is deductive. We can also define deduction by saying that in a deductive argument, the logical relation between the premises and the conclusion is claimed to be 100% supporting.

36. A lexical definition simply reports the way in which a term is already used within a language community. The goal here is to inform someone else of the accepted meaning of the term, so the definition is more or less correct depending upon the accuracy with which it captures that usage. In these pages, my definitions of technical terms of logic are lexical because they are intended to inform you about the way in which these terms are actually employed within the discipline of logic.

37. 35-40 years:

Average Salary

$$= \frac{40+35}{2} = \frac{75}{2} = 37.5 \text{ thousand/month}$$

40-45 years:

$$\text{Average} = \frac{35+35+50+30+45+45}{6}$$

$$= \frac{240}{6} = 40 \text{ thousand/month}$$

45-50 years:

$$\text{Average} = \frac{50+50}{2} = \frac{100}{2}$$

$$= 50 \text{ thousand/month}$$

50-55 years:

$$\text{Average} = \frac{45+60+55}{3} = \frac{160}{3}$$

$$= 53.3 \text{ thousand/month}$$

Hence, the 50-55 class interval has the maximum average salary.

38. Required % = $\frac{7}{20} \times 100$ = 35%.

39. Total age of 20 employees

= 424 + 382 = 806 years

$$\text{Average} = \frac{806}{20} = 40.3 \text{ years.}$$

40. Required % = $\frac{9}{20} \times 100 = 45\%$.

41. 40-50 years:

Total salary = 35 + 35 + 50 + 30 + 45 + 50 + 45 + 50

= 340 thousand

Required average salary = $\frac{340}{8} = 42.5$.

42. Total salary of 20 workers

= (375 + 400) thousand = 775 thousand

Average salary = $\frac{775}{20}$ = 38.75 thousand

Required% = $\frac{11}{20} \times 100 = 55\%$.

43. *Encryption* involves scrambling and perhaps compressing the data prior to transmission; the receiving device is provided with the necessary logic to decrypt and decompress the trasmitted information. Encryption generally resides in firmware included in stand-alone devices, although it can be built into virtually any device. Encryption logic, for example, often is incorporated into routers, which can encrypt data on a packet-by-packet basis. Encryption comes in two basic flavors: private key and public key. *Private key* is a symmetric encryption method that uses the same key to encrypt and decrypt data and requires that the key be kept secret. *Public key* is an asymmetric encryption method with two keys—an encryption (encoding) key that can be used by all authorized network users and a decryption (decoding) key that is kept secret.

44. A computer **keyboard** is one of the primary input devices used with a computer that looks similar to those found on electric typewriters, but with some additional keys. Keyboards allow you to input letters, numbers, and other symbols into a computer that often function as commands.

45. A Gigabyte is approximately 1,000 Megabytes or 1 billion characters. A Gigabyte is still a very common term used these days when referring to disk space or drive storage. 1 Gigabyte of data is almost twice the amount of data that a CD-ROM can hold. But it's about one thousand times the capacity of a 3-1/2 floppy disk. 1 Gigabyte could hold the contents of about 10 yards of books on a shelf. 100 Gigabytes could hold the entire library floor of academic journals.

46. Open source software (OSS) as "software for which the human-readable source code is available for use, study, re-use, modification, enhancement, and re-distribution by the users of that software".

The Internet Explorer Developer Relations Team at Microsoft have hinted at the possibility that the browser may one day become "Open Source".

"Open Source" is a term referring to software that whose source code is available for modification or enhancement by anyone. All other major web browsers (Mozilla Firefox, Google Chrome, Opera and Safari are based on open-source components). Presently, Internet Explorer is the only one of the big 5 browsers to remain entirely "closed source".

47.

2	25	1
2	12	0
2	6	0
2	3	1
	1	

$\therefore (25)_{10} = (11001)_2$.

48. Google Talk is an instant messaging service that provides both text and voice communication. The instant messaging service is colloquially known as "gtalk", "gchat", or "gmessage" to its users, although Google does not endorse those names.

50. Carbon dioxide (CO_2) emissions from fossil fuel burning and cement production increased by 2.3% in 2013, with a total of 9.9 ± 0.5 GtC (billion tonnes of carbon) (36 $GtCO_2$) emitted to the atmosphere, 61% above 1990 emissions (the Kyoto Protocol reference year).

India and China are among the world's biggest contributors to fossil fuel emissions with India's carbon dioxide discharge increasing by a whopping ~ 6 per cent.

52. **Renewable Resources:** These are the resources that are replenished through rapid natural cycles. Common examples of such resources are:
    (*i*) Oxygen in the air, which is replenished through photosynthesis.
    (*ii*) Fresh water, which is replenished through the water cycle.
    (*iii*) All biological products (food, fishes, timber, etc.,) which are replenished through natural cycles of growth and reproduction.
    (*iv*) Solar energy is also considered as renewable as on a human time scale and it is inexhaustible. It is expected that sun will last at least 6.5 billion years.
    (*v*) Some other renewable resources that can be renewed (hours to several decades) through natural processes include forests, grassland grasses, wild animals, fishes, fresh air & water and fertile soil. However, potentially renewable resources can be depleted when resources utilization rate exceeds the natural replacement rate.

53. The Centre for Science and Environment (CSE), which has been demanding adoption of an **Air Quality Index** (AQI) for "an important step forward for building awareness and protecting public health".

    There are six AQI categories, namely: Good, Satisfactory, Moderately polluted, Poor, Very poor and Severe.

    The index considers eight pollutants — PM10, PM2.5, NO_2, SO_2, CO, O_3, NH_3 and Pb (CFC is not included). The likely health implications of the six categories would also be provided with a colour code. CSE said that with this step, India has joined the global league of countries like the US, China, Mexico and France that have implemented smog alert systems.

55. A **joint session** or **joint convention** is, most broadly, when two normally-separate decision-making groups meet together, often in a special session or other extraordinary meeting, for a specific purpose.

    Most often it refers to when both houses of a bicameral legislature sit together. A joint session typically occurs to receive foreign or domestic diplomats or leaders, or to allow both houses to consider bills together.

    In India, if a bill has been rejected by any house of the parliament and if more than six months have elapsed, the President may summon a joint session for purpose of passing the bill. The bill is passed by a simple majority of a joint sitting. Since the lower house (Lok Sabha) has more than twice the members of the upper house (Rajya Sabha), a group commanding a majority in the lower house of the Government of India can pass such a bill even if it was previously rejected by the upper house.

    So far, only three bills - the Dowry Prohibition Act, 1960, the Banking Service Commission Repeal Bill, 1977, and the Prevention of Terrorism Act, 2002 - have been passed at joint sessions.

56. The **Civil Services of India** refer to the civil service and the permanent bureaucracy of the Government of India. The civil service system is the backbone of the administrative machinery of the country.

    Every year, on the 21st of April, the "Civil Service Day" is observed by all Civil Services to re-dedicate and re-commit themselves to the cause of the people. It provides a unique opportunity for introspection as also chalking out future strategies to deal with the challenges being posed by the changing times.

57. **South Asian University** (SAU) is an International University sponsored by the eight

Member States of the South Asian Association for Regional Cooperation (SAARC). The eight countries are : Afghanistan, Bangladesh, Bhutan, India, Maldives, Nepal, Pakistan and Sri Lanka. South Asian University started admitting students in 2010, at a temporary campus at Akbar Bhawan, India. Its permanent campus will be at Maidan Garhi in South Delhi, India, next to Indira Gandhi National Open University (IGNOU). First academic session of the university started in August 2010 with two post-graduate academic programmes, in economics and computer sciences. As of 2014 SAU offered Master's and MPhil/PhD programs in applied mathematics, biotechnology, computer science, development economics, international relations, law and sociology. The degrees of the university are recognized by all the member nations of the SAARC according to an inter-governmental agreement signed by the foreign ministers of the 8 countries.

59. The UGC had chalked out several plans to increase gross enrolment ratio (GER) of students (in the age group of 18 to 22) in higher education. He was optimistic of increasing the GER from the present 19 per cent to 30 per cent by the end of the 12th Five Year Plan (2012-17). The enrolment of candidates for degree courses would be increased from the present 20 million to 29 million by the end of 12th Plan period. The number of students enrolled in distance education would go up from 4.6 million to 6.3 million by 2017.

60. A **Central University** or a **Union University** in India is established by Act of Parliament and are under the purview of the Department of Higher Education in the Union Human Resource Development Ministry. In general, universities in India are recognised by the University Grants Commission (UGC), which draws its power from the *University Grants Commission Act, 1956*. In addition, 15 Professional Councils are established, controlling different aspects of accreditation and coordination. Central universities, in addition, are covered by the *Central Universities Act, 2009*, which regulates their purpose, powers governance etc., and established 12 new universities.

The number of central universities published by the UGC includes 43 central universities as on April 2015.

Previous Years' Paper (Solved)

CBSE-NET (JRF) EXAM DECEMBER, 2014*

PAPER–I

Note : This paper contains **Sixty (60)** multiple choice questions, each question carrying **two (2)** marks. Candidate is expected to answer any **Fifty (50)** questions. In case more than **Fifty (50)** questions are attempted, only the first **Fifty (50)** questions will be evaluated.

1. Namita and Samita are brilliant and studious. Anita and Karabi are obedient and irregular. Babita and Namita are irregular but brilliant. Samita and Kabita are regular and obedient. Who among them is/are brilliant, obedient, regular and studious?

A. Samita alone B. Namita and Samita
C. Kabita alone D. Anita alone

2. Warrior is related to sword, carpenter is related to saw, farmer is related to plough. In the same way, the author is related to

A. Book B. Fame
C. Reader D. Pen

3. Given below is a diagram of three circles A, B and C over-lapping each other. The circle A represents the class of honest people, the circle B represents the class of sincere people and circle C represents the class of politicians. p, q, r, s, U, X, Y represent different regions. Select the code that represents the region indicating the class of honest politicians who are not sincere.

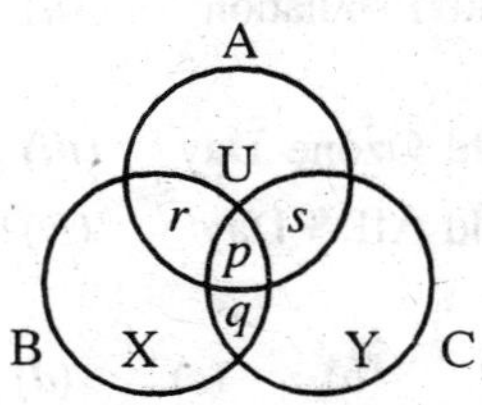

Codes:

A. X B. q
C. p D. s

4. "A man ought no more to value himself for being wiser than a woman if he owes his advantage to a better education, than he ought to boast of his courage for beating a man when his hands were tied."
The above passage is an instance of

A. Deductive argument
B. Hypothetical argument
C. Analogical argument
D. Factual argument

5. By which of the following proposition, the proposition 'wise men are hardly afraid of death' is contradicted?

A. Some wise men are afraid of death
B. All wise men are afraid of death
C. No wise men is afraid of death
D. Some wise men are not afraid of death

6. When in a group of propositions, one proposition is claimed to follow from the others, that group of propositions is called

A. An argument B. A valid argument
C. An explanation D. An invalid argument

Directions (Qs. 7 to 12): *For a country CO_2 emissions (million metric tons) from various sectors are given in the following table. Answer the questions based on the data given:*

CO_2 emissions (million metric tons)

Sector / Year	Power	Industry	Commercial	Agriculture	Domestic
2005	500	200	150	80	100
2006	600	300	200	90	110
2007	650	320	250	100	120
2008	700	400	300	150	150
2009	800	450	320	200	180

* Held on 28-12-2014

7. Which sector has recorded maximum growth in CO_2 emissions during 2005 to 2009?
A. Power
B. Industry
C. Commercial
D. Agriculture

8. By what percentage (%), the total emissions of CO_2 have increased from 2005 to 2009?
A. ~89.32%
B. ~57.62%
C. ~40.32%
D. ~113.12%

9. What is the average annual growth rate of CO_2 emissions in power sector?
A. ~12.57% B. ~16.87%
C. ~30.81% D. ~50.25%

10. What is the percentage contribution of power sector to total CO_2 emissions in the year 2008?
A. ~30.82% B. ~41.18%
C. ~51.38% D. ~60.25%

11. In which year, the contribution (%) of industry to total sectoral CO_2 emissions was minimum?
A. 2005 B. 2006
C. 2007 D. 2009

12. What is the percentage (%) growth of CO_2 emissions from power sector during 2005 to 2009?
A. 60 B. 50
C. 40 D. 80

13. Which one of the following is not a search engine?
A. Google B. Chrome
C. Yahoo D. Bing

14. CSS stands for
A. Cascading Style Sheets
B. Collecting Style Sheets
C. Comparative Style Sheets
D. Comprehensive Style Sheets

15. MOOC stands for
A. Media Online Open Course
B. Massachusetts Open Online Course
C. Massive Open Online Course
D. Myrind Open Online Course

16. Binary equivalent of decimal number 35 is
A. 100011 B. 110001
C. 110101 D. 101011

17. gif, jpg, bmp, png are used as extensions for files which store
A. audio data
B. image data
C. video data
D. text data

18. Symbols A-F are used in which one of the following?
A. Binary number system
B. Decimal number system
C. Hexadecimal number system
D. Octal number system

19. One of the anthropogenic sources of gaseous pollutants chlorofluorocarbons (CFCs) in air is
A. Cement industry
B. Fertiliser industry
C. Foam industry
D. Pesticide industry

20. In terms of total CO_2 emissions from a country, identify the correct sequence:
A. U.S.A. > China > India > Russia
B. China > U.S.A. > India > Russia
C. China > U.S.A. > Russia > India
D. U.S.A. > China > Russia > India

21. Match List-I and List-II and identify the correct code:

List-I	List-II
(*a*) World Health Day	(*i*) 16th September
(*b*) World Population Day	(*ii*) 1st December
(*c*) World Ozone Day	(*iii*) 11th July
(*d*) World AIDS Day	(*iv*) 7th April

Codes:

	(*a*)	(*b*)	(*c*)	(*d*)
A.	(*i*)	(*ii*)	(*iii*)	(*iv*)
B.	(*iv*)	(*iii*)	(*i*)	(*ii*)
C.	(*ii*)	(*iii*)	(*iv*)	(*i*)
D.	(*iii*)	(*iv*)	(*ii*)	(*i*)

22. Which of the anthropogenic activity accounts for more than $\frac{2}{3}$rd of global water consumption?
A. Agriculture
B. Hydropower generation
C. Industry
D. Domestic and Municipal usage

23. Which of the following is ***not*** a renewable natural resource?
A. Clean air B. Fresh water
C. Fertile soil D. Salt

24. The maximum number of fake institutions/ universities as identified by the UGC in the year 2014 are in the State/Union territory of
A. Bihar B. Uttar Pradesh
C. Tamil Nadu D. Delhi

25. Which of the following institutions are empowered to confer or grant degrees under the UGC Act, 1956?
1. A university established by an Act of Parliament.
2. A university established by an Act of Legislature.
3. A university/institution established by a linguistic minority.
4. An institution which is a deemed to be university.

Select the correct answer from the codes given below:
A. 1 and 2 B. 1, 2 and 3
C. 1, 2 and 4 D. 1, 2, 3 and 4

26. Which of the following are the tools of good governance?
1. Social Audit
2. Separation of Powers
3. Citizen's Charter
4. Right to Information

Select the correct answer from the codes given below:
A. 1, 3 and 4
B. 2, 3 and 4
C. 1 and 4
D. 1, 2, 3 and 4

27. The cyclone 'Hudhud' hit the coast of which State?
A. Andhra Pradesh
B. Karnataka
C. Kerala
D. Gujarat

28. The interval between two sessions of parliament must not exceed
A. 3 months B. 6 months
C. 4 months D. 100 days

29. Right to Privacy as a Fundamental Right is implied in
A. Right to Freedom
B. Right to Life and Personal Liberty
C. Right to Equality
D. Right against Exploitation

30. Which of the following organizations deals with 'capacity building program' on Educational Planning?
A. NCERT B. UGC
C. NAAC D. NUEPA

31. Which of the following powers, the President has in relation to Lok Sabha?
1. Summoning
2. Adjournment – sine die
3. Prorogation
4. Dissolution

Select the correct answer from the codes given below:
A. 1 and 4 B. 1, 2 and 3
C. 1, 3 and 4 D. 1, 2, 3 and 4

32. Which of the following is not a prescribed level of teaching?
A. Memory
B. Understanding
C. Reflective
D. Differentiation

33. Maximum participation of students during teaching is possible through
A. Lecture method
B. Demonstration method
C. Inductive method
D. Textbook method

34. Diagnostic evaluation ascertains
A. Students performance at the beginning of instructions
B. Learning progress and failures during instructions
C. Degree of achievement of instructions at the end
D. Causes and remedies of persistent learning problems during instructions

35. Instructional aids are used by the teacher to
A. glorify the class
B. attract the students
C. clarify the concepts
D. ensure discipline

36. Attitude of the teacher that affects teaching pertains to
A. Affective domain
B. Cognitive domain
C. Connative domain
D. Psychomotor domain

37. "Education is the manifestation of perfection already in man" was stated by
A. M.K. Gandhi
B. R.N. Tagore
C. Swami Vivekanand
D. Sri Aurobindo

38. When academicians are called to deliver lecture or presentation to an audience on certain topics or a set of topics of educational nature, it is called
A. Training Program B. Seminar
C. Workshop D. Symposium

39. The core elements of a dissertation are
A. Introduction; Data Collection; Data Analysis; Conclusions and Recommendations
B. Executive Summary; Literature review; Data gathered; Conclusions; Bibliography
C. Research Plan; Research Data; Analysis; References
D. Introduction; Literature Review; Research Methodology; Results; Discussion and Conclusion

40. What is a Research Design?
A. A way of conducting research that is not grounded in theory
B. The choice between using qualitative or quantitative methods
C. The style in which you present your research findings e.g. a graph
D. A framework for every stage of the collection and analysis of data

41. 'Sampling Cases' means
A. Sampling using a sampling frame
B. Identifying people who are suitable for research
C. Literally the researcher's brief case
D. Sampling of people, newspapers, television programmes etc.

42. The frequency distribution of a research data which is symmetrical in shape similar to a normal distribution but center peak is much higher, is
A. Skewed B. Mesokurtic
C. Leptokurtic D. Platykurtic

43. When planning to do as social research, it is better to
A. approach the topic with an open mind
B. do a pilot study before getting stuck into it
C. be familiar with literature on the topic
D. forget about theory because this is a very practical

44. In the classroom, the teacher sends the message either as words or images. The students are really
A. Encoders B. Decoders
C. Agitators D. Propagators

45. Media is known as
A. First Estate B. Second Estate
C. Third Estate D. Fourth Estate

46. The mode of communication that involves a single source transmitting information to a large number of receivers simultaneously, is called
A. Group Communication

B. Mass Communication
C. Intrapersonal Communication
D. Interpersonal Communication

47. A smart classroom is a teaching space which has
(*i*) Smart portion with a touch panel control system
(*ii*) PC/Laptop connection and DVD/VCR player
(*iii*) Document camera and specialized software
(*iv*) Projector and screen
Select the correct answer from the codes given below:
A. (*i*) and (*ii*) only
B. (*ii*) and (*iv*) only
C. (*i*), (*ii*) and (*iii*) only
D. (*i*), (*ii*), (*iii*) and (*iv*)

48. The term 'Yellow Journalism' refers to
A. sensational news about terrorism and violence
B. sensationalism and exaggeration to attract readers/viewers
C. sensational news about arts and culture
D. sensational news prints in yellow paper

49. The next term in the series:
2, 7, 28, 63, 126, ...
is
A. 215 B. 245
C. 276 D. 296

50. The next term in the series:
AB, ED, IH, NM, ...
is
A. TS B. ST
C. TU D. SU

51. If STREAMERS is coded as UVTGALDQR, then KNOWLEDGE will be coded as
A. MQPYLCDFD B. MPQYLDCFD
C. PMYQLDFCD D. YMQPLDDFC

52. A is brother of B. B is the brother of C. C is the husband of D. E is the father of A. D is related to E as
A. Daughter B. Daughter-in-law
C. Sister-in-law D. Sister

53. Two numbers are in the ratio 3 : 5. If 9 is subtracted from the numbers, the ratio becomes 12 : 23. The numbers are
A. 30, 50 B. 36, 60
C. 33, 55 D. 42, 70

54. The mean of the ages of father and his son is 27 years. After 18 years, father will be twice as old as his son. Their present ages are
A. 42, 12 B. 40, 14
C. 30, 24 D. 36, 18

55. Digital Empowerment means
(*i*) Universal digit literacy.
(*ii*) Universal access to all digital resources.
(*iii*) Collaborative digital platform for participative governance.
(*iv*) Probability of all entitlements for individuals through cloud.
Choose the correct answer from the codes given below:
A. (*i*) and (*ii*) only
B. (*ii*) and (*iii*) only
C. (*i*), (*ii*) and (*iii*) only
D. (*i*), (*ii*), (*iii*) and (*iv*)

Directions (Qs. 56 to 60): *Read the following passage carefully and answer questions.*

The literary distaste for politics, however, seems to be focused not so much on the largely murky practice of politics in itself as a subject of literary representation but rather more on how it is often depicted in literature, *i.e.*, on the very politics of such representation. A political novel often turns out to be not merely a novel about politics but a novel with a politics of its own, for it seeks not merely to show us how things are but has fairly definite ideas about how things should be, and precisely what one should think and do in order to make things move in that desired direction. In short, it seeks to convert and enlist the reader to a particular cause or ideology: it often is (in an only too familiar phrase) not literature but propaganda. This is said to violate the very spirit of literature which is to broaden our understanding of the world and the range of our sympathies rather than to narrow them down through partisan commitment. As John Keats said, 'We hate poetry that has a palpable design upon us'.

Another reason why politics does not seem amenable to the highest kind of literary representation seems to arise from the fact that politics by its very nature is constituted of ideas and ideologies. If political situations do not lend themselves to happy literary treatment, political ideas present perhaps an even greater problem in this regard. Literature, it is argued, is about human experiences rather than about intellectual abstractions; it deals in what is called the 'felt reality' of human flesh and blood, and in sap and savour (*rasa*) rather than in arid and lifeless ideas. In an extensive discussion of the matter in her book *Ideas and the Novel,* the American novelist Mary McCarthy observed that 'ideas are still today felt to be unsightly in the novel' though that was not so in 'former days', *i.e.*, in the 18th and 19th centuries. Her formulation of the precise nature of the incompatibility between ideas on the one hand and the novel no the other betrays perhaps a divided conscience in the matter and a sense of dilemma shared by many writers and readers: 'An idea cannot have loose ends, but a novel. I almost think, needs them. Nevertheless, there is enough in common for the novelists to feel .... the attraction of ideas while taking up arms against them – most often with weapons of mockery.'

56. A political novel reveals
A. Reality of the things
B. Writer's perception
C. Particular ideology of the readers
D. The spirit of literature

57. The constructs of politics by its nature is
A. Prevalent political situation
B. Ideas and Ideologies
C. Political propaganda
D. Understanding of human nature

58. Literature deals with
A. Human experiences in politics
B. Intellectual abstractions
C. Dry and empty ideas
D. Felt reality of human life

59. The observation of the novelist, Mary McCarthy reveals
A. unseen felt ideas of today in the novel
B. dichotomy of conscience on political ideas and novels
C. compatibility between idea and novel
D. endless ideas and novels

60. According to the passage, a political novel often turns out to be a
A. Literary distaste for politics
B. Literary representation of politics
C. Novel with its own politics
D. Depiction of murky practice of politics

ANSWERS

1	2	3	4	5	6	7	8	9	10
A	D	D	C	B	A	D	A	A	B
11	**12**	**13**	**14**	**15**	**16**	**17**	**18**	**19**	**20**
A	A	B	A	C	A	B	C	C	B
21	**22**	**23**	**24**	**25**	**26**	**27**	**28**	**29**	**30**
B	A	D	B	C	A	A	B	B	D
31	**32**	**33**	**34**	**35**	**36**	**37**	**38**	**39**	**40**
C	D	B	D	C	A	C	B	D	D
41	**42**	**43**	**44**	**45**	**46**	**47**	**48**	**49**	**50**
D	C	C	B	D	B	D	B	A	A
51	**52**	**53**	**54**	**55**	**56**	**57**	**58**	**59**	**60**
B	B	C	A	D	B	B	D	A	C

SOME SELECTED EXPLANATORY ANSWERS

3. Elements of A = u, r, p, s (honest)
Elements of B = x, r, p, q (sincere)
Elements of C = p, q, s, y (politician)
Hence (honest and politician but not sincere)
p, q, s are sincere.
$\therefore$ Required code is S which is in A and C.

7. Power 800 – 500 = 300

$$\% = \frac{300}{500} \times 100 = 60\%$$

Industry 450 – 200 = 250

$$\% = \frac{250}{200} \times 100 = 125\%$$

Commercial 320 – 150 = 170

$$\% = \frac{170}{150} \times 100$$

$$= \frac{340}{3} = 113\%$$

Agriculture 200 – 80 = 120

$$\% = \frac{120}{80} \times 100 = 150\%$$

Domestic 180 – 100 = 80

$$\% = \frac{80}{100} \times 100 = 80\%$$

Hence, maximum growth in CO_2 is Agriculture.

8. Total emissions of CO_2 in 2005
= 500 + 200 + 150 + 80 + 100
= 1030
Total emissions of CO_2 in 2009
= 800 + 450 + 320 + 200 + 180
= 1950
increased = 1950 – 1030 = 920

$$\% \text{ increased} = \frac{920}{1030} \times 100 = 89.32\%.$$

9. In power sector 2005 to 2006

$$= \frac{100}{500} \times 100 = 20\%$$

$$\text{In 2006 to 2007} = \frac{50}{600} \times 100 = 8.33\%$$

$$\text{In 2007 to 2008} = \frac{50}{650} \times 100 = 7.69\%$$

$$\text{In 2008 to 2009} = \frac{100}{700} \times 100 = 14.28\%$$

Average Annual growth rate

$$= \frac{50.30}{4} = 12.57\%.$$

10. Required % in 2008 $= \frac{700}{1700} \times 100$

$$= \frac{700}{17} = 41.18\%.$$

11. Required year = 2005.

12. Growth of CO_2 from power sector during 2005 to 2009
= 800 – 500 = 300

$$\% \text{ growth} = \frac{300}{500} \times 100 = 60\%.$$

49. 2 7 28 63 126 215

7	28	63	126	215
↓	↓	↓	↓	↓
$2^3 - 1$	$3^3 - 1$	$4^3 - 1$	$5^3 - 1$	$6^3 - 1$

Hence, the next term in the series will be 215.

53. Let the numbers are $3x$ and $5x$
According to the question,

$$\frac{3x-9}{5x-9} = \frac{12}{23}$$

$\Rightarrow$ $69x - 207 = 60x - 108$
$\Rightarrow$ $9x = 99$
$\Rightarrow$ $x = 11$
$\therefore$ Numbers are 33 and 55.

54. Let present age of father = x years
and present age of son = y years

$$x + y = 2 \times 27 = 54$$

$$\Rightarrow \quad x = 54 - y$$

After 18 years, father's age = $(x + 18)$ years
After 18 years, son's age = $(y + 18)$ years
According to the question,

$$x + 18 = 2(y + 18)$$

$$\Rightarrow \quad x + 18 = 2y + 36$$

$$\Rightarrow \quad x - 2y = 18$$

$$\Rightarrow \quad 54 - y - 2y = 18$$

$$\Rightarrow \quad -3y = -36$$

$$\Rightarrow \quad y = 12$$

$$x = 54 - 12 = 42$$

Hence, present age of father
= 42 years
and present age of son
= 12 years.

16. Remainder

$$35 \div 2 = 17 + 1$$

$$17 \div 2 = 8 + 1$$

$$8 \div 2 = 4 + 0$$

$$4 \div 2 = 2 + 0$$

$$2 \div 2 = 1 + 0$$

$$1 \div 2 = 0 + 1$$

$$\therefore \quad 35 = 100011$$

Hence, binary equivalent of decimal number
35 = 100011.

Previous Years' Paper (Solved)

UGC-NET (JRF) EXAM JUNE, 2014*

PAPER–I

Note : This paper contains **Sixty (60)** multiple-choice questions, each question carrying **two (2)** marks. Candidate is expected to answer any **fifty (50)** questions. In case more than **fifty (50)** questions are attempted, only the first **fifty (50)** questions will be evaluated.

1. "If a large diamond is cut up into little bits, it will lose its value just as an army is divided up into small units of soldiers, it loses its strength."
The argument put above may be called as
A. Analogical B. Deductive
C. Statistical D. Causal

2. Given below are some characteristics of logical argument. Select the code which expresses a characteristic which is not of inductive in character.
A. The conclusion is claimed to follow from its premises.
B. The conclusion is based on causal relation.
C. The conclusion conclusively follows from its premises.
D. The conclusion is based on observation and experiment.

3. If two propositions having the same subject and predicate terms can both be true but can not both be false, the relation between those two propositions is called
A. contradictory B. contrary
C. subcontrary D. subaltern

4. One writes all numbers from 50 to 99 without the digits 2 and 7. How many numbers have been written?
A. 32 B. 36
C. 40 D. 38

5. Given below is a diagram of three circles A, B and C enter-related with each other. The circle A represents the class of Indians, the circle B represents the class of scientists and circle C represents the class of politicians. p, q, r, s ... represent different regions. Select the code containing the region that indicates the class of Indian scientists who are not politicians.

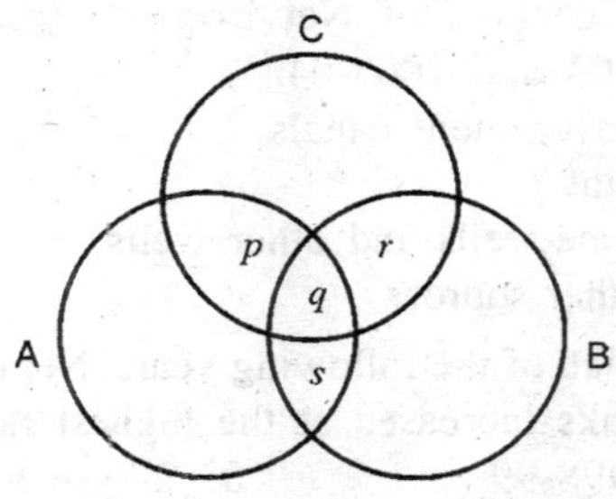

Codes :
A. q and s only B. s only
C. s and r only D. p, q and s only

6. Given below are two premises and four conclusions drawn from those premises. Select the code that expresses conclusion drawn validly from the premises (separately or jointly).

Premises :
(*a*) All dogs are mammals
(*b*) No cats are dogs

Conclusions :
(*i*) No cats are mammals
(*ii*) Some cats are mammals
(*iii*) No dogs are cats
(*iv*) No dogs are non-mammals

Codes :
A. (*i*) only B. (*i*) and (*ii*)
C. (*iii*) and (*iv*) D. (*ii*) and (*iii*)

* Held on 29-06-2014

Read the following table carefully. Based upon this table answer questions from 7 to 11 :

Net area under irrigation by sources in a country

(in Thousand Hectares)

Year	Government canals	Private canals	Tanks	Tube-wells & other wells	Other Sources	Total
1997-98	17117	211	2593	32090	3102	55173
1998-99	17093	212	2792	33988	3326	57411
1999-00	16842	194	2535	34623	2915	57109
2000-01	15748	203	2449	33796	2880	55076
2001-02	15031	209	2179	34906	4347	56672
2002-03	13863	206	1802	34250	3657	53778
2003-04	14444	206	1908	35779	4281	56618
2004-05	14696	206	1727	34785	7453	58867
2005-06	15268	207	2034	35372	7314	60196

7. Find out the source of Irrigation that has registered the maximum improvement in terms of percentage of Net irrigated area during 2002-03 and 2003-04.

A. Government canals
B. Tanks
C. Tube-wells and other wells
D. Other sources

8. In which of the following years, Net irrigation by tanks increased at the highest rate?

A. 1998-99 B. 2000-01
C. 2003-04 D. 2005-06

9. Identify the source of Irrigation that has recorded the maximum incidence of negative growth in terms of Net irrigated area during the years given in the table.

A. Government canals
B. Private canals
C. Tube-wells and other wells
D. Other sources

10. In which of the following years, share of the tube-wells and other wells in the total net irrigated area was the highest?

A. 1998-99 B. 2000-01
C. 2002-03 D. 2004-05

11. Which of the following sources of Irrigation has registered the largest percentage of decline in Net area under irrigation during 1997-98 and 2005-06?

A. Government canals
B. Private canals
C. Tanks
D. Other sources

12. Which one of the following is not a/an image/graphic file format?

A. PNG B. GIF
C. BMP D. GUI

13. The first web browser is

A. Internet Explorer B. Netscape
C. World Wide Web D. Firefox

14. When a computer is booting, BIOS is loaded to the memory by

A. RAM B. ROM
C. CD-ROM D. TCP

15. Which one of the following is not the same as the other three?

A. MAC address B. Hardware address
C. Physical address D. IP address

16. Identify the IP address from the following:

A. 300 · 215 · 317 · 3
B. 302 · 215 @ 417 · 5
C. 202 · 50 · 20 · 148
D. 202 - 50 - 20 - 148

17. The acronym FIP stands for

A. File Transfer Protocol
B. Fast Transfer Protocol
C. File Tracking Protocol
D. File Transfer Procedure

18. Which of the following cities has been worst affected by urban smog in recent times?

A. Paris B. London
C. Los Angeles D. Beijing

19. The primary source of organic pollution in fresh water bodies is

A. run-off urban areas
B. run-off from agricultural forms
C. sewage effluents
D. industrial effluents

20. 'Lahar' is a natural disaster involving

A. eruption of large amount of material
B. strong winds
C. strong water waves
D. strong winds and water waves

21. The population of India is about 1.2 billion. Take the average consumption of energy per person per year in India as 30 Mega Joules. If this consumption is met by carbon based fuels and the rate of carbon emissions per kilojoule is 15 × 106 kgs, the total carbon emissions per year from India will be

A. 54 million metric tons
B. 540 million metric tons
C. 5400 million metric tons
D. 2400 million metric tons

22. The National Disaster Management Authority functions under the Union Ministry of

A. Environment
B. Water Resources
C. Home Affairs
D. Defence

23. Match List-I and List-II and select the correct answer from the codes given below:

List-I	***List-II***
(*a*) Flood	1. Lack of rainfall of sufficient duration
(*b*) Drought	2. Tremors produced by the passage of vibratory waves through the rocks of the earth
(*c*) Earthquake	3. A vent through which molted substances come out
(*d*) Volcano	4. Excess rain and uneven distribution of water

Codes :

	(*a*)	(*b*)	(*c*)	(*d*)
A.	4	1	2	3
B.	2	3	4	1
C.	3	4	2	1
D.	4	3	1	2

24. Which one of the following greenhouse gases has the shortest residence time in the atmosphere?

A. Chlorofluorocarbon
B. Carbon dioxide
C. Methane
D. Nitrous oxide

25. In order to avoid catastrophic consequences of climate change, there is general agreement among the countries of the world to limit the rise in average surface temperature of earth compared to that of pre-industrial times by

A. 1.5 °C to 2 °C
B. 2.0 °C to 3.5 °C
C. 0.5 °C to 1.0 °C
D. 0.25 °C to 0.5 °C

26. Who among the following is the de facto executive head of the Planning Commission?

A. Chairman
B. Deputy Chairman
C. Minister of State for Planning
D. Member Secretary

27. Education as a subject of legislation figures in the

A. Union List B. State List
C. Concurrent List D. Residuary Powers

28. Which of the following are Central Universities?

1. Pondicherry University
2. Vishwa Bharati
3. H.N.B. Garhwal University
4. Kurukshetra University

Select the correct answer from the code given below:

Codes:

A. 1, 2 and 3 B. 1, 3 and 4
C. 2, 3 and 4 D. 1, 2 and 4

29. Consider the following statements and select the correct answer from the code given below:

(*i*) Rajasthan receives the highest solar radiation in the country.
(*ii*) India has the fifth largest installed wind power in the world.
(*iii*) The maximum amount of wind power is contributed by Tamil Nadu.
(*iv*) The primary source of uranium in India is Jaduguda.

Codes :

A. (*i*) and (*ii*) B. (*i*), (*ii*) and (*iii*)
C. (*ii*) and (*iii*) D. (*i*) and (*iv*)

30. Which of the following universities has adopted the meta university concept?
A. Assam University
B. Delhi University
C. Hyderabad University
D. Pondicherry University

31. Which of the following statements are correct about a Central University?
1. Central University is established under an Act of Parliament
2. The President of India acts as the visitor of the University.
3. The President has the power to nominate some members to the Executive Committee or the Board of Management of the University.
4. The President occasionally presides over the meetings of the Executive Committee or Court.

Select the correct answer from the code given below:
A. 1, 2 and 4 B. 1, 3 and 4
C. 1, 2 and 3 B. 1, 2, 3 and 4

32. Consider the statement which is followed by two arguments (*i*) and (*ii*).
Statement : India should have a very strong and powerful Lokpal.
Arguments : (*i*) Yes, it will go a long in eliminating corruption in bureaucracy.
(*ii*) No, it will discourage honest officers from making quick decisions.

Codes:
A. Only argument (*i*) is strong.
B. Only argument (*ii*) is strong.
C. Both the arguments are strong.
D. Neither of the arguments is strong.

33. Which one of the following is the best method of teaching?
A. Lecture B. Discussion
C. Demonstration D. Narration

34. Dyslexia is associated with
A. mental disorder
B. behavioural disorder
C. reading disorder
D. writing disorder

35. The e-content generation for under-graduate courses has been assigned by the Ministry of Human Resource Development to
A. INFLIBNET
B. Consortium for Educational Communication.
C. National Knowledge Commission
D. Indira Gandhi National Open University

36. Classroom communication is normally considered as
A. effective B. cognitive
C. affective D. selective

37. Which one of the following is considered a sign of motivated teaching?
A. Students asking questions
B. Maximum attendance of the students
C. Pin drop silence in the classroom
D. Students taking notes

38. In a thesis, figures and tables are included in
A. the appendix
B. a separate chapter
C. the concluding chapter
D. the text itself

39. A thesis statement is
A. an observation B. a fact
C. an assertion D. a discussion

40. The research approach of Max Weber to understand how people create meanings in natural settings is identified as
A. positive paradigm
B. critical paradigm
C. natural paradigm
D. interpretative paradigm

41. Which one of the following is a non-probability sampling?
A. Simple random B. Purposive
C. Systematic D. Stratified

42. Identify the category of evaluation that assesses the learning progress to provide continuous feedback to the students during instruction.
A. Placement B. Diagnostic
C. Formative D. Summative

43. The research stream of immediate application is

A. Conceptual research
B. Action research
C. Fundamental research
D. Empirical research

44. Who among the following, propounded the concept of paradigm?

A. Peter Haggett B. Von Thunen
C. Thomas Kuhn D. John K. Wright

Read the following passage carefully and answer questions 45 to 49:

Traditional Indian Values must be viewed both from the angle of the individual and from that of the geographically delimited agglomeration of peoples or groups enjoying a common system of leadership which we call the 'State'. The Indian 'State's' special feature is the peaceful, or perhaps mostly peaceful, co-existence of social groups of various historical provenances which mutually adhere in a geographical, economic, and political sense, without ever assimilating to each other in social terms, in ways of thinking, or even in language. Modern Indian law will determine certain rules, especially in relation to the regime of the family, upon the basis of how the loin-cloth is tied, or how the turban is worn, for this may identify the litigants as members of a regional group, and therefore as participants in its traditional law, though their ancestors left the region three or four centuries earlier. The use of the word 'State' above must not mislead us. There was no such thing as a conflict between the individual and the State, atleast before foreign governments became established, just as there was no concept of state 'sovereignty' or of any church-and-state dichotomy.

Modern Indian 'secularism' has an admittedly peculiar feature : It requires the state to make a fair distribution of attention and support amongst all religions. These blessed aspects of India's famed tolerance (Indian kings so rarely persecuted religious groups that the exceptions prove the rule) at once struck Portuguese and other European visitors to the West Coast of India in the sixteenth century, and the impression made upon them in this and other ways gave rise, at one remove, to the basic constitution of Thomas More's Utopia. There is little about modern India that strikes one at once as Utopian : but the insistence upon the inculcation of norms, and the absence of bigotry and institutionalized exploitation of human or natural resources, are two very different features which link the realities of India and her tradition with the essence of all Utopians.

45. The author uses the world 'State' to highlight.

A. Antagonistic relationship between the state and the individual throughout the period of history.
B. Absence of conflict between the state and the individuals upto a point in time.
C. The concept of state sovereignty.
D. Dependence on religion.

46. Which one is the peculiar feature of modern Indian 'Secularism'?

A. No discrimination on religious considerations
B. Total indifference to religion.
C. No space for social identity
D. Disregard for social law

47. The basic construction of Thomas More's Utopia was inspired by

A. Indian tradition of religious tolerance.
B. Persecution of religious groups by Indian rulers.
C. Social inequality in India.
D. European perception of Indian State.

48. What is the striking feature of modern India?

A. A replica of Utopian State
B. Uniform laws
C. Adherence to traditional values
D. Absence of Bigotry

49. Which of the following is a special feature of the Indian State?

A. Peaceful co-existence of people under a common system of leadership.
B. Peaceful co-existence of social groups of different historical provenances attached to each other in a geographical, economic and political sense.
C. Social integration of all groups.
D. Cultural assimilation of all social groups.

50. The Telephone Model of Communication was first developed in the area of
A. Technological theory
B. Dispersion theory
C. Minimal effects theory
D. Information theory

51. The Dada Saheb Phalke Award for 2013 has been conferred on
A. Karan Johar B. Amir Khan
C. Asha Bhonsle D. Gulzar

52. Photographs are not easy to
A. publish B. secure
C. decode D. change

53. The grains that appear on a television set when operated are also referred to as
A. sparks B. green dots
C. snow D. rain drops

54. In circular communication, the encoder becomes a decoder when there is
A. noise B. audience
C. criticality D. feedback

55. Break-down in verbal communication is described as
A. Short circuit B. Contradiction
C. Unevenness D. Entropy

56. In certain coding method, the word QUESTION is encoded as DOMESTIC. In this coding, what is the code word for the word RESPONSE?
A. OMESUCEM B. OMESICSM
C. OMESICEM D. OMESISCM

57. If the series, 4, 5, 8, 13, 14, 17, 22, ... is continued in the same pattern, which one of the following is not a term of this series?
A. 31 B. 32
C. 33 D. 35

58. Complete the series BB, FE, II, ML, PP, ... by choosing one of the following option given:
A. TS B. ST
C. RS D. SR

59. A man started walking from his house towards south. After walking 6 km, he turned to his left and walked 5 km. Then he walked further 3 km after turning left. He then turned to his left and continued his walk for 9 km. How far is he away from his house?
A. 3 km B. 4 km
C. 5 km D. 6 km

60. In a post-office, stamps of three different denominations of ₹ 7, ₹ 8, ₹ 10 are available. The exact amount for which one cannot buy stamps is
A. 19 B. 20
C. 23 D. 29

ANSWERS

1	2	3	4	5	6	7	8	9	10
A	C	C	A	B	C	D	D	A	C
11	**12**	**13**	**14**	**15**	**16**	**17**	**18**	**19**	**20**
C	D	C	B	D	C	A	D	C	A
21	**22**	**23**	**24**	**25**	**26**	**27**	**28**	**29**	**30**
*	C	A	C	A	B	C	A	D	B
31	**32**	**33**	**34**	**35**	**36**	**37**	**38**	**39**	**40**
C	A	C	C	B	B	A	D	C	D
41	**42**	**43**	**44**	**45**	**46**	**47**	**48**	**49**	**50**
B	C	B	C	B	A	A	D	B	D
51	**52**	**53**	**54**	**55**	**56**	**57**	**58**	**59**	**60**
D	C	C	D	D	C	C	A	C	A

SOME SELECTED EXPLANATORY ANSWERS

4. 50 51 (52) 53 54 55 56 (57) 58 59

60 61 (62) 63 64 65 66 (67) 68 69

(70) (71) (72) (73) (74) (75) (76) (77) (78) (79)

80 81 (82) 83 84 85 86 (87) 88 89

90 91 (92) 93 94 95 96 (97) 98 99

$\therefore$ 50 − 18 = 32

He has written 32 numbers.

5.

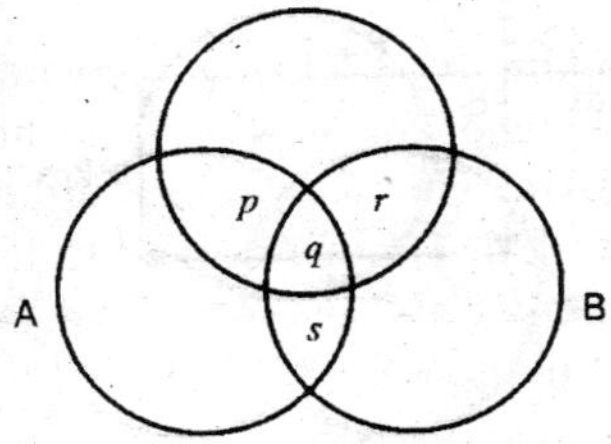

⊙ A represents – Indians

⊙ B represents – Scientists

⊙ C represents – Politicians

p, *q*, *r*, *s*.... represents different regions

Required code is (B) *s* only.

6.

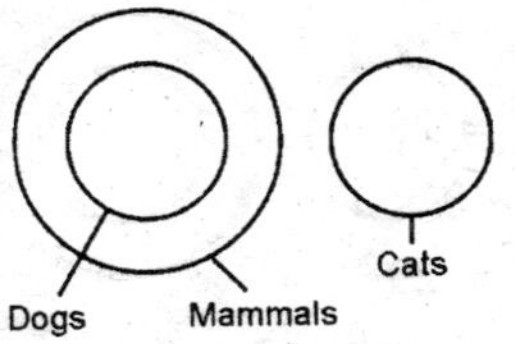

or

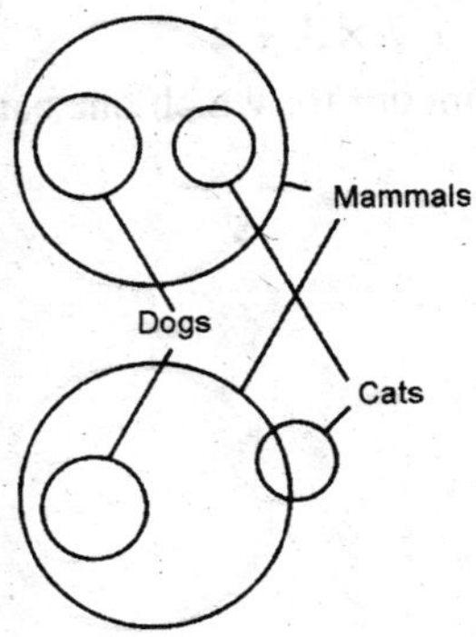

As from premise-II,

No cats are dogs,

So, No dogs are cats.

Again from premise-I

All dogs are mammals

So, No dogs are non-mammals.

7. A. Government canals

= 14444 − 13863 = 581

$$\% = \frac{581}{13863} \times 100 = \frac{58100}{13863} = 4\%$$

B. Tanks = 1908 − 1802 = 106

$$\% = \frac{106}{1802} \times 100 = \frac{10600}{1802} = 5.9\%$$

C. Tube-wells and other wells

= 35779 − 34250 = 1529

$$\% = \frac{1529}{34250} \times 100 = \frac{152900}{34250} = 4\%$$

D. Other sources

= 4281 − 3657 = 624

$$\% = \frac{624}{3657} \times 100 = \frac{62400}{3657} = 17\%$$

Clearly (D) gives maximum.

Hence, correct answer is (D).

8. A. 1998-99 ⇒ 2792 − 2593 = 199

$$\% = \frac{199}{2593} \times 100 = \frac{19900}{2593} = 7\%$$

B. 2000-01 ⇒ 2449 − 2535 = −86

negative sign shows not increase.

C. 2003-04 ⇒ 1908 − 1802 = 106

$$\% = \frac{106}{1802} \times 100 = \frac{10600}{1802} = 5.8\%$$

D. 2005-06 ⇒ 2034 − 1727 = 307

$$\% = \frac{307}{1727} \times 100 = \frac{30700}{1727} = 17\%$$

Hence, 2005-06 net irrigation by tanks increases at the highest rate.

9. Required answer is (A) Government canals.

10. Required year is 2002-03.

11. Required Sources of irrigation is Government canals.

16. The correct format to write IP address is to use dots between each set of digits.

17. FTP stands for file transfer protocol and is a method by which you can transfer files from one computer to another.

18. Beijing along with Tianjin and Hebei province & central and western Shandong province is affected by the worst urban smog in recent times. Bejing has a four-tier alert system, using blue, yellow, orrange and red to indicate the air pollution level. A red alert indicates the most serious air pollution (AQI above 300) for 3 consecutive days. An orange alert indicates heavy to serious air pollution (AQI between 200 and 300) alternately for 3 consecutive days. A yellow alert means severe pollution for 1 day or heavy pollution for 3 consecutive days.

19. The main source of freshwater pollution can be attributed to discharge of untreated waste mainly sewage effluents.

20. Lahar is a natural disaster that involves eruption of large amount of material from volcano. The material flows down from a volcano, typically along a river valley is known as lahar.

56. Q U E S T I O N

↓ ↓ ↓ ↓ ↓ ↓ ↓ ↓

D O M E S T I C

Similarly,

R E S P O N S E

↓ ↓ ↓ ↓ ↓ ↓ ↓ ↓

O M E S I C E M

57.

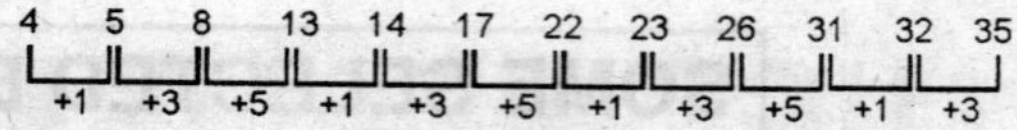

Hence, 33 is not a term of this Series.

58.

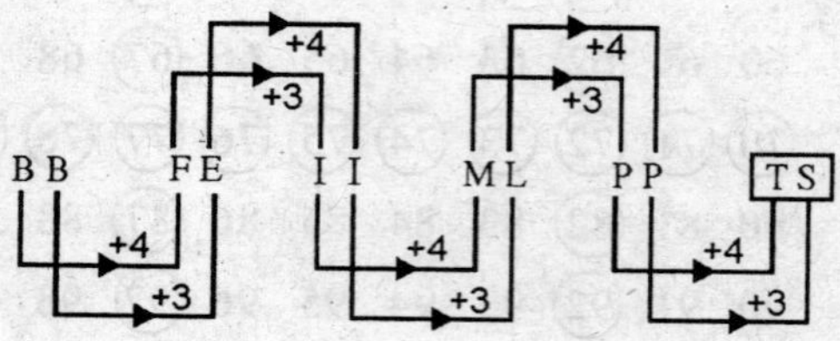

59.

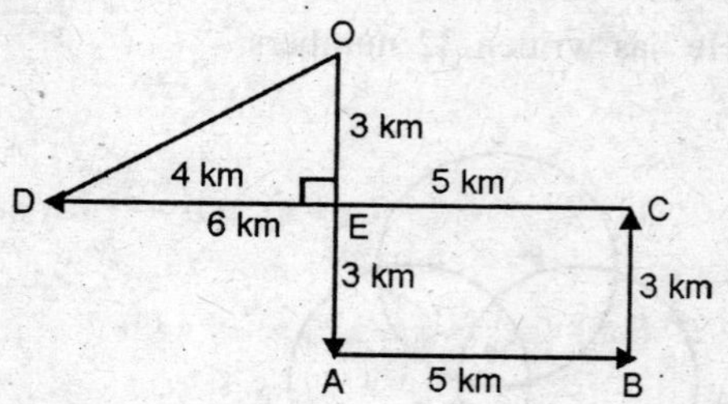

In ΔOED,

$$(OD)^2 = (4)^2 + (3)^2$$

$$= 16 + 9 = 25$$

$$\therefore \quad OD = \sqrt{25} = 5 \text{ km}.$$

Hence, he is 5 km away from his house.

60. B. $20 = 10 \times 2 = 20$

C. $23 = 8 \times 2 + 7 \times 1$

$= 16 + 7 = 23$

D. $29 = 7 \times 3 + 8 \times 1$

$= 21 + 8 = 29$

A. $19 = 7 \times 2 + 5 = 8 \times 2 + 3$

$= 10 \times 1 + 8 \times 1 + 1$

$= 10 \times 1 + 7 \times 1 + 2$

Hence, the exact amount for which one can not buy stamps is 19.

Previous Years' Paper (Solved)

UGC-NET (JRF) EXAM DECEMBER, 2013

PAPER–I

Note: *This paper contains* ***Sixty (60)*** *multiple choice questions, each question carrying* ***two (2)*** *marks. Attempt any* ***Fifty (50)*** *questions.*

1. Which is the main objective of research ?
A. To review the literature
B. To summarize what is already known
C. To get an academic degree
D. To discover new facts or to make fresh interpretation of known facts

2. Sampling error decreases with the
A. decrease in sample size
B. increase in sample size
C. process of randomization
D. process of analysis

3. The principles of fundamental research are used in
A. action research
B. applied research
C. philosophical research
D. historical research

4. Users who use media for their own ends are identified as
A. Passive audience
B. Active audience
C. Positive audience
D. Negative audience

5. Classroom communication can be described as
A. Exploration
B. Institutionalisation
C. Unsignified narration
D. Discourse

6. Ideological codes shape our collective
A. Productions B. Perceptions
C. Consumptions D. Creations

7. In communication, myths have power, but are
A. uncultural. B. insignificant.
C. imprecise. D. unpreferred.

8. The first multi-lingual news agency of India was
A. Samachar
B. API
C. Hindustan Samachar
D. Samachar Bharati

9. Organisational communication can also be equated with
A. intra-personal communication.
B. inter-personal communication.
C. group communication.
D. mass communication.

10. If two propositions having the same subject and predicate terms are such that one is the denial of the other, the relationship between them is called
A. Contradictory B. Contrary
C. Sub-contrary D. Sub-alternation

11. Ananya and Krishna can speak and follow English. Bulbul can write and speak Hindi as Archana does. Archana talks with Ananya also in Bengali. Krishna can not follow Bengali. Bulbul talks with Ananya in Hindi. Who can speak and follow English, Hindi and Bengali?
A. Archana B. Bulbul
C. Ananya D. Krishna

12. A stipulative definition may be said to be
A. Always true
B. Always false
C. Sometimes true, sometimes false
D. Neither true nor false

13. When the conclusion of an argument follows from its premise/premises conclusively, the argument is called
A. Circular argument
B. Inductive argument
C. Deductive argument
D. Analogical argument

14. Saturn and Mars are planets like the earth. They borrow light from the Sun and moves around the Sun as the Earth does. So those planets are inhabited by various orders of creatures as the earth is. What type of argument is contained in the above passage ?
A. Deductive B. Astrological
C. Analogical D. Mathematical

15. Given below are two premises. Four conclusions are drawn from those two premises in four codes. Select the code that states the conclusion validly drawn.
Premises:
(*i*) All saints are religious. (major)
(*ii*) Some honest persons are saints. (minor)
Codes:
A. All saints are honest.
B. Some saints are honest.
C. Some honest persons are religious.
D. All religious persons are honest.

Following table provides details about the Foreign Tourist Arrivals (FTAs) in India from different regions of the world in different years. Study the table carefully and answer questions from 16 to 19 based on this table.

Region	Number of Foreign Tourist Arrivals		
	2007	2008	2009
Western Europe	1686083	1799525	1610086
North America	1007276	1027297	1024469
South Asia	982428	1051846	982633
South East Asia	303475	332925	348495
East Asia	352037	355230	318292
West Asia	171661	215542	201110
Total FTAs in India	5081504	5282603	5108579

16. Find out the region that contributed around 20 per cent of the total foreign tourist arrivals in India in 2009.
A. Western Europe B. North America
C. South Asia D. South East Asia

17. Which of the following regions has recorded the highest negative growth rate of foreign tourist arrivals in India in 2009?
A. Western Europe B. North America
C. South Asia D. West Asia

18. Find out the region that has been showing declining trend in terms of share of foreign tourist arrivals in India in 2008 and 2009.
A. Western Europe B. South East Asia
C. East Asia D. West Asia

19. Identify the region that has shown hyper growth rate of foreign tourist arrivals than the growth rate of the total FTAs in India in 2008.
A. Western Europe B. North America
C. South Asia D. East Asia

20. The post-industrial society is designated as
A. Information society
B. Technology society
C. Mediated society
D. Non-agricultural society

21. The initial efforts for internet based communication was for
A. Commercial communication
B. Military purposes
C. Personal interaction
D. Political campaigns

22. Internal communication within institutions is done through
A. LAN B. WAN
C. EBB D. MMS

23. Virtual reality provides
A. Sharp pictures
B. Individual audio
C. Participatory experience
D. Preview of new films

24. The first virtual university of India came up in
A. Andhra Pradesh B. Maharashtra
C. Uttar Pradesh D. Tamil Nadu

25. Arrange the following books in chronological order in which they appeared. Use the code given below :

(*i*) Limits to Growth
(*ii*) Silent Spring
(*iii*) Our Common Future
(*iv*) Resourceful Earth

Codes:

A. (*i*), (*iii*), (*iv*), (*ii*)
B. (*ii*), (*iii*), (*i*), (*iv*)
C. (*ii*), (*i*), (*iii*), (*iv*)
D. (*i*), (*ii*), (*iii*), (*iv*)

26. Which one of the following continents is at a greater risk of desertification?

A. Africa B. Asia
C. South America D. North America

27. "Women are closer to nature than men." What kind of perspective is this?

A. Realist B. Essentialist
C. Feminist D. Deep ecology

28. Which one of the following is not a matter a global concern in the removal of tropical forests?

A. Their ability to absorb the chemicals that contribute to depletion of ozone layer.
B. Their role in maintaining the oxygen and carbon balance of the earth.
C. Their ability to regulate surface and air temperatures, moisture content and reflectivity.
D. Their contribution to the biological diversity of the planet.

29. The most comprehensive approach to address the problems of man-environment interaction is one of the following:

A. Natural Resource Conservation Approach
B. Urban-industrial Growth Oriented Approach
C. Rural-agricultural Growth Oriented Approach
D. Watershed Development Approach

30. The major source of the pollutant gas, carbon mono-oxide (CO), in urban areas is

A. Thermal power sector
B. Transport sector
C. Industrial sector
D. Domestic sector

31. In a fuel cell driven vehicle, the energy is obtained from the combustion of

A. Methane B. Hydrogen
C. LPG D. CNG

32. Which one of the following Councils has been disbanded in 2013?

A. Distance Education Council (DEC)
B. National Council for Teacher Education (NCTE)
C. National Council of Educational Research and Training (NCERT)
D. National Assessment and Accreditation Council (NAAC)

33. Which of the following statements are correct about the National Assessment and Accreditation Council?

1. It is an autonomous institution.
2. It is tasked with the responsibility of assessing and accrediting institutions of higher education.
3. It is located in Delhi.
4. It has regional offices.

Select the correct answer from the codes given below:

Codes:

A. 1 and 3 B. 1 and 2
C. 1, 2 and 4 D. 2, 3 and 4

34. The power of the Supreme Court of India to decide disputes between two or more States falls under its

A. Advisory Jurisdiction
B. Appellate Jurisdiction
C. Original Jurisdiction
D. Writ Jurisdiction

35. Which of the following statements are correct?

1. There are seven Union Territories in India.
2. Two Union Territories have Legislative Assemblies
3. One Union Territory has a High Court.
4. One Union Territory is the capital of two States.

Select the correct answer from the codes given below :

A. 1 and 3 only B. 2 and 4 only
C. 2, 3 and 4 only D. 1, 2, 3 and 4

36. Which of the following statements are correct about the Central Information Commission?

1. The Central Information Commission is a statutory body.
2. The Chief Information Commissioner and other Information Commissioners are appointed by the President of India.
3. The Commission can impose a penalty upto a maximum of ₹ 25,000/-
4. It can punish an errant officer.

Select the correct answer from the codes given below:

Codes:

A. 1 and 2 only B. 1, 2 and 4
C. 1, 2 and 3 D. 2, 3 and 4

37. Who among the following conducted the CNN-IBN – The Hindu 2013 Election Tracker Survey across 267 constituencies in 18 States?

A. The Centre for the Study of Developing Societies (CSDS)
B. The Association for Democratic Reforms (ADR)
C. CNN and IBN
D. CNN, IBN and The Hindu

38. In certain code TEACHER is written as VGCEJGT. The code of CHILDREN will be

A. EKNJFTGP B. EJKNFTGP
C. KNJFGTP D. None of these

39. A person has to buy both apples and mangoes. The cost of one apple is ₹ 7/- whereas that of a mango is ₹ 5/-. If the person has ₹ 38, the number of apples he can buy is

A. 1 B. 2
C. 3 D. 4

40. A man pointing to a lady said, "The son of her only brother is the brother of my wife". The lady is related to the man as

A. Mother's sister
B. Grand mother
C. Mother-in-law
D. Sister of Father-in-law

41. In this series
6, 4, 1, 2, 2, 8, 7, 4, 2, 1, 5, 3, 8, 6, 2, 2, 7, 1, 4, 1, 3, 5, 8, 6,
how many pairs of successive numbers have a difference of 2 each ?

A. 4 B. 5
C. 6 D. 8

42. The mean marks obtained by a class of 40 students is 65. The mean marks of half of the students is found to be 45. The mean marks of the remaining students is

A. 85 B. 60
C. 70 D. 65

43. Anil is twice as old as Sunita. Three years ago, he was three times as old as Sunita. The present age of Anil is

A. 6 years B. 8 years
C. 12 years D. 16 years

44. Which of the following is a social network?

A. amazon.com B. eBay
C. gmail.com D. Twitter

45. The population information is called parameter while the corresponding sample information is known as

A. Universe B. Inference
C. Sampling design D. Statistics

Read the following passage carefully and answer questions 46 to 51 :

Heritage conservation practices improved worldwide after the International Centre for the Study of the Preservation and Restoration of Cultural Property (ICCROM) was established with UNESCO's assistance in 1959. The inter-governmental organisation with 126 member states has done a commendable job by training more than 4,000 professionals, providing practice standards, and sharing technical expertise. In this golden jubilee year, as we acknowledge its key role in global conservation, an assessment of international practices would be meaningful to the Indian conservation movement. Consistent investment, rigorous attention, and dedicated research and dissemination are some of the positive lessons to imbibe. Countries such as Italy have demonstrated that prioritising heritage with significant budget provision pays. On the other hand, India, which is no less endowed in terms of cultural capital, has a long way to go. Surveys indicate that in addition to the 6,600 protected monuments, there are over 60,000 equally valuable heritage structures that await attention. Besides the small group in the service of Archaeological Survey of India, there are only about 150 trained conservation professionals. In order to overcome this severe shortage the emphasis has been on setting up dedicated labs and training institutions. It would make much better sense for conservation to be made part of mainstream research and engineering institutes, as has been done in Europe. Increasing funding and building institutions are the relatively easy part. The real challenge is to redefine international approaches to address local contexts. Conservation cannot limit itself to enhancing the art-historical value of the heritage structures, which international charters perhaps overemphasise. The effort has to be broad-based : It must also serve as a means to improving the quality of life in the area where the heritage structures are located. The first task therefore is to integrate conservation efforts with sound development plans that take care of people living in the heritage vicinity. Unlike in western countries, many traditional building crafts survive in India, and conservation practices offer an avenue to support them. This has been acknowledged by the Indian National Trust for Art and Cultural Heritage charter for conservation but is yet to receive substantial state support. More strength for heritage conservation can be mobilised by aligning it with the green building movement. Heritage structures are essentially eco-friendly and conservation could become a vital part of the sustainable building practices campaign in future.

46. The outlook for conservation heritage changed

A. after the establishment of the International Centre for the Study of the Preservation and Restoration of Cultural Property.

B. after training the specialists in the field.

C. after extending UNESCO's assistance to the educational institutions.

D. after ASI's measures to protect the monuments.

47. The inter-government organization was appreciated because of

A. increasing number of members to 126.

B. imparting training to professionals and sharing technical expertise.

C. consistent investment in conservation.

D. its proactive role in renovation and restoration.

48. Indian conservation movement will be successful if there would be

A. Financial support from the Government of India.

B. Non-governmental organisations role and participation in the conservation movement.

C. consistent investment, rigorous attention, and dedicated research and dissemination of awareness for conservation.

D. Archaeological Survey of India's meaningful assistance.

49. As per the surveys of historical monuments in India, there is very small number of protected monuments. As per given the total number of monuments and enlisted number of protected monuments, percentage comes to

A. 10 per cent B. 11 per cent

C. 12 per cent D. 13 per cent

50. What should India learn from Europe to conserve our cultural heritage ?

(*i*) There should be significant budget provision to conserve our cultural heritage.

(*ii*) Establish dedicated labs and training institutions.

(*iii*) Force the government to provide sufficient funds.

(*iv*) Conservation should be made part of mainstream research and engineering institutes.

Choose correct answer from the codes given below :

A. (*i*), (*ii*), (*iii*), (*iv*) B. (*i*), (*ii*), (*iv*)

(C. (*i*), (*ii*) D. (*i*), (*iii*), (*iv*)

51. INTACH is known for its contribution for conservation of our cultural heritage. The full form of INTACH is

A. International Trust for Art and Cultural Heritage
B. Intra-national Trust for Art and Cultural Heritage
C. Integrated Trust for Art and Cultural Heritage
D. Indian National Trust for Art and Cultural Heritage

52. While delivering lecture if there is some disturbance in the class, a teacher should

A. keep quiet for a while and then continue.
B. punish those causing disturbance.
C. motivate to teach those causing disturbance.
D. not bother of what is happening in the class.

53. Effective teaching is a function of

A. Teacher's satisfaction.
B. Teacher's honesty and commitment.
C. Teacher's making students learn and understand.
D. Teacher's liking for professional excellence.

54. The most appropriate meaning of learning is

A. Acquisition of skills
B. Modification of behaviour
C. Personal adjustment
D. Inculcation of knowledge

55. Arrange the following teaching process in order :

(*i*) Relate the present knowledge with previous one
(*ii*) Evaluation
(*iii*) Reteaching
(*iv*) Formulating instructional objectives
(*v*) Presentation of instructional materials

A. (*i*), (*ii*), (*iii*), (*iv*), (*v*)
B. (*ii*), (*i*), (*iii*), (*iv*), (*v*)
C. (*v*), (*iv*), (*iii*), (*i*), (*ii*)
D. (*iv*), (*i*), (*v*), (*ii*), (*iii*)

56. CIET stands for

A. Centre for Integrated Education and Technology
B. Central Institute for Engineering and Technology
C. Central Institute for Education Technology
D. Centre for Integrated Evaluation Techniques.

57. Teacher's role at higher education level is to

A. provide information to students.
B. promote self learning in students.
C. encourage healthy competition among students.
D. help students to solve their problems.

58. The Verstehen School of Understanding was popularised by

A. German Social Scientists
B. American Philosophers
C. British Academicians
D. Italian Political Analysts

59. The sequential operations in scientific research are

A. Co-variation, Elimination of Spurious Relations, Generalisation, Theorisation
B. Generalisation, Co-variation, Theorisation, Elimination of Spurious Relations
C. Theorisation, Generalisation, Elimination of Spurious Relations, Co-variation
D. Elimination of Spurious Relations, Theorisation, Generalisation, Co-variation.

60. In sampling, the lottery method is used for

A. Interpretation
B. Theorisation
C. Conceptualisation
D. Randomisation

ANSWERS

1	2	3	4	5	6	7	8	9	10
D	B	B	B	D	B	C	C	C	A
11	**12**	**13**	**14**	**15**	**16**	**17**	**18**	**19**	**20**
C	D	C	C	C	B	D	A	C	A
21	**22**	**23**	**24**	**25**	**26**	**27**	**28**	**29**	**30**
B	A	C	D	C	A	B	A	D	B
31	**32**	**33**	**34**	**35**	**36**	**37**	**38**	**39**	**40**
B	A	B	C	D	C	A	B	D	D
41	**42**	**43**	**44**	**45**	**46**	**47**	**48**	**49**	**50**
C	A	C	D	D	A	B	C	B	B
51	**52**	**53**	**54**	**55**	**56**	**57**	**58**	**59**	**60**
D	C	C	B	D	C	B	A	A	D

SOME SELECTED EXPLANATORY ANSWERS

11.

Language:	Hindi	English	Bengali
Name:	Bulbul	Ananya	Archana
	Archana	Krishna	Ananya
	Ananya		

Hence, Ananya can speak & follow English, Hindi and Bengali.

15.

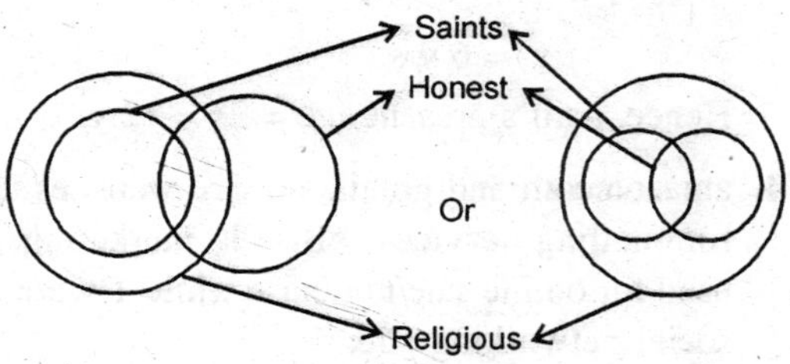

Here, there is no premises given to whether some or all saints are honests.

Hence, clear validly drawn is some honest persons are religious.

16. FTA contribution (in per cent) by different region in year 2009.

$$\text{Western Europe} = \frac{1610086}{5108579} \times 100 = 31.5\%$$

$$\text{North America} = \frac{1024469}{5108579} \times 100 = 20\%$$

$$\text{South Asia} = \frac{982633}{5108579} \times 100 = 19.23\%$$

$$\text{South East Asia} = \frac{348495}{5108579} \times 100 = 6.82\%$$

Hence, North America's contribution is around 20% of the total FTAs.

22. LAN — Local Area Network

This is an interconnection technique use to connect different PC installed within a small area like institutions.

24. The government of Tamil Nadu established the Tamil Virtual University (TVU) on 17 February 2001 as a Society. The university provides internet-based educational resources and opportunities for the Tamil diaspora as well as for others interested in learning the Tamil language and acquiring knowledge of the history, art, literature and culture of the Tamils.

30. Transport contributes to ambient air pollution, one of the most serious poblic health problems.

The main source of ambient air pollution is the combustion of fossil fuels by both stationary and mobile sources. The transportation sector is in general responsible for a significant share of the ambient air pollution in urban areas by emission of carbon monoxide. Ambient air quality problems tend to be most severe in urban areas where both population and pollution sources, particularly automobiles and industry, are most concentrated.

31. A hydrogen vehicle is a vehicle that uses hydrogen as its onboard fuel for motive power. Hydrogen vehicles include hydrogen fueled space rockets, as well as automobiles and other transportation vehicles. The power plants of such vehicles convert the chemical energy of hydrogen to mechanical energy either by burning hydrogen in an internal combustion engine, or by reacting hydrogen with oxygen in a fuel cell to run electric motors. Widespread use of hydrogen for fueling transportation is a key element of a proposed hydrogen economy.

38.

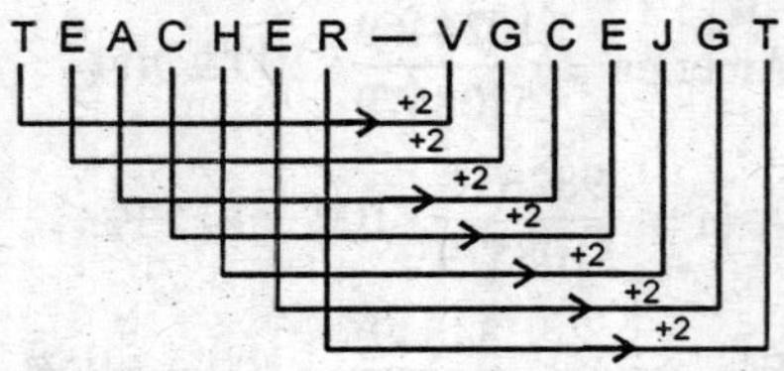

Similarly,

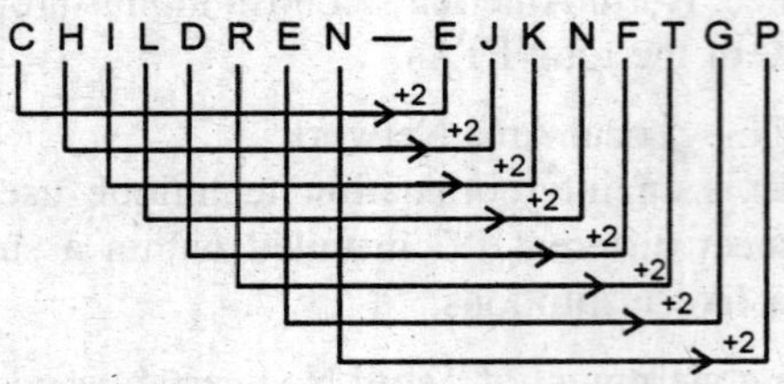

39. Let number of apples and mangoes bought by man is x and y respectively.

then,

$$7x + 5y = 38$$

for x, y an integer number, this is satisfied for $x = 4, y = 2$

Hence, number of apples = 4

41. Such pairs are (6, 4), (4, 2), (5, 3), (8, 6), (3, 5), (8, 6).

42. Total marks obtained by 40 students

$$= 65 \times 40 = 2600$$

Total marks obtained by 20 students

$$= 45 \times 20 = 900$$

Marks obtained by remaining 20 students

$$= 2600 - 900 = 1700$$

So, Average of marks obtained by remaining

$$20 \text{ students} = \frac{1700}{20} = 85.$$

43. Let Sunita's age is x yrs.

Then Anil's age is $2x$ yrs.

According to the question,

$$2x - 3 = 3(x - 3)$$
$$2x - 3 = 3x - 9$$
$$x = 6 \text{ yrs}$$

Hence, Anil's present age = $2x$ = 12 yrs.

44. amazon.com and gmail.com are websites used for mailing services. eBay is marketing site used for online sale/purchase while Twitter is a social networking site.

Previous Years' Paper (Solved)

UGC-NET (JRF) EXAM JUNE, 2013

PAPER–I

Note: *This paper contains* **Sixty (60)** *objective type questions, each question carrying* **two (2)** *marks. Attempt all the questions.*

1. Which one of the following references is written as per Modern Language Association (MLA) format?

A. Hall, Donald. Fundamentals of Electronics, New Delhi : Prentice Hall of India, 2005

B. Hall, Donald, Fundamentals of Electronics, New Delhi : Prentice Hall of India, 2005

C. Hall, Donald, Fundamentals of Electronics, New Delhi – Prentice Hall of India, 2005

D. Hall, Donald. Fundamentals of Electronics. New Delhi : Prentice Hall of India, 2005

2. A workshop is

A. a conference for discussion on a topic.

B. a meeting for discussion on a topic.

C. a class at a college or a university in which a teacher and the students discuss a topic.

D. a brief intensive course for a small group emphasizing the development of a skill or technique for solving a specific problem.

3. A working hypothesis is

A. a proven hypothesis for an argument.

B. not required to be tested.

C. a provisionally accepted hypothesis for further research.

D. a scientific theory.

Read the following passage carefully and answer the questions (4 to 9) :

The Taj Mahal has become one of the world's best known monuments. This domed white marble structure is situated on a high plinth at the southern end of a four-quartered garden, evoking the gardens of paradise, enclosed within walls measuring 305 by 549 metres. Outside the walls, in an area known as Mumtazabad, were living quarters for attendants, markets, serais and other structures built by local merchants and nobles. The tomb complex and the other imperial structures of Mumtazabad were maintained by the income of thirty villages given specifically for the tomb's support. The name Taj Mahal is unknown in Mughal chronicles, but it is used by contemporary Europeans in India, suggesting that this was the tomb's popular name. In contemporary texts, it is generally called simply the Illuminated Tomb (Rauza-i-Munavvara).

Mumtaz Mahal died shortly after delivering her fourteenth child in 1631. The Mughal court was then residing in Burhanpur. Her remains were temporarily buried by the griefstricken emperor in a spacious garden known as Zainabad on the bank of the river Tapti. Six months later her body was transported to Agra, where it was interred in land chosen for the mausoleum. This land, situated south of the Mughal city on the bank of the Jamuna, had belonged to the Kachhwaha rajas since the time of Raja Man Singh and was purchased from the current raja, Jai Singh. Although contemporary chronicles indicate Jai Singh's willing cooperation in this exchange, extant *farmans* (imperial commands) indicate that the final price was not settled until almost two years after the mausoleum's commencement. Jai Singh's further cooperation was insured by imperial orders issued between 1632 and 1637 demanding that he provide stone masons and carts to transport marble from the mines at Makrana, within his "ancestral domain", to Agra where both the Taj Mahal and Shah Jahan's additions to the Agra fort were constructed concurrently.

Work on the mausoleum was commenced early in 1632. Inscriptional evidence indicates much of the tomb was completed by 1636. By 1643, when Shah Jahan most lavishly celebrated the 'Urs ceremony for Mumtaz Mahal', the entire complex was virtually complete.

4. Marble stone used for the construction of the Taj Mahal was brought from the ancestral domain of Raja Jai Singh. The name of the place where mines of marble is

A. Burhanpur B. Makrana
C. Amber D. Jaipur

5. The popular name Taj Mahal was given by

A. Shah Jahan
B. Tourists
C. Public
D. European travellers

6. Point out the true statement from the following:

A. Marble was not used for the construction of the Taj Mahal.
B. Red sand stone is non-visible in the Taj Mahal complex.
C. The Taj Mahal is surrounded by a four-quartered garden known as Chahr Bagh.
D. The Taj Mahal was constructed to celebrate the 'Urs ceremony for Mumtaz Mahal'.

7. In the contemporary texts the Taj Mahal is known

A. Mumtazabad
B. Mumtaz Mahal
C. Zainabad
D. Rauza-i-Munavvara

8. The construction of the Taj Mahal was completed between the period

A. 1632 – 1636 A.D. B. 1630 – 1643 A.D.
C. 1632 – 1643 A.D. D. 1636 – 1643 A.D.

9. The documents indicating the ownership of land, where the Taj Mahal was built, known as

A. Farman
B. Sale Deed
C. Sale-Purchase Deed
D. None of the above

10. In the process of communication, which one of the following is in the chronological order?

A. Communicator, Medium, Receiver, Effect, Message
B. Medium, Communicator, Message, Receiver, Effect
C. Communicator, Message, Medium, Receiver, Effect
D. Message, Communicator, Medium, Receiver, Effect

11. Bengal Gazette, the first Newspaper in India was started in 1780 by

A. Dr. Annie Besant
B. James Augustus Hicky
C. Lord Cripson
D. A.O. Hume

12. Press censorship in India was imposed during the tenure of the Prime Minister

A. Rajeev Gandhi B. Narasimha Rao
C. Indira Gandhi D. Deve Gowda

13. Communication via New media such as computers, teleshopping, internet and mobile telephony is termed as

A. Entertainment
B. Interactive communication
C. Developmental communication
D. Communitarian

14. Classroom communication of a teacher rests on the principle of

A. Infotainment B. Edutainment
C. Entertainment D. Enlightenment

15. ________ is important when a teacher communicates with his/her student.

A. Sympathy B. Empathy
C. Apathy D. Antipathy

16. In a certain code GALIB is represented by HBMJC. TIGER will be represented by

A. UJHFS B. UHJSF
C. JHUSF D. HUJSF

17. In a certain cricket tournament 45 matches were played. Each team played once against each of the other teams. The number of teams participated in the tournament is

A. 8 B. 10
C. 12 D. 14

18. The missing number in the series 40, 120, 60, 180, 90,?, 135 is

A. 110 B. 270
C. 105 D. 210

19. The odd numbers from 1 to 45 which are exactly divisible by 3 are arranged in an ascending order. The number at 6th position is

A. 18 B. 24
C. 33 D. 36

20. The mean of four numbers a, b, c, d is 100. If c = 70, then the mean of the remaining numbers is

A. 30 B. $\frac{85}{2}$
C. $\frac{170}{3}$ D. 110

21. If the radius of a circle is increased by 50%, the perimeter of the circle will increase by

A. 20% B. 30%
C. 40% D. 50%

22. If the statement 'some men are honest' is false, which among the following statements will be true.
Choose the correct code given below :
(*i*) All men are honest.
(*ii*) No men are honest.
(*iii*) Some men are not honest.
(*iv*) All men are dishonest.
Codes :
A. (*i*), (*ii*) and (*iii*)
B. (*ii*), (*iii*) and (*iv*)
C. (*i*), (*iii*) and (*iv*)
D. (*ii*), (*i*) and (*iv*)

23. Choose the proper alternative given in the codes to replace the question mark.
Bee – Honey, Cow – Milk, Teacher – ?

A. Intelligence B. Marks
C. Lessons D. Wisdom

24. P is the father of R and S is the son of Q and T is the brother of P. If R is the sister of S, how is Q related to T?

A. Wife B. Sister-in-law
C. Brother-in-law D. Daughter-in-law

25. A definition put forward to resolve a dispute by influencing attitudes or stirring emotions is called

A. Lexical B. Persuasive
C. Stipulative D. Precisions

26. Which of the codes given below contains only the correct statements?
Statements :
(*i*) Venn diagram is a clear method of notation.
(*ii*) Venn diagram is the most direct method of testing the validity of categorical syllogisms.
(*iii*) In Venn diagram method the premises and the conclusion of a categorical syllogism is diagrammed.
(*iv*) In Venn diagram method the three overlapping circles are drawn for testing a categorical syllogism.
Codes :
A. (*i*), (*ii*) & (*iii*) B. (*i*), (*ii*) & (*iv*)
C. (*ii*), (*iii*) & (*iv*) D. (*i*), (*iii*) & (*iv*)

27. Inductive reasoning presupposes

A. unity in human nature
B. integrity in human nature
C. uniformity in human nature
D. harmony in human nature

Read the table below and based on this table answer questions from 28 to 33 :

Area under Major Horticulture Crops
(in lakh hectares)

Year	*Fruits*	*Vegetables*	*Flowers*	*Total Horticulture Area*
2005–06	53	72	1	187
2006–07	56	75	1	194
2007–08	58	78	2	202
2008–09	61	79	2	207
2009–10	63	79	2	209

28. Which of the following two years have recorded the highest rate of increase in area under the total horticulture?

A. 2005–06 & 2006–07
B. 2006–07 & 2008–09
C. 2007–08 & 2008–09
D. 2006–07 & 2007–08

29. Shares of the area under flowers, vegetables and fruits in the area under total horticulture are respectively :
A. 1, 38 and 30 percent
B. 30, 38 and 1 percent
C. 38, 30 and 1 percent
D. 35, 36 and 2 percent

30. Which of the following has recorded the highest rate of increase in area during 2005–06 to 2009–10?
A. Fruits B. Vegetables
C. Flowers D. Total horticulture

31. Find out the horticultural crop that has recorded an increase of area by around 10 percent from 2005–06 to 2009–10
A. Fruits B. Vegetables
C. Flowers D. Total horticulture

32. What has been the share of area under fruits, vegetables and flowers in the area under total horticulture in 2007–08?
A. 53 percent B. 68 percent
C. 79 percent D. 100 percent

33. In which year, area under fruits has recorded the highest rate of increase?
A. 2006–07 B. 2007–08
C. 2008–09 D. 2009–10

34. 'www' stands for
A. work with web B. word wide web
C. world wide web D. worth while web

35. A hard disk is divided into tracks which is further subdivided into
A. Clusters B. Sectors
C. Vectors D. Heads

36. A computer program that translates a program statement by statement into machine language is called a/an
A. Compiler B. Simulator
C. Translator D. Interpreter

37. A Gigabyte is equal to
A. 1024 Megabytes B. 1024 Kilobytes
C. 1024 Terabytes D. 1024 Bytes

38. A Compiler is a software which converts
A. characters to bits
B. high level language to machine language
C. machine language to high level language
D. words to bits

39. Virtual memory is
A. an extremely large main memory.
B. an extremely large secondary memory.
C. an illusion of extremely large main memory.
D. a type of memory used in super computers.

40. The phrase 'tragedy of commons' is in the context of
A. tragic event related to damage caused by release of poisonous gases.
B. tragic conditions of poor people.
C. degradation of renewable free access resources.
D. climate change.

41. Kyoto Protocol is related to
A. Ozone depletion B. Hazardous waste
C. Climate change D. Nuclear energy

42. Which of the following is a source of emissions leading to the eventual formation of surface ozone as a pollutant?
A. Transport sector
B. Refrigeration and Airconditioning
C. Wetlands
D. Fertilizers

43. The smog in cities in India mainly consists of
A. Oxides of sulphur
B. Oxides of nitrogen and unburnt hydrocarbons
C. Carbon monoxide and SPM
D. Oxides of sulphur and ozone

44. Which of the following types of natural hazards have the highest potential to cause damage to humans?
A. Earthquakes
B. Forest fires
C. Volcanic eruptions
D. Droughts and Floods

45. The percentage share of renewable energy sources in the power production in India is around
A. 2–3% B. 22–25%
C. 10–12% D. < 1%

46. In which of the following categories the enrolment of students in higher education in 2010–11 was beyond the percentage of seats reserved?
- A. OBC students
- B. SC students
- C. ST students
- D. Woman students

47. Which one of the following statements is not correct about the University Grants Commission (UGC)?
- A. It was established in 1956 by an Act of Parliament.
- B. It is tasked with promoting and coordinating higher education.
- C. It receives Plan and Non-plan funds from the Central Government.
- D. It receives funds from State Governments in respect of State Universities.

48. Consider the statement which is followed by two arguments (I) and (II) :

Statement : Should India switch over to a two party system?

Arguments : (I) Yes, it will lead to stability of Government.

(II) No, it will limit the choice of voters.

- A. Only argument (I) is strong.
- B. Only argument (II) is strong.
- C. Both the arguments are strong.
- D. Neither of the arguments is strong.

49. Consider the statement which is followed by two arguments (I) and (II) :

Statement : Should persons with criminal background be banned from contesting elections?

Arguments : (I) Yes, it will decriminalise politics.

(II) No, it will encourage the ruling party to file frivolous cases against their political opponents.

- A. Only argument (I) is strong.
- B. Only argument (II) is strong.
- C. Both the arguments are strong.
- D. Neither of the arguments is strong.

50. Which of the following statement(s) is/are correct about a Judge of the Supreme Court of India?
1. A Judge of the Supreme Court is appointed by the President of India.
2. He holds office during the pleasure of the President.
3. He can be suspended, pending an inquiry.
4. He can be removed for proven misbehaviour or incapacity.

Select the correct answer from the codes given below :

Codes :

A. 1, 2 and 3	B. 1, 3 and 4
C. 1 and 3	D. 1 and 4

51. In the warrant of precedence, the Speaker of the Lok Sabha comes next only to
- A. The President
- B. The Vice-President
- C. The Prime Minister
- D. The Cabinet Ministers

52. The black-board can be utilised best by a teacher for
- A. putting the matter of teaching in black and white
- B. making the students attentive
- C. writing the important and notable points
- D. highlighting the teacher himself

53. Nowadays the most effective mode of learning is
- A. self study
- B. face-to-face learning
- C. e-learning
- D. blended learning

54. At the primary school stage, most of the teachers should be women because they
- A. can teach children better than men.
- B. know basic content better than men.
- C. are available on lower salaries.
- D. can deal with children with love and affection.

55. Which one is the highest order of learning?
- A. Chain learning
- B. Problem-solving learning
- C. Stimulus-response learning
- D. Conditioned-reflex learning

56. A person can enjoy teaching as a profession when he
A. has control over students.
B. commands respect from students.
C. is more qualified than his colleagues.
D. is very close to higher authorities.

57. "A diagram speaks more than 1000 words." The statement means that the teacher should
A. use diagrams in teaching.
B. speak more and more in the class.
C. use teaching aids in the class.
D. not speak too much in the class.

58. A research paper
A. is a compilation of information on a topic.
B. contains original research as deemed by the author.
C. contains peer-reviewed original research or evaluation of research conducted by others.
D. can be published in more than one journal.

59. Which one of the following belongs to the category of good "research ethics"?
A. Publishing the same paper in two research journals without telling the editors.
B. Conducting a review of the literature that acknowledges the contributions of other people in the relevant field or relevant prior work.
C. Trimming outliers from a data set without discussing your reasons in a research paper.
D. Including a colleague as an author on a research paper in return for a favour even though the colleague did not make a serious contribution to the paper.

60. Which of the following sampling methods is not based on probability?
A. Simple Random Sampling
B. Stratified Sampling
C. Quota Sampling
D. Cluster Sampling

ANSWERS

1	2	3	4	5	6	7	8	9	10
D	D	C	B	D	C	D	C	A	C
11	**12**	**13**	**14**	**15**	**16**	**17**	**18**	**19**	**20**
B	C	B	B	B	A	B	B	C	D
21	**22**	**23**	**24**	**25**	**26**	**27**	**28**	**29**	**30**
D	B	D	B	B	B	C	D	A	C
31	**32**	**33**	**34**	**35**	**36**	**37**	**38**	**39**	**40**
B	B	A	C	B	D	A	B	C	C
41	**42**	**43**	**44**	**45**	**46**	**47**	**48**	**49**	**50**
C	A	B	D	C	A	D	C	A	D
51	**52**	**53**	**54**	**55**	**56**	**57**	**58**	**59**	**60**
C	C	D	D	D	B	C	C	B	C

SOME SELECTED EXPLANATORY ANSWERS

16.

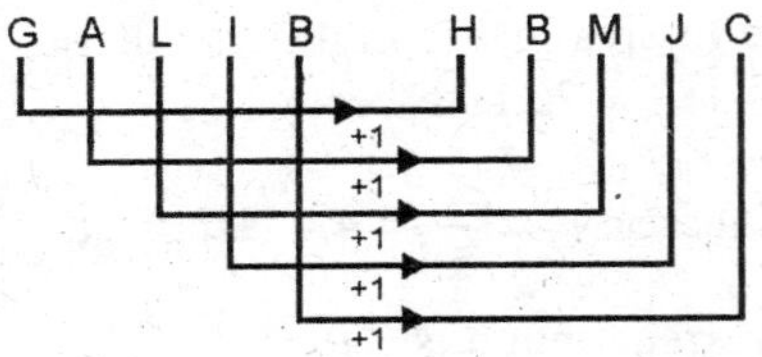

Similarly,

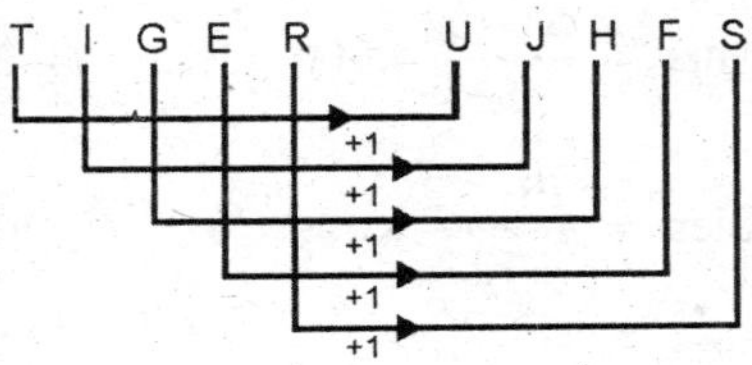

17. Let number of teams participated in the tournament are n

then, number of game played by,

first team $= (n-1)$

Second team $= (n-2)$

....

....

....

$(n-1)^{th}$ team $= 1$

According to the question,

$(n-1)+(n-2)+(n-3)+ \ldots +1 = 45$

This is equivalent to, Selection of two teams out of n teams ${}^nc_2$

$$\therefore \quad {}^nc_2 = 45$$

$$\frac{n(n-1)}{2} = 45$$

$$\text{or,} \quad n(n-1) = 90$$

$$n^2 - n - 90 = 0$$

$$(n-10)(n+9) = 0$$

$$\Rightarrow \quad n = 10.$$

18.

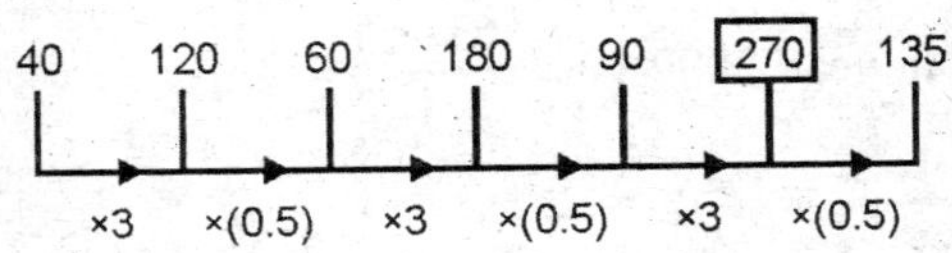

19. Odd numbers from 1 to 45 which are exactly divisible by 3 are following.

3, 9, 15, 21, ..., 45

This is an arthmetic series with first term $a = 3$, and common difference $d = 6$

Sixth term of this series

$$t_6 = a + (6-1).d$$
$$= 3 + 5 \times 6 = 33.$$

20. Mean of four numbers $\dfrac{a+b+c+d}{4} = 100$

$$\text{or,} \quad a+b+c+d = 400$$

$$\text{or,} \quad a+b+70+d = 400$$

$$a+b+d = 400-70 = 330$$

$$\text{Mean} = \frac{a+b+d}{3} = \frac{330}{3}$$
$$= 110.$$

21. Perimeter of circle $(p) = 2\pi r$

when radius (r) increased by 50%

$$r' = r + \frac{r \times 50}{100} = \frac{3r}{2}$$

$$\text{New Perimeter } (p') = 2\pi r'$$
$$= 3\pi r$$

Increase in perimeter

$$p' - p = 3\pi r - 2\pi r = \pi r$$

$$\text{Percentage increment} = \frac{\pi r}{2\pi r} \times 100 = 50\%.$$

23. Bee give us honey and Cow gives milk, similarly from teacher we get wisdom.

24.

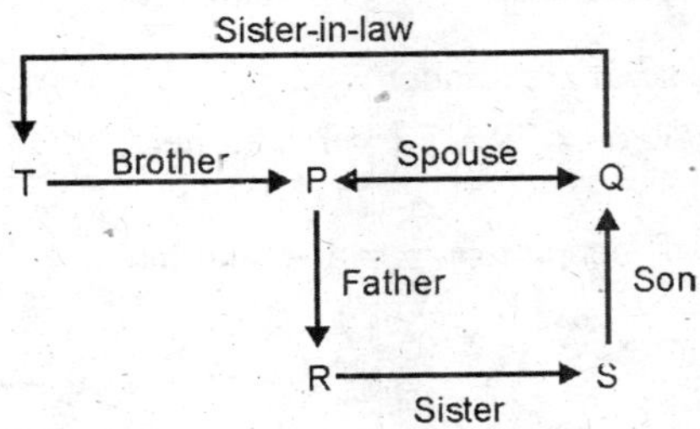

28. Increase in total horticulture area

from 2005-06 & 2006-07

194 – 187 = 7 Lakh hect.

from 2006-07 & 2007-08

202 – 194 = 8 Lakh hect.

from 2007-08 & 2008-09

207 – 202 = 5 Lakh hect.

from 2006-07 & 2008-09

207 – 194 = 13 Lakh hect.

Hence, highest rate of increase is registered in 2006-07 & 2007-08.

29. Total horticultural area

= 187 + 194 + 202 + 207 + 209 = 999 lakh hect.

Total flowers area

= 1 + 1 + 2 + 2 + 2 = 8 lakh hect.

Percentage area under flowers

$$= \frac{8}{999} \times 100 \cong 0.8\%$$

Total area under Vegetation

= 72 + 75 + 78 + 79 + 79 = 383 Lakh hect.

Percentage area under vegetation

$$= \frac{383}{999} \times 100 \cong 38.3\%$$

Total area under Fruits

= 53 + 56 + 58 + 61 + 63 = 291 Lakh hect.

Percentage area under fruits

$$= \frac{291}{999} \times 100 \cong 29.1\%$$

Hence, Correct option is (A).

30. Increase in area under

Fruits = 63 – 53 = 10 lakh hect.

Rate of increase = $\frac{10}{5} = 2$ lakh hect

Increase in area under

Vegetables = 79 – 72 = 7 lakh hect.

Rate of increase = $\frac{7}{5}$ = 1.4 lakh hect.

Increase in area under flowers

= 2 – 1 = 1 Lakh hect.

Rate of increase = $\frac{1}{5}$ = 0.2 lakh hect.

Increase in area under total horticulture

= 209 – 187 = 22 lakh hect.

Rate of increase = $\frac{22}{5}$ = 4.4 lakh hect.

Hence correct option is (D).

31. Percentage increase in area under

$$\text{fruits} = \frac{63-53}{53} \times 100 = 18.89\% \cong 20\%$$

$$\text{Vegetables} = \frac{79-72}{72} \times 100 = 9.77\% \cong 10\%$$

$$\text{Flowers} = \frac{2-1}{1} \times 100 = 100\%$$

Total horticulture

$$= \frac{209-187}{187} \times 100$$

$$= 11.7\% \cong 12\%$$

Hence, correct option is (B).

32. Area under fruits, vegetables and flowers in year 2007 – 08

= 58 + 78 + 2 = 138 lakh hect.

Area under horticulture in year 2007 – 08

= 202 lakh hect.

Percentage of area = $\frac{138}{202} \times 100$ = 68.33%.

33. Rate of increase of area under flowers

in year 2006-07 = $\frac{56-53}{1} = 3$

in year 2007-08 = $\frac{58-56}{1} = 2$

in year 2008-09 = $\frac{61-58}{1} = 3$

in year 2009-10 = $\frac{63-61}{1} = 2.$

Previous Years' Paper (Solved)

UGC-NET (JRF) EXAM DECEMBER, 2012

PAPER–I

Note : This paper contains **sixty (60)** multiple-choice questions, each question carrying **two (2)** marks. Candidate is expected to answer any **fifty (50)** questions. In case more than **fifty (50)** questions are attempted, only the first **fifty (50)** questions will be evaluated.

1. The English word 'Communication' is derived from the words:
A. Communis and Communicare
B. Communist and Commune
C. Communism and Communalism
D. Communion and Common sense

2. Chinese Cultural Revolution leader Mao Zedong used a type of communication to talk to the masses is known as:
A. Mass line communication
B. Group communication
C. Participatory communication
D. Dialogue communication

3. Conversing with the spirits and ancestors is termed as:
A. Transpersonal communication
B. Intrapersonal communication
C. Interpersonal communication
D. Face-to-face communication

4. The largest circulated daily newspaper among the following is:
A. The Times of India
B. The Indian Express
C. The Hindu
D. The Deccan Herald

5. The Pioneer of the silent feature film in India was:
A. K.A. Abbas B. Satyajit Ray
C. B.R. Chopra D. Dada Sahib Phalke

6. Classroom communication of a teacher rests on the principle of:
A. Infotainment B. Edutainment
C. Entertainment D. Power equation

7. The missing number in the series :
0, 6, 24, 60, 120, ?, 336, is:
A. 240 B. 220
C. 280 D. 210

8. A group of 7 members having a majority of boys is to be formed out of 6 boys and 4 girls. The number of ways the group can be formed is:
A. 80 B. 100
C. 90 D. 110

9. The number of observations in a group is 40. The average of the first 10 members is 4.5 and the average of the remaining 30 members is 3.5. The average of the whole group is:
A. 4 B. 15/2
C. 15/4 D. 6

10. If MOHAN is represented by the code KMFYL, then COUNT will be represented by:
A. AMSLR B. MSLAR
C. MASRL D. SAMLR

11. The sum of the ages of two persons A and B is 50. 5 years ago, the ratio of their ages was 5/3. The present age of A and B are:
A. 30, 20 B. 35, 15
C. 38, 12 D. 40, 10

12. Let *a* means minus (–), *b* means multiplied by (×), C means divided by (÷) and D means plus (+). The value of 90 D 9 *a* 29 C 10 *b* 2 is:
A. 8 B. 10
C. 12 D. 14

13. Consider the Assertion-I and Assertion-II and select the right code given below :
Assertion-I : Even Bank-lockers are not safe. Thieves can break them and take away your

wealth. But thieves can not go to heaven. So you should keep your wealth in heaven.

Assertion-II : The difference of skin-colour of beings is because of the distance from the sun and not because of some permanent traits. Skin-colour is the result of body's reaction to the sun and its rays.

Codes :

A. Both the assertions-I and II are forms of argument.

B. The assertion-I is an argument but the assertion-II is not.

C. The assertion-II is an argument but the assertion-I is not.

D. Both the assertions are explanations of facts.

14. By which of the following proposition, the proposition 'some men are not honest' is contradicted?

A. All men are honest

C. Some men are honest

B. No men are honest

D. All of the above

15. A stipulative definition is:

A. always true

B. always false

C. sometimes true sometimes false

D. neither true nor false

16. Choose the appropriate alternative given in the codes to replace the question mark.

Examiner – Examinee, Pleader – Client, Preceptor – ?

A. Customer B. Path-finder

C. Perceiver D. Disciple

17. If the statement 'most of the students are obedient' is taken to be true, which one of the following pair of statements can be claimed to be true?

I. All obedient persons are students.

II. All students are obedient.

III. Some students are obedient.

IV. Some students are not disobedient.

Codes:

A. I & II B. II & III

C. III & IV D. II & IV

18. Choose the right code :

A deductive argument claims that :

I. The conclusion does not claim something more than that which is contained in the premises.

II. The conclusion is supported by the premise/premises conclusively.

III. If the conclusion is false, then premise/premises may be either true or false.

IV. If premise/combination of premises is true, then conclusion must be true.

Codes:

A. I and II B. I and III

C. II and III D. All of the above

Direction (Qs. 19 to 24): *On the basis of the data given in the following table, give answers to questions.*

Government Expenditures on Social Services

(As per cent of total expenditure)

S.I. No.	Items	2007-08	2008-09	2009-10	2010-11
	Social Services	11.06	12.94	13.06	14.02
(a)	Education, sports & youth affairs	4.02	4.04	3.96	4.46
(b)	Health & family welfare	2.05	1.91	1.90	2.03
(c)	Water supply, housing, etc,	2.02	2.31	2.20	2.27
(d)	Information & broadcasting	0.22	0.22	0.20	0.22
(e)	Welfare to SC/ST & OBC	0.36	0.35	0.41	0.63
(f)	Labour and employment	0.27	0.27	0.22	0.25
(g)	Social welfare & nutrition	0.82	0.72	0.79	1.06
(h)	North-eastern areas	0.00	1.56	1.50	1.75
(i)	Other social services	1.29	1.55	1.87	1.34
	Total Government expenditure	100.00	100.00	100.00	100.00

19. How many activities in the social services are there where the expenditure has been less than 5 per cent of the total expenditures incurred on the social services in 2008-09?

A. One B. Three
C. Five D. All of the above

20. In which year, the expenditures on the social services have increased at the highest rate?

A. 2007-08 B. 2008-09
C. 2009-10 D. 2010-11

21. Which of the following activities remains almost stagnant in terms of share of expenditures?

A. North-eastern areas
B. Welfare to SC/ST & OBC
C. Information & broadcasting
D. Social welfare and nutrition

22. Which of the following item's expenditure share is almost equal to the remaining three items in the given years?

A. Information & broadcasting
B. Welfare to SC/ST and OBC
C. Labour and employment
D. Social welfare & nutrition

23. Which of the following items of social services has registered the highest rate of increase in expenditures during 2007-08 to 2010-11?

A. Education, sports & youth affairs
B. Welfare to SC/ST & OBC
C. Social welfare & nutrition
D. Overall social services

24. Which of the following items has registered the highest rate of decline in terms of expenditure during 2007-08 to 2009-10?

A. Labour and employment
B. Health & family welfare
C. Social welfare & nutrition
D. Education, sports & youth affairs

25. ALU stands for:

A. American Logic Unit
B. Alternate Local Unit
C. Alternating Logic Unit
D. Arithmetic Logic Unit

26. A Personal Computer uses a number of chips mounted on a circuit board called:

A. Microprocessor B. System Board
C. Daughter Board D. Mother Board

27. Computer Virus is a:

A. Hardware B. Bacteria
C. Software D. None of these

28. Which one of the following is correct?

A. $(17)_{10} = (17)_{16}$
B. $(17)_{10} = (17)_8$
C. $(17)_{10} = (10111)_2$
D. $(17)_{10} = (10001)_2$

29. The file extension of MS-Word document in Office 2007 is ....

A. .pdf B. .doc
C. .docx D. .txt

30. .... is a protocol used by e-mail clients to download e-mails to your computer.

A. TCP B. FTP
C. SMTP D. POP

31. Which of the following is a source of methane?

A. Wetlands
B. Foam Industry
C. Thermal Power Plants
D. Cement Industry

32. 'Minamata disaster' in Japan was caused by pollution due to:

A. Lead B. Mercury
C. Cadmium D. Zinc

33. Biomagnification means increase in the:

A. concentration of pollutants in living organisms
B. number of species
C. size of living organisms
D. biomass

34. Nagoya Protocol is related to:

A. Climate change B. Ozone depletion
C. Hazardous waste D. Biodiversity

35. The second most important source after fossil fuels contributing to India's energy needs is:

A. Solar energy C. Nuclear energy
B. Hydropower D. Wind energy

36. In case of earthquakes, an increase of magnitude 1 on Richter Scale implies:

A. a ten-fold increase in the amplitude of seismic waves.
B. a ten-fold increase in the energy of the seismic waves.
C. two-fold increase in the amplitude of seismic waves.
D. two-fold increase in the energy of seismic waves.

37. Which of the following is not a measure of Human Development Index?

A. Literacy Rate B. Gross Enrolment
C. Sex Ratio D. Life Expectancy

38. India has the highest number of students in colleges after:

A. the U.K.
B. the U.S.A.
C. Australia
D. Canada

39. Which of the following statement(s) is/are not correct about the Attorney General of India?

1. The President appoints a person, who is qualified to be a Judge of a High Court, to be the Attorney General of India.
2. He has the right of audience in all the Courts of the country.
3. He has the right to take part in the proceedings of the Lok Sabha and the Rajya Sabha.
4. He has a fixed tenure.

Select the correct answer from the codes given below :

Codes:

A. 1 and 4 B. 2, 3 and 4
C. 3 and 4 D. 3 only

40. Which of the following prefix President Pranab Mukherjee desires to be discontinued while interacting with Indian dignitaries as well as in official notings?

1. His Excellency 2. Mahamahim
3. Hon'ble 4. Shri/Smt.

Select the correct answer from the codes given below:

Codes:

A. 1 and 3 B. 2 and 3
C. 1 and 2 D. 1, 2 and 3

41. Which of the following can be done under conditions of financial emergency?

1. State Legislative Assemblies can be abolished.
2. Central Government can acquire control over the budget and expenditure of States.
3. Salaries of the Judges of the High Courts and the Supreme Court can be reduced.
4. Right to Constitutional Remedies can be suspended.

Select the correct answer from the codes given below :

Codes :

A. 1, 2 and 3 B. 2, 3 and 4
C. 1 and 2 D. 2 and 3

42. Match List-I with List-II and select the correct answer from the codes given below :

List-I	List-II
(a) Poverty Reduction Programme	(i) Mid-day Meals
(b) Human Development Scheme	(ii) Indira Awas Yojna (IAY)
(c) Social Assistance Scheme	(iii) National Old Age Pension (NOAP)
(d) Minimum Need Scheme	(iv) MNREGA

Codes :

	(a)	(b)	(c)	(d)
A.	(iv)	(i)	(iii)	(ii)
B.	(ii)	(iii)	(iv)	(ii)
C.	(iii)	(iv)	(i)	(ii)
D.	(iv)	(iii)	(ii)	(i)

43. For an efficient and durable learning, learner should have:

A. ability to learn only
B. requisite level of motivation only
C. opportunities to learn only
D. desired level of ability and motivation

44. Classroom communication must be:

A. Teacher centric B. Student centric
C. General centric D. Textbook centric

45. The best method of teaching is to:
A. impart information
B. ask students to read books
C. suggest good reference material
D. initiate a discussion and participate in it

46. Interaction inside the classroom should generate:
A. Argument B. Information
C. Ideas D. Controversy

47. "Spare the rod and spoil the child", gives the message that:
A. punishment in the class should be banned.
B. corporal punishment is not acceptable.
C. undesirable behaviour must be punished.
D. children should be beaten with rods.

48. The type of communication that the teacher has in the classroom, is termed as:
A. Interpersonal
B. Mass communication
C. Group communication
D. Face-to-face communication

49. Which one of the following is an indication of the quality of a research journal?
A. Impact factor B. h-index
C. g-index D. i10-index

50. Good 'research ethics' means:
A. Not disclosing the holdings of shares/ stocks in a company that sponsors your research.
B. Assigning a particular research problem to one Ph.D./research student only.
C. Discussing with your colleagues confidential data from a research paper that you are reviewing for an academic journal.
D. Submitting the same research manuscript for publishing in more than one journal.

51. Which of the following sampling methods is based on probability?
A. Convenience sampling
B. Quota sampling
C. Judgement sampling
D. Stratified sampling

52. Which one of the following references is written according to American Psychological Association (APA) format?
A. Sharma, V. (2010). Fundamentals of Computer Science.
New Delhi : Tata McGraw Hill
B. Sharma, V. 2010. Fundamentals of Computer Science.
New Delhi : Tata McGraw Hill
C. Sharma. V. 2010. Fundamentals of Computer Science,
New Delhi : Tata McGraw Hill
D. Sharma, V. (2010), Fundamentals of Computer Science,
New Delhi : Tata McGraw Hill

53. Arrange the following steps of research in correct sequence:
1. Identification of research problem
2. Listing of research objectives
3. Collection of data
4. Methodology
5. Data analysis
6. Results and discussion
A. 1 – 2 – 3 – 4 – 5 – 6
B. 1 – 2 – 4 – 3 – 5 – 6
C. 2 – 1 – 3 – 4 – 5 – 6
D. 2 – 1 – 4 – 3 – 5 – 6

54. Identify the **incorrect** statement :
A. A hypothesis is made on the basis of limited evidence as a starting point for further investigations.
B. A hypothesis is a basis for reasoning without any assumption of its truth.
C. Hypothesis is a proposed explanation for a phenomenon.
D. Scientific hypothesis is a scientific theory.

Directions (Qs. 50 to 60) : *Read the following passage carefully and answer the questions:*

The popular view of towns and cities in developing countries and of urbanization process is that despite the benefits and comforts it brings, the emergence of such cities connotes environmental degradation, generation of slums and squatters, urban poverty, unemployment, crimes, lawlessness, traffic chaos etc. But what is the reality? Given the unprecedental increase in urban population over the last 50 years from 300 million in 1950 to 2 billion in 2000 in developing countries, the wonder really is how well the world has coped, and not how badly.

In general, the urban quality of life has improved in terms of availability of water and sanitation, power, health and education, communication and transport. By way of illustration, a large number of urban residents have been provided with improved water in urban areas in Asia's largest countries such as China, India, Indonesia and Philippines. Despite that, the access to improved water in terms of percentage of total urban population seems to have declined during the last decade of 20th century, though in absolute numbers, millions of additional urbanites, have been provided improved services. These countries have made significant progress in the provision of sanitation services too, together, providing for an additional population of more than 293 million citizens within a decade (1990-2000). These improvements must be viewed against the backdrop of rapidly increasing urban population, fiscal crunch and strained human resources and efficient and quality-oriented public management.

55. The popular view about the process of urbanization in developing countries is:
A. Positive B. Negative
C. Neutral D. Unspecified

56. The average annual increase in the number of urbanites in developing countries, from 1950 to 2000 A.D. was close to:
A. 30 million B. 40 million
C. 50 million D. 60 million

57. The reality of urbanization is reflected in:
A. How well the situation has been managed.
B. How badly the situation has gone out of control.
C. How fast has been tempo of urbanization.
D. How fast the environment has degraded.

58. Which one of the following is not considered as an indicator of urban quality of life?
A. Tempo of urbanization
B. Provision of basic services
C. Access to social amenities
D. All of the above

59. The author in this passage has tried to focus on
A. Extension of Knowledge
B. Generation of Environmental Consciousness
C. Analytical Reasoning
D. Descriptive Statement

60. In the above passage, the author intends to state:
A. The hazards of the urban life
B. The sufferings of the urban life
C. The awareness of human progress
D. The limits to growth

ANSWERS

1	2	3	4	5	6	7	8	9	10
A	D	A	A	D	B	D	B	C	A
11	**12**	**13**	**14**	**15**	**16**	**17**	**18**	**19**	**20**
A	D	A	A	D	C	C	D	D	D
21	**22**	**23**	**24**	**25**	**26**	**27**	**28**	**29**	**30**
C	D	D	B	D	D	C	D	B	D
31	**32**	**33**	**34**	**35**	**36**	**37**	**38**	**39**	**40**
A	B	A	D	C	A	C	B	D	C
41	**42**	**43**	**44**	**45**	**46**	**47**	**48**	**49**	**50**
C	A	D	B	D	C	C	C	A	A
51	**52**	**53**	**54**	**55**	**56**	**57**	**58**	**59**	**60**
D	A	B	D	B	A	A	A	D	D

SOME SELECTED EXPLANATORY ANSWERS

7. 0, 6, 24, 60, 120, x, 336.

Let missing term is x

Now,

$$\frac{0}{6}, \frac{6}{24}, \frac{24}{60}, \frac{60}{120}, \frac{120}{x}, \frac{x}{336}$$

$$= 0, \frac{1}{4}, \frac{2}{5}, \frac{3}{6}, \frac{120}{x}, \frac{x}{336}$$

From the pattern

$\frac{120}{x}$ should be $\frac{4}{7}$

so, $\frac{120}{x} = \frac{4}{7}$ or, $x = 210$.

8. The group must formed by 4, 5 or 6 boys and 3, 2 or 1 girls

the required number of ways

when group formed by 4 boys and 3 girls

Number of ways for this selection

$$^6C_4 \times {^4C_3}$$

when group formed by 5 boys and 2 girls

Number of ways for this selection

$$^6C_5 \times {^4C_2}$$

when group formed by 6 boys and 1 girl

the number of ways for this selection

$$^6C_6 \times {^4C_1}$$

total number of ways

$= {^6C_4} \times {^4C_3} + {^6C_5} \times {^4C_2} + {^6C_6} \times {^4C_1}$

$= 15 \times 4 + 6 \times 6 + 1 \times 4$

$= 60 + 36 + 4 = 100.$

9. Observation of first 10 members

$= 4.5 \times 10 = 45$

observation of last 30 members

$= 3.5 \times 30 = 105$

total observation done by 40 members

$= 45 + 105 = 150$

Average observation $= \frac{150}{40} = \frac{15}{4}$.

11. Let present age of A is x and B is y.

According to the question

$$x + y = 50 \quad ...(i)$$

5 years ago, ratio of their age

$$\frac{x-5}{y-5} = \frac{5}{3}$$

$$3(x - 5) = 5(y - 5)$$

or, $\quad 3x - 5y = -10 \quad ...(ii)$

from (i) and (ii)

$$8x = 250 - 10$$

$$x = \frac{240}{8} = 30$$

$$y = 20$$

Present Age of A = 30 years

Present Age of B = 20 years.

12. $(90 + 9 - 29) \div 10 \times 2$

$= (99 - 29) \div 10 \times 2$

$= 70 \div 10 \times 2$

$= 7 \times 2 = 14.$

28. $(10001)_2 = 1 \times 2^4 + 0 \times 2^3 + 0 \times 2^2 + 0 \times 2^1 + 1 \times 2^0$

$= 16 + 0 + 0 + 0 + 1 = 17$

so, $(17)^{10} = (10001)_2$.

Previous Years' Paper (Solved)

UGC-NET (JRF) EXAM JUNE, 2012

PAPER–I

Note : This paper contains **sixty (60)** multiple-choice questions, each question carrying **two (2)** marks. Candidate is expected to answer any **fifty (50)** questions. In case more than **fifty (50)** questions are attempted, only the first **fifty (50)** questions will be evaluated.

1. Video-Conferencing can be classified as one of the following types of communication:
(A) Visual one way
(B) Audio-Visual one way
(C) Audio-Visual two way
(D) Visual two way

2. MC National University of Journalism and Communication is located at:
(A) Lucknow (B) Bhopal
(C) Chennai (D) Mumbai

3. All India Radio (A.I.R.) for broadcasting was named in the year:
(A) 1926 (B) 1936
(C) 1946 (D) 1956

4. In India for broadcasting TV programmes which system is followed?
(A) NTCS (B) PAL
(C) NTSE (D) SECAM

5. The term 'DAVP' stands for:
(A) Directorate of Advertising & Vocal Publicity
(B) Division of Audio-Visual Publicity
(C) Department of Audio-Visual Publicity
(D) Directorate of Advertising & Visual Publicity

6. The term "TRP" is associated with TV shows stands for:
(A) Total Rating Points
(B) Time Rating Points
(C) Thematic Rating Points
(D) Television Rating Points

7. Which is the number that comes next in the following sequence?
2, 6, 12, 20, 30, 42, 56, _____
(A) 60 (B) 64
(C) 72 (D) 70

8. Find the next letter for the series YVSP ....
(A) N (B) M
(C) O (D) L

9. Given that in a code language, '645' means 'day is warm'; '42' means 'warm spring' and '634' means 'spring is sunny'; which digit represents 'sunny'?
(A) 3 (B) 2
(C) 4 (D) 5

10. The basis of the following classification is: 'first President of India', 'author of *Godan*', 'books in my library', 'blue things' and 'students who work hard'
(A) Common names
(B) Proper names
(C) Descriptive phrases
(D) Indefinite description

11. In the expression 'Nothing is larger than itself' the relation 'is larger than' is:
(A) antisymmetric

(B) asymmetrical
(C) intransitive
(D) irreflexive

12. **Assertion (A) :** There are more laws on the books today than ever before, and more crimes being committed than ever before.
Reason (R) : Because to reduce crime we must eliminate the laws.
Choose the correct answer from below:
(A) (A) is true, (R) is doubtful and (R) is not the correct explanation of (A).
(B) (A) is false, (R) is true and (R) is the correct explanation of (A).
(C) (A) is doubtful, (R) is doubtful and (R) is not the correct explanation of (A).
(D) (A) is doubtful, (R) is true and (R) is not the correct explanation of (A).

13. If the proposition "All men are not mortal" is true then which of the following inferences is correct? Choose from the code given below:
1. "All men are mortal" is true.
2. "Some men are mortal" is false.
3. "No men are mortal" is doubtful.
4. "All men are mortal" is false.

Code :
(A) 1, 2 and 3 (B) 2, 3 and 4
(C) 1, 3 and 4 (D) 1 and 3

14. Determine the nature of the following definition:
"Abortion" means the ruthless murdering of innocent beings.
(A) Lexical (B) Persuasive
(C) Stipulative (D) Theoretical

15. Which one of the following is **not** an argument?
(A) Devadutt does not eat in the day so he must be eating at night.
(B) If Devadutt is growing fat and if he does not eat during the day, he will be eating at night.
(C) Devadutt eats in the night so he does not eat during the day.
(D) Since Devadutt does not eat in the day, he must be eating in the night.

16. Venn diagram is a kind of diagram to:
(A) represent and assess the validity of elementary inferences of syllogistic form.
(B) represent but not assess the validity of elementary inferences of syllogistic form.
(C) represent and assess the truth of elementary inferences of syllogistic form.
(D) assess but not represent the truth of elementary inferences of syllogistic form.

17. Reasoning by analogy leads to:
(A) certainty
(B) definite conclusion
(C) predictive conjecture
(D) surety

18. Which of the following statements are false? Choose from the code given below:
1. Inductive arguments always proceed from the particular to the general.
2. A cogent argument must be inductively strong.
3. A valid argument may have a false premise and a false conclusion.
4. An argument may legitimately be spoken of as 'true' or 'false'.

Code :
(A) 2, 3 and 4 (B) 1 and 3
(C) 2 and 4 (D) 1 and 2

19. Six persons A, B, C, D, E and F are standing in a circle. B is between F and C, A is between E and D, F is to the left of D. Who is between A and F?
(A) B (B) C
(C) D (D) E

20. The price of petrol increases by 25%. By what percentage must a customer reduce the consumption so that the earlier bill on the petrol does not alter?
(A) 20% (B) 25%
(C) 30% (D) 33.33%

21. If Ram knows that y is an integer greater than 2 and less than 7 and Hari knows that y is an integer greater than 5 and less than 10, then they may correctly conclude that
(A) y can be exactly determined
(B) y may be either of two values

(C) y may be any of three values
(D) there is no value of y satisfying these conditions

22. Four pipes can fill a reservoir in 15, 20, 30 and 60 hours respectively. The first one was opened at 6 AM, second at 7 AM, third at 8 AM and the fourth at 9 AM. When will the reservoir be filled?
(A) 11 AM (B) 12 Noon
(C) 1 PM (D) 1:30 PM

The total electricity generation in a country is 97 GW. The contribution of various energy sources is indicated in percentage terms in the Pie Chart given below:

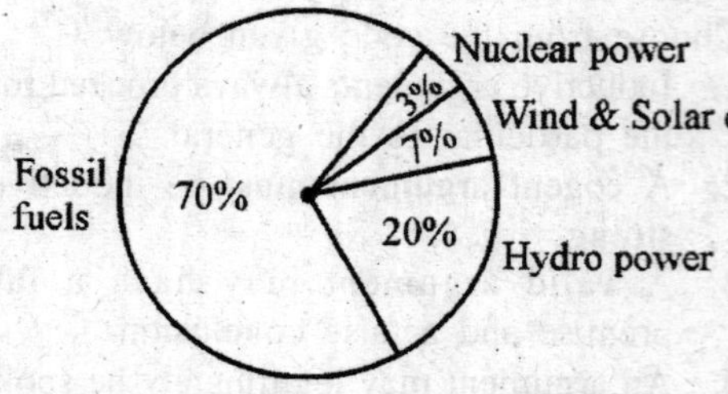

23. What is the contribution of wind and solar power in absolute terms in the electricity generation?
(A) 6.79 GW (B) 19.4 GW
(C) 9.7 GW (D) 29.1 GW

24. What is the contribution of renewable energy sources in absolute terms in the electricity generation?
(A) 29.1 GW (B) 26.19 GW
(C) 67.9 GW (D) 97 GW

25. TCP/IP is necessary if one is to connect to the:
(A) Phone lines
(B) LAN
(C) Internet
(D) Server

26. Each character on the keyboard of computer has an ASCII value which stands for:
(A) American Stock Code for Information Interchange
(B) American Standard Code for Information Interchange
(C) African Standard Code for Information Interchange
(D) Adaptable Standard Code for Information Change

27. Which of the following is not a programming language?
(A) Pascal
(B) Microsoft Office
(C) Java
(D) C++

28. Minimum number of bits required to store any 3 digit decimal number is equal to:
(A) 3 (B) 5
(C) 8 (D) 10

29. Internet explorer is a type of
(A) Operating System
(B) Compiler
(C) Browser
(D) IP address

30. POP3 and IMAP are e-mail accounts in which:
(A) One automatically gets one's mail everyday
(B) One has to be connected to the server to read or write one's mail
(C) One only has to be connected to the server to send and receive e-mail
(D) One does not need any telephone lines

31. Irritation in eyes is caused by the pollutant:
(A) Sulphur di-oxide
(B) Ozone
(C) PAN
(D) Nitrous oxide

32. Which is the source of chlorofluorocarbons?
(A) Thermal power plants
(B) Automobiles
(C) Refrigeration and Airconditioning
(D) Fertilizers

33. Which of the following is not a renewable natural resource?
(A) Clean air (B) Fertile soil
(C) Fresh water (D) Salt

34. Which of the following parameters is not used as a pollution indicator in water?

(A) Total dissolved solids
(B) Coliform count
(C) Dissolved oxygen
(D) Density

35. S and P waves are associated with:
(A) floods
(B) wind energy
(C) earthquakes
(D) tidal energy

36. Match Lists I and II and select the correct answer from the codes given below:

List-I	***List-II***
(i) Ozone hole	*(a)* Tsunami
(ii) Greenhouse effect	*(b)* UV radiations
(iii) Natural hazards	*(c)* Methane
(iv) Sustainable development	*(d)* Eco-centrism

Codes :

	(i)	*(ii)*	*(iii)*	*(iv)*
(A)	*(b)*	*(c)*	*(a)*	*(d)*
(B)	*(c)*	*(b)*	*(a)*	*(d)*
(C)	*(d)*	*(c)*	*(a)*	*(b)*
(D)	*(d)*	*(b)*	*(c)*	*(a)*

37. Indian Institute of Advanced Study is located at:
(A) Dharmshala
(B) Shimla
(C) Solan
(D) Chandigarh

38. Indicate the number of Regional Offices of National Council of Teacher Education.
(A) 04 (B) 05
(C) 06 (D) 08

39. Which of the following rights was considered the "Heart and Soul" of the Indian Constitution by Dr. B.R. Ambedkar?
(A) Freedom of Speech
(B) Right to Equality
(C) Right to Freedom of Religion
(D) Right to Constitutional Remedies

40. Who among the following created the office of the District Collector in India?
(A) Lord Cornwallis
(B) Warren Hastings
(C) The Royal Commission on Decentralisation
(D) Sir Charles Metcalf

41. The Fundamental Duties of a citizen include:
1. Respect for the Constitution, the National Flag and the National Anthem
2. To develop the scientific temper.
3. Respect for the Government.
4. To protect Wildlife.

Choose the correct answer from the codes given below:
Codes :
(A) 1, 2 and 3 (B) 1, 2 and 4
(C) 2, 3 and 4 (D) 1, 3, 4 and 2

42. The President of India takes oath:
(A) to uphold the sovereignty and integrity of India.
(B) to bear true faith and allegiance to the Constitution of India.
(C) to uphold the Constitution and Laws of the country.
(D) to preserve, protect and defend the Constitution and the law of the country.

43. If you get an opportunity to teach a visually challenged student along with normal students, what type of treatment would you like to give him in the class?
(A) Not giving extra attention because majority may suffer.
(B) Take care of him sympathetically in the class-room.
(C) You will think that blindness is his destiny and hence you cannot do anything.
(D) Arrange a seat in the front row and try to teach at a pace convenient to him.

44. Which of the following is not a characteristic of a good achievement test?
(A) Reliability (B) Objectivity
(C) Ambiguity (D) Validity

45. Which of the following does not belong to a projected aid?
(A) Overhead projector
(B) Blackboard

(C) Epidiascope
(D) Slide projector

46. For a teacher, which of the following methods would be correct for writing on the blackboard?
(A) Writing fast and as clearly as possible.
(B) Writing the matter first and then asking students to read it.
(C) Asking a question to students and then writing the answer as stated by them.
(D) Writing the important points as clearly as possible.

47. A teacher can be successful if he/she:
(A) helps students in becoming better citizens
(B) imparts subject knowledge to students
(C) prepares students to pass the examination
(D) presents the subject matter in a well organized manner

48. Dynamic approach to teaching means:
(A) Teaching should be forceful and effective
(B) Teachers should be energetic and dynamic
(C) The topics of teaching should not be static, but dynamic
(D) The students should be required to learn through activities

49. The research that aims at immediate application is:
(A) Action Research
(B) Empirical Research
(C) Conceptual Research
(D) Fundamental Research

50. When two or more successive footnotes refer to the same work which one of the following expressions is used?
(A) ibid (B) et.al
(C) op.cit : (D) loc.cit.

51. Nine year olds are taller than seven year olds. This is an example of a reference drawn from:
(A) Vertical study
(B) Cross-sectional study
(C) Time series study
(D) Experimental study

52. Conferences are meant for:
(A) Multiple target groups
(B) Group discussions
(C) Show-casing new Research
(D) All the above

53. Ex Post Facto research means:
(A) The research is carried out after the incident
(B) The research is carried out prior to the incident
(C) The research is carried out along with the happening of an incident.
(D) The research is carried out keeping in mind the possibilities of an incident.

54. Research ethics do not include:
(A) Honesty (B) Subjectivity
(C) Integrity (D) Objectivity

Directions (Qs. 55 to 60): *Read the following passage carefully and answer the questions:*

James Madison said, "A people who mean to be their own governors must arm themselves with power that knowledge gives." In India, the Official Secrets Act, 1923 was a convenient smokescreen to deny members of the public access to information. Public functioning has traditionally been shrouded in secrecy. But in a democracy in which people govern themselves, it is necessary to have more openness. In the maturing of our democracy, right to information is a major step forward; it enables citizens to participate fully in the decision-making process that affects their lives so profoundly. It is in this context that the address of the Prime Minister in the Lok Sabha is significant. He said, "I would only like to see that everyone, particularly our civil servants, should see the Bill in a positive spirit; not as a draconian law for paralyzing Government, but as an instrument for improving Government-Citizen interface resulting in a friendly, caring and effective Government functioning for the good of our People." He further said, "This is an innovative Bill, where there will be scope to review its functioning as we gain experience. Therefore, this is a piece of legislation, whose working will be kept under constant reviews."

The Commission, in its Report, has dealt with the application of the Right to Information in Executive, Legislature and Judiciary. The judiciary could be a pioneer in implementing the Act in letter and spirit because much of the work that the Judiciary does is open to public scrutiny, Government of India has sanctioned an e-governance project in the Judiciary for about ₹ 700 crores which would bring about systematic classification, standardization and categorization of records. This would help the judiciary to fulfil its mandate under the Act. Similar capacity building would be required in all other public authorities. The transformation from non-transparency to transparency and public accountability is the responsibility of all three organs of State.

55. A person gets power:
(A) by acquiring knowledge
(B) from the Official Secrets Act, 1923
(C) through openings
(D) by denying public information

56. Right to Information is a major step forward to:
(A) enable citizens to participate fully in the decision-making process
(B) to make the people aware of the Act
(C) to gain knowledge of administration
(D) to make the people Government friendly

57. The Prime Minister considered the Bill:
(A) to provide power to the civil servants
(B) as an instrument for improving Government-citizen interface resulting in a friendly, caring and effective Government
(C) a draconian law against the officials
(D) to check the harassment of the people

58. The Commission made the Bill effective by:
(A) extending power to the executive authorities
(B) combining the executive and legislative power
(C) recognizing Judiciary a pioneer in implementing the act in letter and spirit
(D) educating the people before its implementation

59. The Prime Minister considered the Bill innovative and hoped that
(A) It could be reviewed based on the experience gained on its functioning.
(B) The civil servants would see the Bill in a positive spirit.
(C) It would not be considered as a draconian law for paralyzing Government
(D) All the above

60. The transparency and public accountability is the responsibility of three organs of the State. These three organs are:
(A) Lok Sabha, Rajya Sabha and Judiciary
(B) Lok Sabha, Rajya Sabha and Executive
(C) Judiciary, Legislature and the Commission
(D) Legislature, Executive and Judiciary

ANSWERS

1	2	3	4	5	6	7	8	9	10
(C)	(B)	(B)	(B)	(D)	(A)	(C)	(B)	(A)	(C)
11	**12**	**13**	**14**	**15**	**16**	**17**	**18**	**19**	**20**
(D)	(A)	(B)	(B)	(B)	(A)	(C)	(C)	(C)	(A)
21	**22**	**23**	**24**	**25**	**26**	**27**	**28**	**29**	**30**
(A)	(C)	(A)	(B)	(C)	(B)	(B)	(D)	(C)	(C)
31	**32**	**33**	**34**	**35**	**36**	**37**	**38**	**39**	**40**
(C)	(C)	(D)	(D)	(C)	(A)	(B)	(A)	(D)	(B)
41	**42**	**43**	**44**	**45**	**46**	**47**	**48**	**49**	**50**
(B)	(D)	(D)	(C)	(B)	(D)	(A)	(D)	(A)	(A)
51	**52**	**53**	**54**	**55**	**56**	**57**	**58**	**59**	**60**
(B)	(D)	(A)	(B)	(A)	(A)	(B)	(C)	(D)	(D)

SOME SELECTED EXPLANATORY ANSWERS

1. Video-conferencing is the conduct of a video-conference by a set of tele-communication technologies which allow two or more locations to communicate by simultaneous two-way video and audio transmissions. It has also been called visual collaboration and is a type of groupware.
2. Makhanlal Chaturvedi National University of Journalism and Communication, officially known as MC Rashtriya Patrakarita Vishwa-vidyalaya is a government University located in Bhopal, Madhya Pradesh. It was set up by the Act 15 of 1990 of the Madhya Pradesh Legislative Assembly. This University was formally inaugurated by Dr. Shankar Dayal Sharma, the then Vice President of India, on 16th January, 1990.
3. In June 1923, the Radio Club of Bombay made the first ever broadcast in the country. This was followed by the setting up of the Calcutta Radio Club five month later. The first radio station of the Indian Broadcasting Company (IBC) at Bombay (now Mumbai), formally inaugurated by the then Viceroy of India, Lord Irwin, on January 23, 1927, heralded the beginning of organised broadcasting in India. Interestingly, this was the year in which the British Broadcasting Corporation (BBC) was formed. The IBC was liquidated in 1930.
4. PAL (Phase Alternating Line) is a analogue television colour encoding system used in broadcast television systems in many countries. Other common analogue television systems are NTSC (National Television System Committee) and SECAM (Sequential Couleur Avec Memoire).

   North America, most of South America, Japan, South Korea and Taiwan adopted NTSC. Most of Western Europe, India, Iceland, Australia, parts of Africa and the Middle East, and a few countries in South America adopted PAL. SECAM was mainly adopted in France, Eastern Europe and parts of Africa.
5. The Directorate of Advertising & Visual Publicity (DAVP) is the nodal agency to undertake multi-media advertising and publicity for various Ministries and Departments of Governments of India. Some of the Autonomous Bodies also route their advertisements through DAVP. As a service agency, it endeavours to Communicate at grass roots level on behalf of various Central Government Ministries.

7. 2 → 6 → 12 → 20 → 30 → 42 → 56 → **72**

   +(2×2) +(2×3) +(2×4) +(2×5) +(2×6) +(2×7) +(2×8)

8. Y → V → S → P → M

   –3 –3 –3 –3

14. **Persuasive Definitions:** The purpose of a persuasive definition is to convince us to believe that something is the case and to get us to act accordingly. Frequently definitions of words like "freedom," "democracy," and "communism," are of this type. (E.g., taxation is the means by which bureaucrats rip off the people who have elected them.) While these sorts of definitions might be emotionally useful, we should avoid them when we are attempting to be logical.

    Theoretical Definitions: Theoretical definitions are designed to explain a theory. Whether they are correct or not will depend, largely, on whether the theory they are an integral part of is correct. Newton's famous formula "F = ma" (*i.e.*, Force = mass x acceleration), provides a good example of such a definition.

    Stipulative Definitions: Stipulative definitions are frequently provided when we need to refer to a complex idea, but there simply is no word for that idea. A word is selected and assigned a meaning without any pretense that this is what that word really means. (E.g., by "a blue number" we mean any number greater than 17 but less than 36.)

Lexical Definitions: Unlike stipulative definitions, lexical definitions do attempt to capture the real meaning of a word and so can be either correct or incorrect. When we tell someone that "intractable" means not easily governed, or obstinate, this is the kind of definition we are providing. Roughly, lexical definitions are the kinds of definitions found in dictionaries.

20. Let the price of petrol be ₹ 100 per litre. Let the user use 1 litre of petrol. Therefore, his expense on petrol = 100 × 1 = ₹ 100
Now, the price of petrol increases by 25%.
Therefore, the new price of petrol = ₹ 125.
As he has to maintain his expenditure on petrol constant, he will be spending only ₹ 100 on petrol.
Let 'x' be the number of litres of petrol he will use at the new price.
Therefore,

$$125 \times x = 100$$

$$\Rightarrow x = \frac{100}{125} = \frac{4}{5} = 0.8 \text{ litres}$$

He has cut down his petrol consumption by

$$0.2 \text{ litres} = \frac{0.2}{1} \times 100 = 20\%.$$

22. Upto 9 A.M. 1st pipe has worked for 3 hrs; 2nd pipe for 2 hrs. and 3rd pipe for 1 hr.

$\therefore$ Part filled up to 9 A.M.

$$= 3 \times \frac{1}{15} + 2 \times \frac{1}{20} + \frac{1}{30}$$

$$= \frac{1}{5} + \frac{1}{10} + \frac{1}{30}$$

$$= \frac{1}{3}$$

Unfilled part at 9 A.M. $= 1 - \frac{1}{3} = \frac{2}{3}$

From 9 A.M. onwards all four pipes are functioning.
Part filled (by all four pipes) in 1 hr.

$$= \frac{1}{15} + \frac{1}{20} + \frac{1}{30} + \frac{1}{60} = \frac{1}{6}$$

$\therefore$ $\frac{2}{3}$ of reservoir will be filled up in

$$6 \times \frac{2}{3} = 4 \text{ hr.}$$

Counting 4 hrs. from 9 A.M. reservoir will be full at 1.00 P.M.

23. Contribution of wind and solar power in absolute terms $= 97 \times \frac{7}{100} = 6.79$ GW.

24. Contribution of renewable energy sources in absolute terms $= \frac{97 \times 27}{100} = 26.19$ GW.

25. TCP/IP is the communication protocol for communication between computers on the Internet.
TCP/IP stands for Transmission Control Protocol/Internet Protocol.
TCP/IP defines how electronic devices (like computers) should be connected to the Internet, and how data should be transmitted between them.

26. ASCII stands for the "American Standard Code for Information Interchange". It was designed in the early 60's, as a standard character-set for computers and hardware devices like teleprinters and tapedrives.
ASCII is a 7-bit character set containing 128 characters.
It contains the numbers from 0-9, the uppercase and lowercase English letters from A to Z, and some special characters.
The character-sets used in modern computers, HTML, and Internet are all based on ASCII.

29. Internet Explorer is a free web browser from Microsoft.
Internet Explorer was released in 1995 and is one of the most popular browsers today.

30. POP3 stands for a Post Office Protocol version 3. The POP3 protocol is designed to allow the users to retrieve e-mail messages when they are connected to the e-mail server (via Internet, Ethernet or VPN network connection). Once the e-mail messages are downloaded from the server they can be modified, read and manipulated offline.

The IMAP (Internet Message Access Protocol) is a newer and modern alternative to the POP3 protocol. Unlike it, the IMAP allows the users to work with their messages in both online and offline modes. The IMAP-capable e-mail client programs retrieve the messages' headers from the server and can store local copies of the messages in a local (temporary) cache. All the messages are left on the server until they are deleted by the user. This mechanism allows multiple e-mail clients to access a single mailbox and is often used for corporate/business e-mails (*e.g.* sales@company-domain.com).

31. Peroxyacyl nitrates (PANs) are powerful respiratory and eye irritants present in photochemical smog.

35. There are two types of seismic waves, *body waves* and *surface waves*. Body waves travel through the interior of the Earth, while surface waves travel only within the top surface layers. Most earthquakes take place at depths of less than 80 km below the Earth's surface. There are two types of body waves, *P waves* and *S waves*. P waves bunch together and then spread apart when they move. It is a bit like the movement of an inch worm or a slinky. S waves are like rolling ocean waves or like when you snap a rope. The oscillations are in a waveform.

37. The Indian Institute of Advanced Study (IIAS) is a prestigious research institute based in Shimla. It was set up by the Ministry of Education, Government of India in 1964 and it started functioning from October 20, 1965. The building that houses the Institute was originally built as a home for Lord Dufferin, Viceroy of India from 1884-1888 and was called the Viceregal Lodge. It housed all the subsequent viceroys and governors general of India. It occupied the Observatory Hill, one of the seven hills that Shimla is built upon.

38. NCTE has 4 Regional offices which are as follows:

1. Eastern Regional Committee (ERC) located at Bhubaneshwar.
2. Southern Regional Committee (SRC) located at Bangalore.
3. Western Regional Committee (WRC) located at Bhopal.
4. Northern Regional Committee (NRC) located at Jaipur.

39. Right to Constitutional Remedies (Article 32) was regarded as the heart and soul of the Indian Constitution by Dr. B.R. Ambedkar.

45. **Non-projected Aids:** Visual instructional devices which are simply presented without any projection equipment are non-projected aids. **Examples:** blackboard, chart, etc.

Projected Aids: Visual instructional devices which are shown with a projector are called projected aids. **Examples:** slides, filmstrip, silent films, cartoons, etc. projected through an opaque projector (epidiascope), or an over head projector.

50. Ibid is a contraction of *ibidem*, a Latin word meaning "the same place." This term is most commonly used for footnoting in scholarly texts, allowing the author to say "ibid" instead of citing a lengthy title. In legal texts, people may use "id," a shortening of "idem," a word which means "as mentioned previously."

53. *Ex-post facto* research is systematic empirical inquiry in which the scientist does not have direct control of independent variables because their manifestations have already occurred or because they are inherently not manipulated.

Previous Years' Paper (Solved)

UGC-NET (JRF) EXAM DECEMBER, 2011

PAPER–I

Note : This paper contains **Sixty (60)** multiple-choice questions, each question carrying **two (2)** marks. Candidate is expected to answer any **Fifty (50)** questions. In case more than **Fifty (50)** questions are attempted, only the first **Fifty (50)** questions will be evaluated.

1. Photo bleeding means
A. Photo cropping
B. Photo placement
C. Photo cutting
D. Photo colour adjustment

2. While designing communication strategy feed-forward studies are conducted by
A. Audience B. Communicator
C. Satellite D. Media

3. In which language the newspapers have highest circulation ?
A. English B. Hindi
C. Bengali D. Tamil

4. Aspect ratio of TV Screen is
A. 4 : 3 B. 3 : 4
C. 2 : 3 D. 2 : 4

5. Communication with oneself is known as
A. Organisational Communication
B. Grapewine Communication
C. Interpersonal Communication
D. Intrapersonal Communication

6. The term 'SITE' stands for
A. Satellite Indian Television Experiment
B. Satellite International Television Experiment
C. Satellite Instructional Television Experiment
D. Satellite Instructional Teachers Education

7. What is the number that comes next in the sequence ?
2, 5, 9, 19, 37, ___
A. 76 B. 74
C. 75 D. 50

8. Find the next letter for the series MPSV.....
A. X B. Y
C. Z D. A

9. If '367' means 'I am happy'; '748' means 'you are sad' and '469' means 'happy and sad' in a given code, then which of the following represents 'and' in that code ?
A. 3 B. 6
C. 9 D. 4

10. The basis of the following classification is 'animal', 'man', 'house', 'book', and 'student':
A. Definite descriptions
B. Proper names
C. Descriptive phrases
D. Common names

11. Assertion (A) : The coin when flipped next time will come up tails.

Reason (R) : Because the coin was flipped five times in a row, and each time it came up heads.

Choose the correct answer from below :
A. Both (A) and (R) are true, and (R) is the correct explanation of (A).

B. Both (A) and (R) are false, and (R) is the correct explanation of (A).
C. (A) is doubtful, (R) is true, and (R) is not the correct explanation of (A).
D. (A) is doubtful, (R) is false, and (R) is the correct explanation of (A).

12. The relation 'is a sister of ' is
A. non-symmetrical
B. symmetrical
C. asymmetrical
D. transitive

13. If the proposition "Vegetarians are not meat eaters" is false, then which of the following inferences is correct ? Choose from the codes given below :
1. "Some vegetarians are meat eaters" is true.
2. "All vegetarians are meat eaters" is doubtful.
3. "Some vegetarians are not meat eaters" is true.
4. "Some vegetarians are not meat eaters" is doubtful.

Codes:
A. 1, 2 and 3 B. 2, 3 and 4
C. 1, 3 and 4 D. 1, 2 and 4

14. Determine the nature of the following definition :
'Poor' means having an annual income of ₹ 10,000.
A. persuasive B. precising
C. lexical D. stipulative

15. Which one of the following is not an argument ?
A. If today is Tuesday, tomorrow will be Wednesday.
B. Since today is Tuesday, tomorrow will be Wednesday.
C. Ram insulted me so I punched him in the nose.
D. Ram is not at home, so he must have gone to town.

16. Venn diagram is a kind of diagram to
A. represent and assess the truth of elementary inferences with the help of Boolean Algebra of classes.
B. represent and assess the validity of elementary inferences with the help of Boolean Algebra of classes.
C. represent but not assess the validity of elementary inferences with the help of Boolean Algebra of classes.
D. assess but not represent the validity of elementary inferences with the help of Boolean Algebra of classes.

17. Inductive logic studies the way in which a premise may
A. support and entail a conclusion
B. not support but entail a conclusion
C. neither support nor entail a conclusion
D. support a conclusion without entailing it

18. Which of the following statements are true ? Choose from the codes given below.
1. Some arguments, while not completely valid, are almost valid.
2. A sound argument may be invalid.
3. A cogent argument may have a probably false conclusion.
4. A statement may be true or false.

Codes:
A. 1 and 2 B. 1, 3 and 4
C. 4 alone D. 3 and 4

19. If the side of the square increases by 40%, then the area of the square increases by
A. 60 % B. 40 %
C. 196 % D. 96 %

20. There are 10 lamps in a hall. Each one of them can be switched on independently. The number of ways in which hall can be illuminated is
A. 10^2 B. 1023
C. 2^{10} D. 10 !

21. How many numbers between 100 and 300 begin or end with 2 ?
A. 100 B. 110
C. 120 D. 180

22. In a college having 300 students, every student reads 5 newspapers and every newspaper is read by 60 students. The number of newspapers required is

A. at least 30 B. at most 20
C. exactly 25 D. exactly 5

The total CO_2 emissions from various sectors are 5 mmt. In the Pie Chart given below, the percentage contribution to CO_2 emissions from various sectors is indicated.

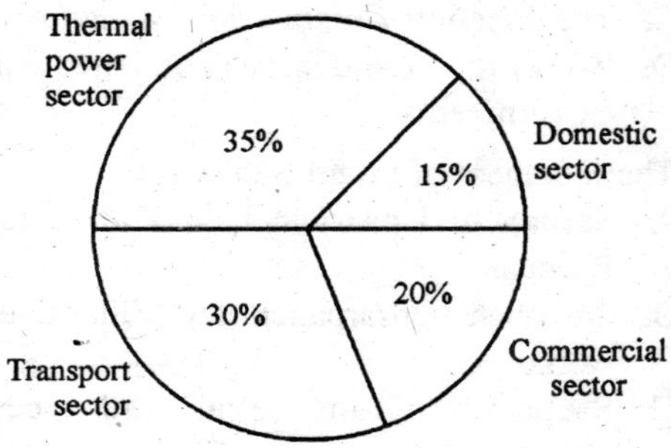

23. What is the absolute CO_2 emission from domestic sector ?
A. 1.5 mmt B. 2.5 mmt
C. 1.75 mmt D. 0.75 mmt

24. What is the absolute CO_2 emission for combined thermal power and transport sectors?
A. 3.25 mmt B. 1.5 mmt
C. 2.5 mmt D. 4 mmt

25. Which of the following operating system is used on mobile phones?
A. Windows Vista B. Android
C. Windows XP D. All of the above

26. If $(y)_x$ represents a number y in base x, then which of the following numbers is smallest of all?
A. $(1111)_2$ B. $(1111)_8$
C. $(1111)_{10}$ D. $(1111)_{16}$

27. High level programming language can be converted to machine language using which of the following?
A. Oracle B. Compiler
C. Mat lab D. Assembler

28. HTML is used to create
A. machine language program
B. high level program
C. web page
D. web server

29. The term DNS stands for
A. Domain Name System
B. Defense Nuclear System
C. Downloadable New Software
D. Dependent Name Server

30. IPv4 and IPv6 are addresses used to identify computers on the internet. Find the correct statement out of the following :
A. Number of bits required for IPv4 address is more than number of bits required for IPv6 address.
B. Number of bits required for IPv4 address is same as number of bits required for IPv6 address.
C. Number of bits required for IPv4 address is less than number of bits required for IPv6 address.
D. Number of bits required for IPv4 address is 64.

31. Which of the following pollutants affects the respiratory tract in humans?
A. Carbon monoxide
B. Nitric oxide
C. Sulphur di-oxide
D. Aerosols

32. Which of the following pollutants is not emitted from the transport sector?
A. Oxides of nitrogen
B. Chlorofluorocarbons
C. Carbon monoxide
D. Poly aromatic hydrocarbons

33. Which of the following sources of energy has the maximum potential in India?
A. Solar energy
B. Wind energy
C. Ocean thermal energy
D. Tidal energy

34. Which of the following is not a source of pollution in soil ?
A. Transport sector
B. Agriculture sector
C. Thermal power plants
D. Hydropower plants

35. Which of the following is ***not*** a natural hazard?

A. Earthquake B. Tsunami
C. Flash floods D. Nuclear accident

36. Ecological footprint represents

A. area of productive land and water to meet the resources requirement
B. energy consumption
C. CO_2 emissions per person
D. forest cover

37. The aim of value education to inculcate in students is

A. the moral values
B. the social values
C. the political values
D. the economic values

38. Indicate the number of Regional Offices of University Grants Commission of India.

A. 10 B. 07
C. 08 D. 09

39. One-rupee currency note in India bears the signature of

A. The President of India
B. Finance Minister of India
C. Governor, Reserve Bank of India
D. Finance Secretary of Government of India

40. Match the List – I with the List – II and select the correct answer from the codes given below:

List – I (Commissions and Committees)	List – II (Year)
(*a*) First Administrative Reforms Commission	(*i*) 2005
(*b*) Paul H. Appleby Committee I	(*ii*) 1962
(*c*) K. Santhanam Committee	(*iii*) 1966
(*d*) Second Administrative Reforms Commission	(*iv*) 1953

Codes :

	(*a*)	(*b*)	(*c*)	(*d*)
A.	(i)	(iii)	(ii)	(iv)
B.	(iii)	(iv)	(ii)	(i)
C.	(iv)	(ii)	(iii)	(i)
D.	(ii)	(i)	(iv)	(iii)

41. Constitutionally the registration and recognition of political parties is the function performed by

A. The State Election Commission of respective States
B. The Law Ministry of Government of India
C. The Election Commission of India
D. Election Department of the State Governments

42. The members of Gram Sabha are

A. Sarpanch, Upsarpanch and all elected Panchas
B. Sarpanch, Upsarpanch and Village level worker
C. Sarpanch, Gram Sevak and elected Panchas
D. Registered voters of Village Panchayat

43. By which of the following methods the true evaluation of the students is possible?

A. Evaluation at the end of the course.
B. Evaluation twice in a year.
C. Continuous evaluation.
D. Formative evaluation.

44. Suppose a student wants to share his problems with his teacher and he visits the teacher's house for the purpose, the teacher should

A. contact the student's parents and solve his problem.
B. suggest him that he should never visit his house.
C. suggest him to meet the principal and solve the problem.
D. extend reasonable help and boost his morale.

45. When some students are deliberately attempting to disturb the discipline of the class by making mischief, what will be your role as a teacher?

A. Expelling those students.
B. Isolate those students.
C. Reform the group with your authority.
D. Giving them an opportunity for introspection and improve their behaviour.

46. Which of the following belongs to a projected aid?
   A. Blackboard B. Diorama
   C. Epidiascope D. Globe
47. A teacher is said to be fluent in asking questions, if he can ask
   A. meaningful questions
   B. as many questions as possible
   C. maximum number of questions in a fixed time
   D. many meaningful questions in a fixed time
48. Which of the following qualities is most essential for a teacher ?
   A. He should be a learned person.
   B. He should be a well dressed person.
   C. He should have patience.
   D. He should be an expert in his subject.
49. A hypothesis is a
   A. law B. canon
   C. postulate D. supposition
50. Suppose you want to investigate the working efficiency of nationalised bank in India, which one of the following would you follow?
   A. Area Sampling
   B. Multi-stage Sampling
   C. Sequential Sampling
   D. Quota Sampling
51. Controlled group condition is applied in
   A. Survey Research
   B. Historical Research
   C. Experimental Research
   D. Descriptive Research
52. Workshops are meant for
   A. giving lectures
   B. multiple target groups
   C. showcase new theories
   D. hands on training/experience
53. Which one of the following is a research tool?
   A. Graph B. Illustration
   C. Questionnaire D. Diagram
54. Research is not considered ethical if it
   A. tries to prove a particular point.
   B. does not ensure privacy and anonymity of the respondent.
   C. does not investigate the data scientifically.
   D. is not of a very high standard.

Directions (Qs. 55 to 60): *Read the following passage carefully and answer the questions.*

The catalytic fact of the twentieth century is uncontrollable development, consumerist society, political materialism, and spiritual devaluation. This inordinate development has led to the transcendental 'second reality' of sacred perception that biologically transcendence is a part of human life. As the century closes, it dawns with imperative vigour that the 'first reality' of enlightened rationalism and the 'second reality' of the Beyond have to be harmonised in a worthy state of man. The *de facto* values describe what we are, they portray the 'is' of our ethic, they are *est* values (Latin *est* means is). The ideal values tell us what we ought to be, they are *esto* values (Latin *esto* 'ought to be'). Both have to be in the ebb and flow of consciousness. The ever new science and technology and the ever-perennial faith are two modes of one certainty, that is the wholeness of man, his courage to be, his share in Being.

The materialistic foundations of science have crumbled down. Science itself has proved that matter is energy, processes are as valid as facts, and affirmed the non-materiality of the universe. The encounter of the 'two cultures', the scientific and the humane, will restore the normal vision, and will be the bedrock of a 'science of understanding' in the new century. It will give new meaning to the ancient perception that quantity (measure) and quality (value) coexist at the root of nature. Human endeavours cannot afford to be humanistically irresponsible.

55. The problem raised in the passage reflects overall on
   A. Consumerism
   B. Materialism
   C. Spiritual devaluation
   D. Inordinate development
56. The '*de facto*' values in the passage means
   A. What is B. What ought to be
   C. What can be D. Where it is

57. According to the passage, the 'first reality' constitutes
A. Economic prosperity
B. Political development
C. Sacred perception of life
D. Enlightened rationalism

58. Encounter of the 'two cultures', the scientific and the human implies
A. Restoration of normal vision
B. Universe is both material and non-material
C. Man is superior to nature
D. Co-existence of quantity and quality in nature

59. The contents of the passage are
A. Descriptive B. Prescriptive
C. Axiomatic D. Optional

60. The passage indicates that science has proved that
A. universe is material
B. matter is energy
C. nature has abundance
D. humans are irresponsible

ANSWERS

1	2	3	4	5	6	7	8	9	10
A	B	B	A	D	C	C	B	C	D
11	**12**	**13**	**14**	**15**	**16**	**17**	**18**	**19**	**20**
C	B	A	B	A	B	D	D	D	B
21	**22**	**23**	**24**	**25**	**26**	**27**	**28**	**29**	**30**
B	C	D	A	B	A	B	C	A	C
31	**32**	**33**	**34**	**35**	**36**	**37**	**38**	**39**	**40**
A	B	B	D	D	A	A	B	D	B
41	**42**	**43**	**44**	**45**	**46**	**47**	**48**	**49**	**50**
C	D	D	D	D	C	D	C	D	B
51	**52**	**53**	**54**	**55**	**56**	**57**	**58**	**59**	**60**
C	D	C	B	C	A	D	A	A	B

SOME SELECTED EXPLANATORY ANSWERS

7.
$2 \times 2 + 1 = 5$
$5 \times 2 - 1 = 9$
$9 \times 2 + 1 = 19$
$19 \times 2 - 1 = 37$
$\therefore \quad 37 \times 2 + 1 = \boxed{75}$

8. M P S V Y

M →(+2)→ P →(+2)→ S →(+2)→ V →(+2)→ Y

9.
I am happy = 367 ...(1)
You are sad = 748 ...(2)
Happy and sad = 469 ...(3)

From (1) and (3)
Happy = 6
and from (2) and (3)
Sad = 4
$\therefore$ and = 9

19. Let the side of the square be 100 m.
$\therefore$ Area = side^2 = 10000 m^2
After increase, side of the square = 100 + 40
= 140 cm

$\therefore$ Area = 140 × 140 = 19600 cm^2

$\therefore$ Percentage increase = $\frac{19600-10000}{10000} \times 100$

$= \frac{9600 \times 100}{10000} = 96\%$

21. The required numbers are—
Numbers from 200 to 299
And 102, 112, 122, 132, 142, 152, 162, 172, 182, 192
Hence total required number = 100 + 10
= 110

22. Here we suppose group of 5 students as 1 unit.

so, number of units = $\frac{300}{60} = 5$ units

Now, each unit requires sets of papers

Total requirement = 5 × 5 = $\boxed{25}$

23. Domestic sector emission = $5 \times \frac{15}{100}$

= 0.75 mmt.

24. Combined % of emission of CO_2 from thermal and transport sector = 30 + 35 = 65%

Required emission = $5 \times \frac{65}{100}$ = 3.25 mmt.

26. $(1111)_2 = 2^3 + 2^2 + 2^1 + 2^0 = \boxed{15}$

Previous Years' Paper (Solved)

UGC-NET (JRF) EXAM JUNE, 2011

PAPER–I

Note : This paper contains **sixty (60)** multiple-choice questions, each question carrying **two (2)** marks. Candidate is expected to answer any **fifty (50)** questions. In case more than **fifty (50)** questions are attempted, only the first **fifty (50)** questions will be evaluated.

1. A research paper is a brief report of research work based on
A. Primary Data only
B. Secondary Data only
C. Both Primary and Secondary Data
D. None of the above

2. Newton gave three basic laws of motion. This research is categorized as
A. Descriptive Research
B. Sample Survey
C. Fundamental Research
D. Applied Research

3. A group of experts in a specific area of knowledge assembled at a place and prepared a syllabus for a new course. The process may be termed as
A. Seminar B. Workshop
C. Conference D. Symposium

4. In the process of conducting research ''Formulation of Hypothesis'' is followed by
A. Statement of Objectives
B. Analysis of Data
C. Selection of Research Tools
D. Collection of Data

Read the following passage carefully and answer questions from 5 to 10:

All historians are interpreters of text if they be private letters, Government records or parish birthlists or whatever. For most kinds of historians, these are only the necessary means to understanding something other than the texts themselves, such as a political action or a historical trend, whereas for the intellectual historian, a full understanding of his chosen texts is itself the aim of his enquiries. Of course, the intellectual history is particularly prone to draw on the focus of other disciplines that are habitually interpreting texts for purposes of their own, probing the reasoning that ostensibly connects premises and conclusions. Furthermore, the boundaries with adjacent subdisciplines are shifting and indistinct : the history of art and the history of science both claim a certain autonomy, partly just because they require specialised technical skills, but both can also be seen as part of a wider intellectual history, as is evident when one considers, for example, the common stock of knowledge about cosmological beliefs or moral ideals of a period.

Like all historians, the intellectual historian is a consumer rather than a producer of 'methods'. His distinctiveness lies in which aspect of the past he is trying to illuminate, not in having exclusive possession of either a corpus of evidence or a body of techniques. That being said, it does seem that the label 'intellectual history' attracts a disproportionate share of misunderstanding.

It is alleged that intellectual history is the history of something that never really mattered. The long dominance of the historical profession by political historians bred a kind of philistinism, an unspoken belief that power and its exercise was 'what mattered'. The prejudice was reinforced by the assertion that political action was never really the outcome of principles or ideas that were 'more flapdoodle'. The legacy of this precept is still discernible in the tendency to require ideas to have 'licensed' the political class before they can be deemed worthy of intellectual attention, as if there were some reasons why the history of art or science, of philosophy or literature, were somehow of interest and significance than the history of Parties or Parliaments. Perhaps in recent years the mirror-image of this philistinism has been more common in the claim that ideas of any one is of systematic expression or sophistication do not matter, as if they were only held by a minority.

Answer the following questions :

5. An intellectual historian aims to fully understand
   A. the chosen texts of his own
   B. political actions
   C. historical trends
   D. his enquiries
6. Intellectual historians do not claim exclusive possession of
   A. conclusions
   B. any corpus of evidence
   C. distinctiveness
   D. habitual interpretation
7. The misconceptions about intellectual history stem from
   A. a body of techniques
   B. the common stock of knowledge
   C. the dominance of political historians
   D. cosmological beliefs
8. What is philistinism?
   A. Reinforcement of prejudice
   B. Fabrication of reasons
   C. The hold of land-owning classes
   D. Belief that power and its exercise matter
9. Knowledge of cosmological beliefs or moral ideas of a period can be drawn as part of
   A. literary criticism
   B. history of science
   C. history of philosophy
   D. intellectual history
10. The claim that ideas of any one is of systematic expression do not matter, as if they were held by a minority, is
    A. to have a licensed political class
    B. political action
    C. a philosophy of literature
    D. the mirror-image of philistinism
11. Public communication tends to occur within a more
    A. complex structure
    B. political structure
    C. convenient structure
    D. formal structure
12. Transforming thoughts, ideas and messages into verbal and non-verbal signs is referred to as
    A. channelisation B. mediation
    C. encoding D. decoding
13. Effective communication needs a supportive
    A. economic environment
    B. political environment
    C. social environment
    D. multi-cultural environment
14. A major barrier in the transmission of cognitive data in the process of communication is an individual's
    A. personality C. expectation
    B. social status D. coding ability
15. When communicated, institutionalised stereotypes become
    A. myths B. reasons
    C. experiences D. convictions
16. In mass communication, selective perception is dependent on the receiver's
    A. competence B. pre-disposition
    C. receptivity D. ethnicity
17. Determine the relationship between the pair of words NUMERATOR : DENOMINATOR and then select the pair of words from the following which have a similar relationship :
    A. fraction : decimal
    B. divisor : quotient
    C. top : bottom
    D. dividend : divisor

18. Find the wrong number in the sequence
125, 127, 130, 135, 142, 153, 165

A. 130 B. 142
C. 153 D. 165

19. If HOBBY is coded as IOBY and LOBBY is coded as MOBY; then BOBBY is coded as

A. BOBY B. COBY
C. DOBY D. OOBY

20. The letters in the first set have certain relationship. On the basis of this relationship, make the right choice for the second set :
K/T : 11/20 : : J/R : ?

A. 10/8 B. 10/18
C. 11/19 D. 10/19

21. If A = 5, B = 6, C = 7, D = 8 and so on, what do the following numbers stand for?
17, 19, 20, 9, 8

A. Plane B. Moped
C. Motor D. Tonga

22. The price of oil is increased by 25%. If the expenditure is not allowed to increase, the ratio between the reduction in consumption and the original consumption is

A. 1 : 3 B. 1 : 4
C. 1 : 5 D. 1 : 6

23. How many 8's are there in the following sequence which are preceded by 5 but not immediately followed by 3?
5 8 3 7 5 8 6 3 8 5 4 5 8 4 7 6
5 5 8 3 5 8 7 5 8 2 8 5

A. 4 B. 5
C. 7 D. 3

24. If a rectangle were called a circle, a circle a point, a point a triangle and a triangle a square, the shape of a wheel is

A. Rectangle B. Circle
C. Point D. Triangle

25. Which one of the following methods is best suited for mapping the distribution of different crops as provided in the standard classification of crops in India?

A. Pie diagram
B. Chorochromatic technique
C. Isopleth technique
D. Dot method

26. Which one of the following does not come under the methods of data classification?

A. Qualitative B. Normative
C. Spatial D. Quantitative

27. Which one of the following is not a source of data?

A. Administrative records
B. Population census
C. GIS
D. Sample survey

28. If the statement 'some men are cruel' is false which of the following statements/statement are/is true?

(*i*) All men are cruel.
(*ii*) No men are cruel.
(*iii*) Some men are not cruel.

A. (*i*) and (*iii*) B. (*i*) and (*ii*)
C. (*ii*) and (*iii*) D. (*iii*) only

29. The octal number system consists of the following symbols:

A. 0 – 7 B. 0 – 9
C. 0 – 9, A – F D. None of the above

30. The binary equivalent of $(-19)_{10}$ in signed magnitude system is

A. 11101100 B. 11101101
C. 10010011 D. None of these

31. DNS in internet technology stands for

A. Dynamic Name System
B. Domain Name System
C. Distributed Name System
D. None of these

32. HTML stands for

A. Hyper Text Markup Language
B. Hyper Text Manipulation Language
C. Hyper Text Managing Links
D. Hyper Text Manipulating Links

33. Which of the following is type of LAN?

A. Ethernet B. Token Ring
C. FDDI D. All of the above

34. Which of the following statements is true?

A. Smart cards do not require an operating system.
B. Smart cards and PCs use some operating system.

C. COS is smart card operating system.
D. The communication between reader and card is in full duplex mode.

35. The Ganga Action Plan was initiated during the year
A. 1986 C. 1988
B. 1990 D. 1992

36. Identify the correct sequence of energy sources in order of their share in the power sector in India:
A. Thermal > nuclear > hydro > wind
B. Thermal > hydro > nuclear > wind
C. Hydro > nuclear > thermal > wind
D. Nuclear > hydro > wind > thermal

37. Chromium as a contaminant in drinking water in excess of permissible levels, causes
A. Skeletal damage
B. Gastrointestinal problem
C. Dermal and nervous problems
D. Liver/Kidney problems

38. The main precursors of winter smog are
A. N_2O and hydrocarbons
B. NO_x and hydrocarbons
C. SO_2 and hydrocarbons
D. SO_2 and ozone

39. Flash floods are caused when
A. the atmosphere is convectively unstable and there is considerable vertical wind-shear
B. the atmosphere is stable
C. the atmosphere is convectively unstable with no vertical windshear
D. winds are catabatic

40. In mega cities of India, the dominant source of air pollution is
A. transport sector
B. thermal power
C. municipal waste
D. commercial sector

41. The first Open University in India was set up in the State of
A. Andhra Pradesh
B. Delhi
C. Himachal Pradesh
D. Tamil Nadu

42. Most of the Universities in India are funded by
A. the Central Government
B. the State Governments
C. the University Grants Commission
D. Private bodies and Individuals

43. Which of the following organizations looks after the quality of Technical and Management education in India?
A. NCTE
B. MCI
C. AICTE
D. CSIR

44. Consider the following statements : Identify the statement which implies natural justice.
A. The principle of natural justice is followed by the Courts.
B. Justice delayed is justice denied.
C. Natural justice is an inalienable right of a citizen
D. A reasonable opportunity of being heard must be given.

45. The President of India is
A. the Head of State
B. the Head of Government
C. both A and B
D. None of the above

46. Who among the following holds office during the pleasure of the President of India?
A. Chief Election Commissioner
B. Comptroller and Auditor General of India
C. Chairman of the Union Public Service Commission
D. Governor of a State

Questions 47 to 49 are based upon the following diagram in which there are three interlocking circles A, P and S where A stands for Artists, circle P for Professors and circle S for Sportspersons.

Different regions in the figure are lettered from a to f :

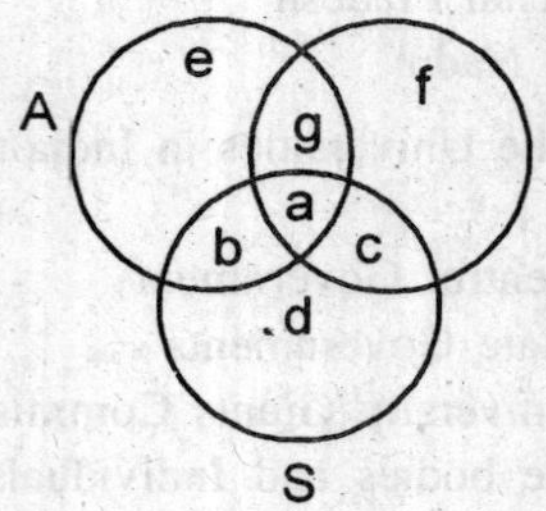

47. The region which represents artists who are neither sportsmen nor professors.

A. d B. e

C. b D. g

48. The region which represents professors, who are both artists and sportspersons.

A. a B. c

C. d D. g

49. The region which represents professors, who are also sportspersons, but not artists.

A. e B. f

C. c D. g

Questions 50 to 52 are based on the following data :

Measurements of some variable X were made at an interval of 1 minute from 10 A.M. to 10:20 A.M. The data, thus, obtained is as follows :

X : 60, 62, 65, 64, 63, 61, 66, 65, 70, 68
63, 62, 64, 69, 65, 64, 66, 67, 66, 64

50. The value of X, which is exceeded 10% of the time in the duration of measurement, is

A. 69 B. 68

C. 67 D. 66

51. The value of X, which is exceeded 90% of the time in the duration of measurement, is

A. 63 B. 62

C. 61 D. 60

52. The value of X, which is exceeded 50% of the time in the duration of measurement, is

A. 66 B. 65

C. 64 D. 63

53. For maintaining an effective discipline in the class, the teacher should

A. Allow students to do what they like.

B. Deal with the students strictly.

C. Give the students some problem to solve.

D. Deal with them politely and firmly.

54. An effective teaching aid is one which

A. is colourful and good looking

B. activates all faculties

C. is visible to all students

D. easy to prepare and use

55. Those teachers are popular among students who

A. develop intimacy with them

B. help them solve their problems

C. award good grades

D. take classes on extra tuition fee

56. The essence of an effective classroom environment is

A. a variety of teaching aids

B. lively student-teacher interaction

C. pin-drop silence

D. strict discipline

57. On the first day of his class, if a teacher is asked by the students to introduce himself, he should

A. ask them to meet after the class

B. tell them about himself in brief

C. ignore the demand and start teaching

D. scold the student for this unwanted demand

58. Moral values can be effectively inculcated among the students when the teacher

A. frequently talks about values

B. himself practices them

C. tells stories of great persons

D. talks of Gods and Goddesses

59. The essential qualities of a researcher are

A. spirit of free enquiry

B. reliance on observation and evidence

C. systematization or theorizing of knowledge
D. All of the above

60. Research is conducted to
I. Generate new knowledge
II. Not to develop a theory
III. Obtain research degree
IV. Reinterpret existing knowledge

Which of the above are correct?
A. I, III & II B. III, II & IV
C. II, I & III D. I, III & IV

ANSWERS

1	2	3	4	5	6	7	8	9	10
C	C	B	C	A	B	C	D	D	D
11	**12**	**13**	**14**	**15**	**16**	**17**	**18**	**19**	**20**
D	C	D	C	D	B	D	D	B	B
21	**22**	**23**	**24**	**25**	**26**	**27**	**28**	**29**	**30**
B	C	A	C	A	B	A	B	A	D
31	**32**	**33**	**34**	**35**	**36**	**37**	**38**	**39**	**40**
B	A	D	C	A	B	D	C	A	A
41	**42**	**43**	**44**	**45**	**46**	**47**	**48**	**49**	**50**
A	C	C	D	B	D	B	A	C	C
51	**52**	**53**	**54**	**55**	**56**	**57**	**58**	**59**	**60**
B	D	D	B	B	B	B	B	D	D

SOME SELECTED EXPLANATORY ANSWERS

18.

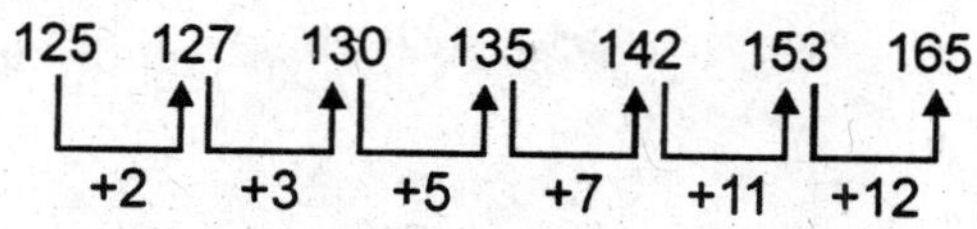

Except 12, all others are odd numbers.

19. ∵

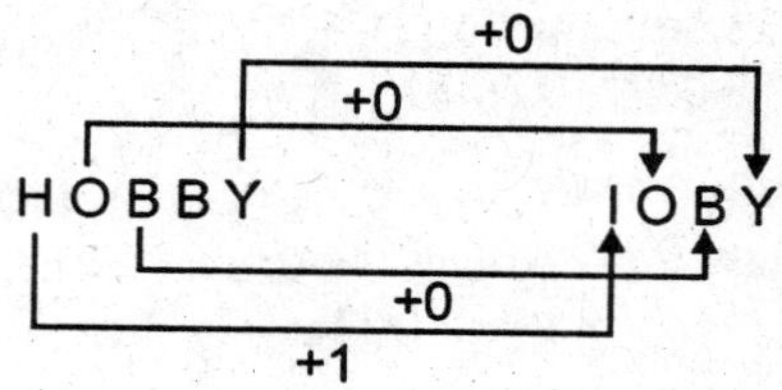

and

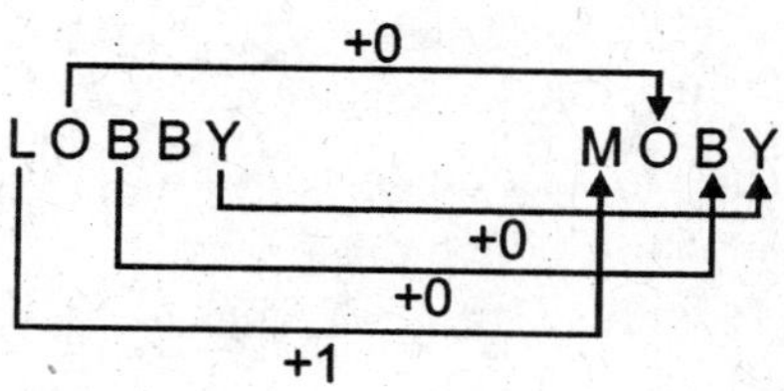

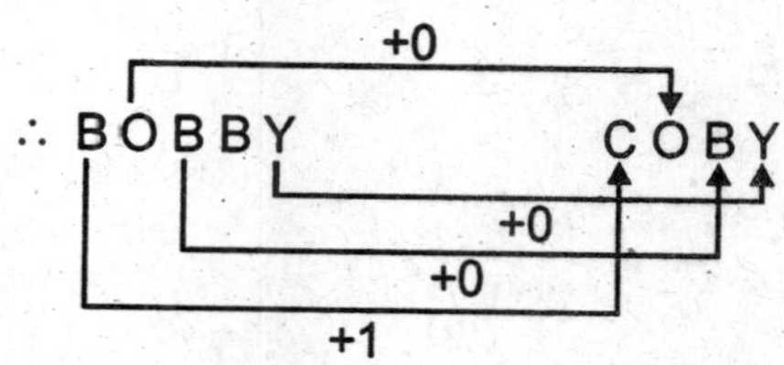

20.

A	B	C	D	E	F	G	H	I	J
1	2	3	4	5	6	7	8	9	10
K	L	M	N	O	P	Q	R	S	T
11	12	13	14	15	16	17	18	19	20
U	V	W	X	Y	Z				
21	22	23	24	25	26				

∵ K → 11
and T → 20
∴ J → 10
R → 18

21. ∵ A = 5, B = 6, C = 7, D = 8,
∴ E = 9, F = 10, G = 11, H = 12, I = 13,

J = 14, K = 15, L = 16, M = 17, N = 18, O = 19, P = 20, Q = 21, R = 22, S = 23 ....

Therefore, 17 = M
19 = O
20 = P
9 = E
8 = D

23. There are four 8's in the sequence which are preceded by 5 but not immediately followed by 3.

24. Since

□ → ○ → · → △ → □

Rectangle circle point triangle square

∴ The shape of a wheel is Point.

29. An octal number is a number that consists of any of the following eight symbols – 0, 1, 2, 3, 4, 5, 6 and 7.

Hints : 47 to 49

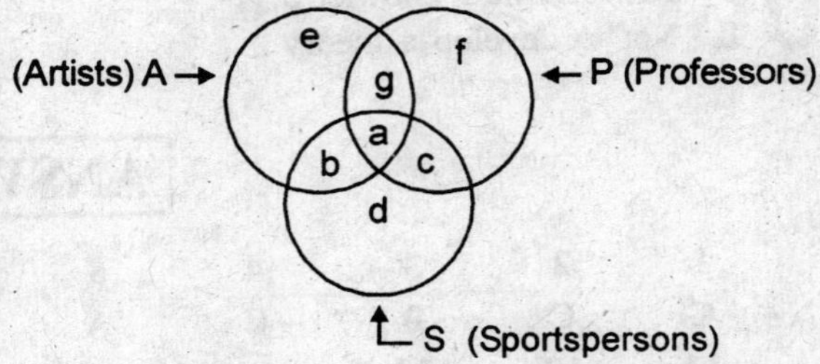

47. 'e' represents artists who are neither sportsmen nor professors.

48. 'a' represents professors, who are both artists and sportspersons.

49. 'c' represents professors, who are also sports persons but not artists.

Previous Years' Paper (Solved)

UGC-NET (JRF) EXAM DECEMBER, 2010

PAPER–I

Note : This paper contains **sixty** (60) multiple-choice questions, each question carrying **two** (2) marks. Candidate is expected to answer any **fifty** (50) questions. In case more than **fifty** **(50)** questions are attempted, only the first **fifty (50)** questions will be evaluated.

1. Which of the following variables cannot be expressed in quantitative terms?
   A. Socio-economic Status
   B. Marital Status
   C. Numerical Aptitude
   D. Professional Attitude

2. A doctor studies the relative effectiveness of two drugs of dengue fever. His research would be classified as
   A. Descriptive Survey
   B. Experimental Research
   C. Case Study
   D. Ethnography

3. The term 'phenomenology' is associated with the process of
   A. Qualitative Research
   B. Analysis of Variance
   C. Correlational Study
   D. Probability Sampling

4. The 'Sociogram' technique is used to study
   A. Vocational Interest
   B. Professional Competence
   C. Human Relations
   D. Achievement Motivation

Read the following passage carefully and answer questions from 5 to 10.

It should be remembered that the nationalist movement in India, like all nationalist movements, was essentially a bourgeois movement. It represented the natural historical stage of development, and to consider it or to criticise it as a working-class movement is wrong. Gandhi represented that movement and the Indian masses in relation to that movement to a supreme degree, and he became the voice of Indian people to that extent. The main contribution of Gandhi to India and the Indian masses has been through the powerful movements which he launched through the National Congress. Through nation-wide action he sought to mould the millions, and largely succeeded in doing so, and changing them from a demoralised, timid and hopeless mass, bullied and crushed by every dominant interest, and incapable of resistance, into a people with self-respect and self-reliance, resisting tyranny, and capable of united action and sacrifice for a larger cause.

Gandhi made people think of political and economic issues and every village and every bazaar hummed with argument and debate on the new ideas and hopes that filled the people. That was an amazing psychological change. The time was ripe for it, of course, and circumstances and world conditions worked for this change. But a great leader is necessary to take advantage of circumstances and conditions. Gandhi was that leader, and he released many of the bonds that imprisoned and disabled our minds, and none of us who experienced it can ever forget that great feeling of release and exhilaration that came over the Indian people.

Gandhi has played a revolutionary role in India of the greatest importance because he knew how to make the most of the objective conditions and could reach the heart of the masses, while groups with a more advanced ideology functioned largely in the air because they did not fit in with those conditions and could therefore not evoke any substantial response from the masses.

It is perfectly true that Gandhi, functioning in the nationalist plane, does not think in terms of the conflict of classes, and tries to compose their differences. But the action he has indulged and taught the people has inevitably raised mass consciousness tremendously and made social issues vital. Gandhi and the Congress must be judged by the policies they pursue and the action they indulge in. But behind this, personality counts and colours those policies and activities. In the case of very exceptional person like Gandhi the question of personality becomes especially important in order to understand and appraise him. To us he has represented the spirit and honour of India, the yearning of her sorrowing millions to be rid of their innumerable burdens, and an insult to him by the British Government or others has been an insult to India and her people.

5. Which one of the following is true of the given passage?
   A. The passage is a critique of Gandhi's role in Indian movement for independence.
   B. The passage hails the role of Gandhi in India's freedom movement.
   C. The author is neutral on Gandhi's role in India's freedom movement.
   D. It is an account of Indian National Congress's support to the working-class movement.

6. The change that the Gandhian movement brought among the Indian masses was
   A. Physical B. Cultural
   C. Technological D. Psychological

7. To consider the nationalist movement or to criticise it as a working-class movement was wrong because it was a
   A. historical movement
   B. voice of the Indian people
   C. bourgeois movement
   D. movement represented by Gandhi

8. Gandhi played a revolutionary role in India because he could
   A. preach morality
   B. reach the heart of Indians
   C. see the conflict of classes
   D. lead the Indian National Congress

9. Groups with advanced ideology functioned in the air as they did not fit in with
   A. objective conditions of masses
   B. the Gandhian ideology
   C. the class consciousness of the people
   D. the differences among masses

10. The author concludes the passage by
    A. criticising the Indian masses
    B. the Gandhian movement
    C. pointing out the importance of the personality of Gandhi
    D. identifying the sorrows of millions of Indians

11. Media that exist in an interconnected series of communication – points are referred to as
    A. Networked media
    B. Connective media
    C. Nodal media
    D. Multimedia

12. The information function of mass communication is described as
    A. diffusion B. publicity
    C. surveillance D. diversion

13. An example of asynchronous medium is
    A. Radio B. Television
    C. Film D. Newspaper

14. In communication, connotative words are
    A. explicit C. abstract
    B. simple D. cultural

15. A message beneath a message is labelled as
    A. embedded text B. internal text
    C. inter-text D. sub-text

16. In analog mass communication, stories are
    A. static B. dynamic
    C. interactive D. exploratory

17. Determine the relationship between the pair of words ALWAYS : NEVER and then select from the following pair of words which have a similar relationship
A. often : rarely
B. frequently : occasionally
C. constantly : frequently
D. intermittently : casually

18. Find the wrong number in the sequence
52, 51, 48, 43, 34, 27, 16
A. 27 B. 34
C. 43 D. 48

19. In a certain code, PAN is written as 31 and PAR as 35, then PAT is written in the same code as
A. 30 B. 37
C. 39 D. 41

20. The letters in the first set have certain relationship. On the basis of this relationship, make the right choice for the second set :
AF : IK : : LQ : ?
A. MO B. NP
C. OR D. TV

21. If 5472 = 9, 6342 = 6, 7584 = 6, what is 9236?
A. 2 B. 3
C. 4 D. 5

22. In an examination, 35% of the total students failed in Hindi, 45% failed in English and 20% in both. The percentage of those who passed in both subjects is
A. 10 B. 20
C. 30 D. 40

23. Two statements I and II given below are followed by two conclusions (a) and (b). Supposing the statements are true, which of the following conclusions can logically follow?

Statements :
I. Some flowers are red.
II. Some flowers are blue.

Conclusions :
(a) Some flowers are neither red nor blue.
(b) Some flowers are both red and blue.
A. Only (a) follows.
B. Only (b) follows.
C. Both (a) and (b) follows.
D. Neither (a) nor (b) follows.

24. If the statement 'all students are intelligent' is true, which of the following statements are false?
(*i*) No students are intelligent.
(*ii*) Some students are intelligent.
(*iii*) Some students are not intelligent.
A. (*i*) and (*ii*)
B. (*i*) and (*iii*)
C. (*ii*) and (*iii*)
D. (*i*) only

25. A reasoning where we start with certain particular statements and conclude with a universal statement is called
A. Deductive Reasoning
B. Inductive Reasoning
C. Abnormal Reasoning
D. Transcendental Reasoning

26. What is the smallest number of ducks that could swim in this formation — two ducks in front of a duck, two ducks behind a duck and a duck between two ducks?
(a) 5 (b) 7
(c) 4 (d) 3

27. Mr. A, Miss B, Mr. C and Miss D are sitting around a table and discussing their trades.
(*i*) Mr. A sits opposite to the cook.
(*ii*) Miss B sits right to the barber.
(*iii*) The washerman sits right to the barber.
(*iv*) Miss D sits opposite to Mr. C.
What are the trades of A and B?
(a) Tailor and barber
(b) Barber and cook
(c) Tailor and cook
(d) Tailor and washerman

28. Which one of the following methods serve to measure correlation between two variables?
(a) Scatter Diagram
(b) Frequency Distrubution
(c) Two-way table
(d) Coefficient of Rank Correlation

29. Which one of the following is not an Internet Service Provider (ISP)?
(a) MTNL (b) BSNL
(c) ERNET India (d) Infotech India Ltd.

30. The hexadecimal number system consists of the symbols
(a) 0 – 7 (b) 0 – 9, A – F
(c) 0 – 7, A – F (d) None of these

31. The binary equivalent of $(-15)_{10}$ is (2's complement system is used)
A. 11110001 B. 11110000
C. 10001111 D. None of these

32. 1 GB is equal to
A. 2^{30} bits B. 2^{30} bytes
C. 2^{20} bits D. 2^{20} bytes

33. The set of computer programs that manage the hardware/software of a computer is called
A. Compiler system
B. Operation system
C. Operating system
D. None of these

34. S/MIME in Internet technology stands for
A. Secure Multipurpose Internet Mail Extension
B. Secure Multimedia Internet Mail Extension
C. Simple Multipurpose Internet Mail Extension
D. Simple Multimedia Internet Mail Extension

35. Which of the following is **not** covered in 8 missions under the Climate Action Plan of Government of India?
A. Solar power
C. Waste to energy conversion
B. Afforestation
D. Nuclear energy

36. The concentration of Total Dissolved Solids (TDS) in drinking water should not exceed
A. 500 mg/L B. 400 mg/L
C. 300 mg/L D. 200 mg/L

37. 'Chipko movement was first started by
A. Arundhati Roy
B. Medha Patkar
C. Ila Bhatt
D. Sunderlal Bahuguna

38. The constitutents of photochemical smog responsible for eye irritation are
A. SO_2 and O_3
B. SO_2 and NO_2
C. HCHO and PAN
D. SO_2 and SPM

39. **Assertion (A) :** Some carbonaceous aerosols may be carcinogenic.

Reason (R) : They may contain polycyclic aromatic hydrocarbons (PAHs).
A. Both (A) and (R) are correct and (R) is the correct explanation of (A).
B. Both (A) and (R) are correct but (R) is not the correct explanation of (A).
C. (A) is correct, but (R) is false.
D. (A) is false, but (R) is correct.

40. Volcanic eruptions affect
A. atmosphere and hydrosphere
B. hydrosphere and biosphere
C. lithosphere, biosphere and atmosphere
D. lithosphere, hydrosphere and atmosphere

41. India's first Defence University is in the State of
A. Haryana B. Andhra Pradesh
C. Uttar Pradesh D. Punjab

42. Most of the Universities in India
A. conduct teaching and research only
B. affiliate colleges and conduct examinations
C. conduct teaching/research and examinations
D. promote research only

43. Which one of the following is not a Constitutional Body?
A. Election Commission
B. Finance Commission
C. Union Public Service Commission
D. Planning Commission

44. Which one of the following statements is not correct?
A. Indian Parliament is supreme.
B. The Supreme Court of India has the power of judicial review.

C. There is a division of powers between the Centre and the States.
D. There is a Council of Ministers to aid and advise the President.

45. Which one of the following statements reflects the republic character of Indian democracy?
A. Written constitution
B. No State religion
C. Devolution of power to local Government institutions
D. Elected President and directly or indirectly elected Parliament

46. Who among the following appointed by the Governor can be removed by only the President of India?
A. Chief Minister of a State
B. A member of the State Public Service Commission
C. Advocate-General
D. Vice-Chancellor of a State University

47. If two small circles represent the class of the 'men' and the class of the 'plants and the big circle represents 'mortality', which one of the following figures represent the proposition 'All men are mortal.'?

A. 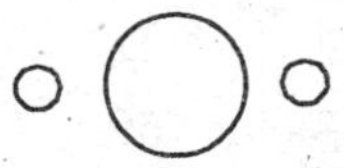
B. 
C. 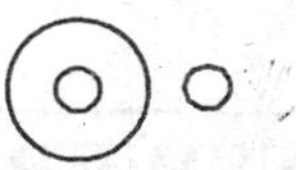
D. 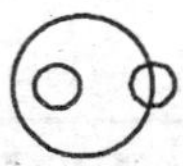

The following table presents the production of electronic items (TVs and LCDs) in a factory during the period from 2006 to 2010. Study the table carefully and answer the questions from **48** to **52** :

Year	2006	2007	2008	2009	2010
TVs	6000	9000	13000	11000	8000
LCDs	7000	9400	9000	10000	12000

48. In which year, the total production of electronic items is maximum?
A. 2006 B. 2007
C. 2008 D. 2010

49. What is the difference between averages of production of LCDs and TVs from 2006 to 2008?
A. 3000 B. 2867
C. 3015 D. None of these

50. What is the year in which production of TVs is half the production of LCDs in the year 2010?
(a) 2007 (b) 2006
(c) 2009 (d) 2008

51. What is the ratio of production of LCDs in the years 2008 and 2010?
A. 4 : 3 B. 3 : 4
C. 1 : 3 D. 2 : 3

52. What is the ratio of production of TVs in the years 2006 and 2007?
A. 6 : 7 B. 7 : 6
C. 2 : 3 D. 3 : 2

53. Some students in a class exhibit great curiosity for learning. It may be because such children
A. Are gifted
B. Come from rich families
C. Show artificial behaviour
D. Create indiscipline in the class

54. The most important quality of a good teacher is
A. Sound knowledge of subject matter
B. Good communication skills
C. Concern for students' welfare
D. Effective leadership qualities

55. Which one of the following is appropriate in respect of teacher-student relationship?
A. Very informal and intimate
B. Limited to classroom only
C. Cordial and respectful
D. Indifferent

56. The academic performance of students can be improved if parents are encouraged to
A. supervise the work of their wards
B. arrange for extra tuition
C. remain unconcerned about it
D. interact with teachers frequently

57. In a lively classroom situation, there is likely to be
A. occasional roars of laughter
B. complete silence
C. frequent teacher-student dialogue
D. loud discussion among students

58. If a parent approaches the teacher to do some favour to his/her ward in the examination, the teacher should
A. try to help him
B. ask him not to talk in those terms
C. refulse politely and firmly
D. ask him rudely to go away

59. Which of the following phrases is not relevant to describe the meaning of research as a process?
A. Systematic Activity
B. Objective Observation
C. Trial and Error
D. Problem Solving

60. Which of the following is not an example of a continuous variable?
A. Family size
B. Intelligence
C. Height
D. Attitude

ANSWERS

1	**2**	**3**	**4**	**5**	**6**	**7**	**8**	**9**	**10**
D	B	A	C	B	D	C	B	A	C
11	**12**	**13**	**14**	**15**	**16**	**17**	**18**	**19**	**20**
A	C	D	D	D	A	A	B	B	D
21	**22**	**23**	**24**	**25**	**26**	**27**	**28**	**29**	**30**
A	B	C	D	B	A	C	D	D	B
31	**32**	**33**	**34**	**35**	**36**	**37**	**38**	**39**	**40**
D	B	C	A	D	A	D	B	A	D
41	**42**	**43**	**44**	**45**	**46**	**47**	**48**	**49**	**50**
A	C	D	B	D	B	C	C	D	B
51	**52**	**53**	**54**	**55**	**56**	**57**	**58**	**59**	**60**
B	C	A	B	C	D	C	C	C	C

SOME SELECTED EXPLANATORY ANSWERS

18. 52 51 48 43 34 27 16

–1 –3 –5 –9 –7 –11

Only 9 is divisible by 3 and rest are not divisible by any number.

19. ∵

A	B	C	D	E	F	G	H	I
1	2	3	4	5	6	7	8	9
J	K	L	M	N	O	P	Q	R
10	11	12	13	14	15	16	17	18

S	T	U	V	W	X	Y	Z
19	20	21	22	23	24	25	26

∵ PAN $\Rightarrow 16 + 1 + 14 = 31$

PAR $\Rightarrow 16 + 1 + 18 = 35$

∴ PAT $\Rightarrow 16 + 1 + 20 = \boxed{37}$.

21. ∵ $5472 \Rightarrow 5 + 4 + 7 + 2 = 18 \Rightarrow 1 + 8 = 9$

$6342 \Rightarrow 6 + 3 + 4 + 2 = 15 \Rightarrow 1 + 5 = 6$

$7584 \Rightarrow 7 + 5 + 8 + 4 = 24 \Rightarrow 2 + 4 = 6$

∴ $9236 \Rightarrow 9 + 2 + 3 + 6 = 20 \Rightarrow 2 + 0 = 2$

UGC-NET (JRF)

PREVIOUS PAPERS (SOLVED) (COMPULSORY)

Previous Paper (Solved)

UGC-NET (JRF) EXAM
JUNE, 2010

PAPER–I

Note : This paper contains **sixty** (60) multiple-choice questions, each question carrying **two** (2) marks. Candidate is expected to answer any **fifty** (50) questions. In case more than 50 questions are attempted, only the first 50 questions will be evaluated.

1. Which one of the following is the most important quality of a good teacher ?

A. Punctuality and sincerity
B. Content mastery
C. Content mastery and reactive
D. Content mastery and sociable

2. The primary responsibility for the teacher's adjustment lies with

A. The children
B. The principal
C. The teacher himself
D. The community

3. As per the NCTE norms, what should be the staff strength for a unit of 100 students at B.Ed, level ?

A. 1 + 7 B. 1 + 9
C. 1 + 10 D. 1 + 5

4. Research has shown that the most frequent symptom of nervous instability among teachers is

A. Digestive upsets
B. Explosive behaviour
C. Fatigue
D. Worry

5. Which one of the following statements is correct ?

A. Syllabus is an annexure to the curriculum.
B. Curriculum is the same in all educational institutions.
C. Curriculum includes both formal, and informal education.
D. Curriculum does not include methods of evaluation.

6. A successful teacher is one who is

A. Compassionate and disciplinarian
B. Quite and reactive
C. Tolerant and dominating
D. Passive and active

Read the following passage carefully and answer the questions 7 to 12.

The phrase "What is it like ?" stands for a fundamental thought process. How does one go about observing and reporting on things and events that occupy segments of earth space ? Of all the infinite variety of phenomena on the face of the earth, how does one decide what phenomena to observe ? There is no such thing as a complete description of the earth or any part of it, for every microscopic point on the earth's surface differs from every other such point. Experience shows that the things observed are already familiar, because they are like phenomena that occur at home or because they resemble the abstract images and models developed in the human mind.

How are abstract images formed ? Humans alone among the animals possess language; their words symbolize not only specific things but also mental images of classes of things. People can remember what they have seen or experienced because they attach a word symbol to them.

During the long record of our efforts to gain more and more knowledge about the face of the earth as the human habitat, there has been a continuing interplay between things and events. The direct observation through the senses is described as a percept; the mental image is described as a concept. Percepts are what some people describe as reality, in contrast to mental images, which are theoretical, implying that they are not real.

The relation of Percept to Concept is not as simple as the definition implies. It is now quite clear that people of different cultures or even individuals in the same culture develop different mental images of reality and what they perceive is a reflection of these preconceptions. The direct observation of things and events on the face of the earth is so clearly a function of the mental images of the mind of the observer that the whole idea of reality must be reconsidered.

Concepts determine what the observer perceives, yet concepts are derived from the generalizations of previous percepts. What happens is that the educated observer is taught to accept a set of concepts and then sharpens or changes these concepts during a professional career. In any one field of scholarship, professional opinion at one time determines what concepts and procedures are acceptable, and these form a kind of model of scholarly behaviour.

7. The problem raised in the passage reflects on
A. thought process
B. human behaviour
C. cultural perceptions
D. professional opinion

8. According to the passage, human beings have mostly in mind
A. Observation of things
B. Preparation of mental images
C. Expression through language
D. To gain knowledge

9. Concept means
A. A mental image
B. A reality
C. An idea expressed in language form
D. All the above

10. The relation of Percept to Concept is
A. Positive B. Negative
C. Reflective D. Absolute

11. In the passage, the earth is taken as
A. The Globe
B. The Human Habitat
C. A Celestial Body
D. A Planet

12. Percept means
A. Direct observation through the senses
B. A conceived idea
C. Ends of a spectrum
D. An abstract image

13. Action research means
A. A longitudinal research
B. An applied research
C. A research initiated to solve an immediate problem
D. A research with socio-economic objective

14. Research is
A. Searching again and again
B. Finding solution to any problem
C. Working in a scientific way to search for truth of any problem
D. None of the above

15. A common test in research demands much priority on
A. Reliability B. Useability
C. Objectivity D. All of the above

16. Which of the following is the first step in starting the research process ?
A. Searching sources of information to locate problem.
B. Survey of related literature
C. Identification of problem
D. Searching for solutions to the problem

17. If a researcher conducts a research on finding out which administrative style contributes more to institutional effectiveness ? This will be an example of
A. Basic Research
B. Action Research
C. Applied Research
D. None of the above

18. Normal Probability Curve should be
A. Positively skewed
B. Negatively skewed
C. Leptokurtic skewed
D. Zero skewed

19. In communication, a major barrier to reception of messages is
A. audience attitude
B. audience knowledge
C. audience education
D. audience income

20. Post-modernism is associated with
A. newspapers B. magazines
C. radio D. television

21. Didactic communication is
A. intra-personal B. inter-personal
C. organisational D. relational

22. In communication, the language is
A. the non-verbal code
B. the verbal code
C. the symbolic code
D. the iconic code

23. Identify the correct sequence of the following:
A. Source, channel, message, receiver
B. Source, receiver, channel, message
C. Source, message, receiver, channel
D. Source, message, channel, receiver

24. **Assertion** A.: Mass media promote a culture of violence in the society.

Reason (R) : Because violence sells in the market as people themselves are violent in character.
A. Both A. and (R) are true and (R) is the correct explanation of A..
B. Both A. and (R) are true, but (R) is not the correct explanation of A..
C. A. is true, but (R) is false.
D. Both A. and (R) are false.

25. When an error of 1% is made in the length of a square, the percentage error in the area of a square will be
A. 0 B. 1/2
C. 1 D. 2

26. On January 12, 1980, it was a Saturday. The day of the week on January 12, 1979 was
A. Thursday B. Friday
C. Saturday D. Sunday

27. If water is called food, food is called tree, tree is called earth, earth is called world, which of the following grows a fruit ?
A. Water B. Tree
C. World D. Earth

28. E is the son of A, D is the son of B, E is married to C, C is the daughter of B. How is D related to E ?
A. Brother B. Uncle
C. Father-in-law D. Brother-in-law

29. If INSURANCE is coded as ECNARUSNI, how HINDRANCE will be coded ?
A. CADNHIWCE B. HANODEINR
C. AENIRHDCN D. ECNARDNIH

30. Find the next number in the following series:
2, 5, 10, 17, 26, 37, 50, ?
A. 63 B. 65
C. 67 D. 69

31. Which of the following is an example of circular argument ?
A. God created man in his image and man created God in his own image.
B. God is the source of a scripture and the scripture is the source of our knowledge of God.
C. Some of the Indians are great because India is great.
D. Rama is great because he is Rama.

32. Lakshmana is a morally good person because
A. he is religious B. he is educated
C. he is rich D. he is rational

33. Two statements I and II given below are followed by two conclusions (a) and (b). Supposing the statements are true, which of the following conclusions can logically follow ?
I. Some religious people are morally good.
II. Some religious people are rational.

Conclusions :
(a) Rationally religious people are good morally.

(b) Non-rational religious persons are not morally good.

A. Only (a) follows.
B. Only (b) follows.
C. Both (a) and (b) follow.
D. Neither (a) nor (b) follows.

34. Certainty is
A. an objective fact
B. emotionally satisfying
C. logical
D. ontological

Questions from 35 to 36 are based on the following diagram in which there are three intersecting circles I, S and P where circle I stands for Indians, circle S stands for scientists and circle P for politicians. Different regions of the figure are lettered from a to g.

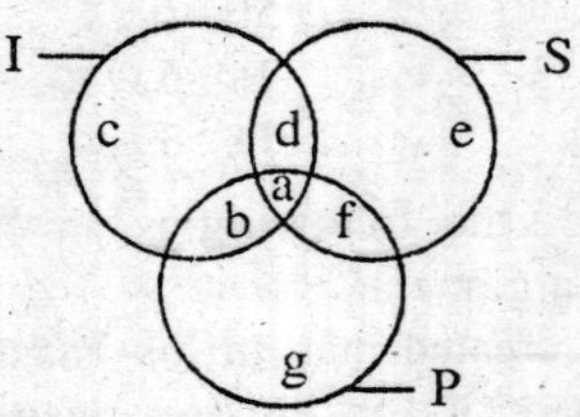

35. The region which representsn o n - I n d i a n scientists who are politicians.

A. f B. d
C. a D. c

36. The region which represents politicians who are Indians as well as scientists.

A. b B. c
C. a D. d

A. an objective fact

37. The population of a city is plotted as a function of time (years) in graphic form below:

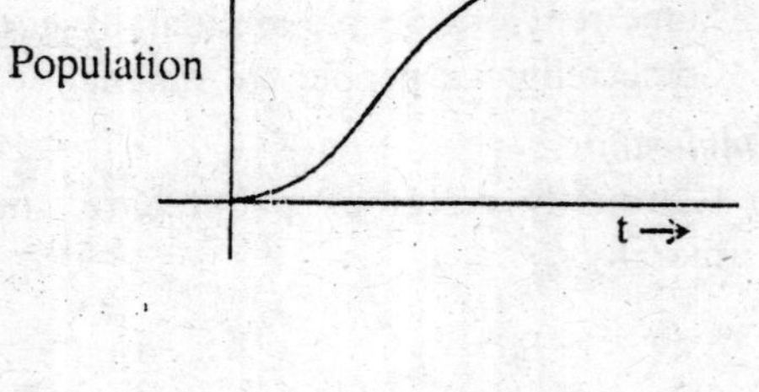

Which of the following inference can be drawn from above plot ?

A. The population increases exponentially.
The population increases in parabolic fashion.
The population initially increases in a linear fashion and then stabilizes.
The population initially increases exponentially and then stabilizes.

In the following chart, the price of logs is shown in per cubic metre and that of Plywood and Saw Timber in per tonnes. Study the chart and answer the following questions 38, 39 and 40.

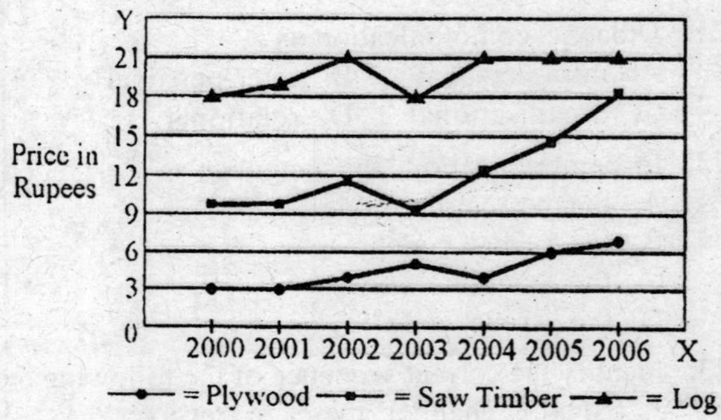

38. Which product shows the maximum percentage increase in price over the period?
A. Saw timber
B. Plywood
C. Log
D. None of the above

39. What is the maximum percentage increase in price per cubic metre of log ?

A. 6 B. 12
C. 18 D. None of these

40. In which year the prices of two products increased and that of the third increased ?

A. 2000 B. 2002
C. 2003 D. 2006

41. Which one of the following is the oldest Archival source of data in India ?
A. National Sample Surveys
B. Agricultural Statistics
C. Census
D. Vital Statistics

42. In a large random data set following normal distribution, the ratio (%) of number of data points which are in the range of (mean ± standard deviation) to the total number of data points, is

A. ~ 50% B. ~ 67%
C. ~ 97% D. ~ 47%

43. Which number system is usually followed in a typical 32-bit computer?

A. 2 B. 8
C. 10 D. 16

44. Which one of the following is an example of Operating System ?

A. Microsoft Word
B. Microsoft Excel
C. Microsoft Access
D. Microsoft Windows

45. Which one of the following represent the binary equivalent of the decimal number 23?

A. 01011 B. 10111
C. 10011 D. None of the above

46. Which one of the following is different from other members?

A. Google B. Windows
C. Linux D. Mac

47. Where does a computer add and compare its data?

A. CPU B. Memory
C. Hard disk D. Floppy disk

48. Computers on an internet are identified by

A. e-mail address
B. street address
C. IP address
D. None of the above

49. The Right to Information Act, 2005 makes the provision of

A. Dissemination of all types of information by all Public authorities to any person.
B. Establishment of Central, State and District Level Information Commissions as an appellate body.
C. Transparency and accountability in Public authorities.
D. All of the above

50. Which type of natural hazards cause maximum damage to property and lives?

A. Hydrological
B. Hydro-meteorological
C. Geological
D. Geo-chemical

51. Dioxins are produced from

A. Wastelands
B. Power plants
C. Sugar factories
D. Combustion of plastics

52. The slogan "A tree for each child" was coined for

A. Social forestry programme
B. Clean Air programme
C. Soil conservation programme
D. Environmental protection programme

53. The main constituents of biogas are

A. Methane and Carbon di-oxide
B. Methane and Nitric oxide
C. Methane, Hydrogen and Nitric oxide
D. Methane and Sulphur di-oxide

54. **Assertion (A):** In the world as a whole, the environment has degraded during past several decades.

Reason (R) : The population of the world has been growing significantly.

A. A. is correct, (R) is correct and (R) is the correct explanation of A..
B. A. is correct, (R) is correct and (R) is not the correct explanation of A..
C. A. is correct, but (R) is false.
D. A. is false, but (R) is correct.

55. Climate change has implications for

1. soil moisture 2. forest fires
3. biodiversity 4. ground water

Identify the correct combination according to the code :

Codes :

A. 1 and 3 B. 1, 2 and 3
C. 1, 3 and 4 D. 1, 2, 3 and 4

56. The accreditation process by National Assessment and Accreditation Council (NAAC) differs from that of National Board of Accreditation (NBA) in terms of
A. Disciplines covered by both being the same, there is duplication of efforts.
B. One has institutional grading approach and the other has programme grading approach.
C. Once get accredited by NBA or NAAC, the institution is free from renewal of grading, which is not a progressive decision.
D. This accreditation amounts to approval of minimum standards in the quality of education in the institution concerned.

57. Which option is not correct ?
A. Most of the educational institutions of National repute in scientific and technical sphere fall under 64th entry of Union list.
B. Education, in general, is the subject of concurrent list since 42nd Constitutional Amendment Act 1976.
C. Central Advisory Board on Education (CABE) was first established in 1920.
D. India had implemented the right to Free and Compulsory Primary Education in 2002 through 86th Constitutional Amendment.

58. Which statement is not correct about the "National Education Day" of India ?
A. It is celebrated on 5th September every year.
B. It is celebrated on 11th November every year.
C. It is celebrated in the memory of India's first Union Minister of Education, Dr. Abul Kalam Azad.
D. It is being celebrated since 2008.

59. Match List-I with List-II and select the correct answer from the codes given below:

List -1 (Articles of the Constitution)	List - II (Institutions)
(a) Article 280	(i) Administrative Tribunals
(b) Article 324	(ii) Election Commission of India
(c) Article 323	(iii) Finance Commission at Union level
(d) Article 315	(iv) Union Public Service Commission

Codes :

	(a)	(b)	(c)	(d)
A.	(i)	(ii)	(iii)	(iv)
B.	(iii)	(ii)	(i)	(iv)
C.	(ii)	(iii)	(iv)	(i)
D.	(ii)	(iv)	(iii)	(i)

60. Deemed Universities declared by UGC under Section 3 of the UGC Act 1956, are not permitted to
A. offer programmes in higher education and issue degrees.
B. give affiliation to any institute of higher education.
C. open off-campus and off-shore campus anywhere in the country and overseas respectively without the permission of the UGC.
D. offer distance education programmes without the approval of the Distance Education Council.

ANSWERS

1	2	3	4	5	6	7	8	9	10
B	C	C	B	C	A	C	A	A	C
11	**12**	**13**	**14**	**15**	**16**	**17**	**18**	**19**	**20**
B	A	C	C	D	C	C	D	C	D
21	**22**	**23**	**24**	**25**	**26**	**27**	**28**	**29**	**30**
B	B	D	D	D	B	C	D	D	B

31	32	33	34	35	36	37	38	39	40
B	A	D	C	A	C	D	C	D	B
41	**42**	**43**	**44**	**45**	**46**	**47**	**48**	**49**	**50**
C	B	A	D	B	B	A	C	D	C
51	**52**	**53**	**54**	**55**	**56**	**57**	**58**	**59**	**60**
D	D	A	B	D	C	A	A	B	B

SOME SELECTED EXPLANATORY ANSWERS

29. Since, I N S U R A N C E → E C N A R U S N I

Therefore, H I N D R A N C E → E C N A R D N I H

30. 2 → 5 → 10 → 17 → 26 → 37 → 50 → 65

(+3, +5, +7, +9, +11, +13, +15)

48. Computers on an internet are identified by IP address.

53. Main constituents of biogas are: Methane and Carbon di-oxide.

Previous Paper (Solved)

UGC-NET (JRF) EXAM DECEMBER, 2009

PAPER–I

Note : This paper contains **sixty** (60) multiple-choice questions, each question carrying **two** (2) marks. Candidate is expected to answer any **fifty** (50) questions. In case more than 50 questions are attempted, only the first 50 questions will be evaluated.

1. The University which telecasts interaction educational programmes through its own channel is
A. Osmania University
B. University of Pune
C. Annamalai University
D. Indira Gandhi National University (IGNOU)

2. Which of the following skills are needed for present day teacher to adjust effectively with the classroom teaching?
1. Knowledge of technology
2. Use of technology in teaching learning
3. Knowledge of students' needs
4. Content mastery

A. 1 & 3 B. 2 & 3
C. 2, 3 & 4 D. 2 & 4

3. Who has signed as MOU for Accreditation of Teacher Education Institutions in India?
A. NAAC and UGC
B. NCTE and NAAC
C. UGC and NCTE
D. NCTE and IGNOU

4. The primary duty of the teacher is to
A. raise the intellectual standard of the students
B. improve the physical standard of the students
C. help all round development of the students
D. imbibe value system in the students

5. Micro teaching is more effective
A. during the preparation for teaching-practice
B. during the teaching-practice
C. after the teaching-practice
D. always

6. What quality the students like the most in a teacher ?
A. Idealist philosophy
B. Compassion
C. Discipline
D. Entertaining

7. A null hypothesis is
A. when there is no difference between the variables
B. the same as research hypothesis
C. subjective in nature
D. when there is difference between the variables

8. The research which is exploring new facts through the study of the past is called
A. Philosophical research
B. Historical research
C. Mythological research
D. Content analysis

9. Action research is
A. An applied research
B. A research carried out to solve immediate problems
C. A longitudinal research
D. Simulative research

10. The process <u>not</u> needed in Experimental Researches is
A. Observation B. Manipulation
C. Controlling D. Content Analysis

11. Manipulation is always a part of
A. Historical research
B. Fundamental research
C. Descriptive research
D. Experimental research

12. Which correlation co-efficient best explains the relationship between creativity and intelligence ?
A. 1.00 B. 0.6
C. 0.5 D. 0.3

Read the following passage and answer the Question Nos. 13 to 18 :

The decisive shift in British Policy really came about under mass pressure in the autumn and winter of 1945 to 46 - the months which Perderel Moon while editing Wavell's Journal has perceptively described as 'The Edge of a Volcano'. Very foolishly, the British initially decided to hold public trials of several hundreds of the 20,000 I.N.A. prisoners (as well as dismissing from service and detaining without trial no less than 7,000). They compounded the folly by holding the first trial in the Red Fort, Delhi in November 1945, and putting on the dock together a Hindu, a Muslim and a Sikh (P.K. Sehgal, Shah Nawaz, Gurbaksh Singh Dhillon). Bhulabhai Desai, Tejbahadur Sapru and Nehru appeared for the defence (the latter putting on his barrister's gown after 25 years), and the Muslim League also joined the countrywide protest. On 20 November, an Intelligence Bureau note admitted that "there has seldom been a matter which has attracted so much Indian public interest and, it is safe to say, sympathy ... this particular brand of sympathy cuts across communal barriers.' A journalist (B. Shiva Rao) visiting the Red Fort prisoners on the same day reported that 'There is not the slightest feeling among them of Hindu and Muslim ... A majority of the men now awaiting trial in the Red Fort is Muslim. Some of these men are bitter that Mr. Jinnah is keeping alive a controversy about Pakistan.' The British became extremely nervous about the I.N.A. spirit spreading to the Indian Army, and in January the Punjab Governor reported that a Lahore reception for released I.N.A. prisoners had been attended by Indian soldiers in uniform.

13. Which heading is more appropriate to assign to the above passage ?
A. Wavell's Journal
B. Role of Muslim League
C. I.N.A. Trials
D. Red Fort Prisoners

14. The trial of P.K. Sehgal, Shah Nawaz and Gurbaksh Singh Dhillon symbolises
A. communal harmony
B. threat to all religious persons
C. threat to persons fighting for the freedom
D. British reaction against the natives

15. I.N.A. stands for
A. Indian National Assembly
B. Indian National Association
C. Inter-national Association
D. Indian National Army

16. 'There has seldom been a matter which has attracted so much Indian Public Interest and, it is safe to say, sympathy ... this particular brand of sympathy cuts across communal barriers.' Who sympathises to whom and against whom ?
A. Muslims sympathised with Shah Nawaz against the British
B. Hindus sympathised with P.K. Sehgal against the British
C. Sikhs sympathised with Gurbaksh Singh Dhillon against the British
D. Indians sympathised with the persons who were to be trialled

17. The majority of people waiting for trial outside the Red Fort and criticising Jinnah were the
A. Hindus
B. Muslims
C. Sikhs
D. Hindus and Muslims both

18. The sympathy of Indian soldiers in uniform with the released I.N.A. prisoners at Lahore indicates

A. Feeling of Nationalism and Fraternity
B. Rebellious nature of Indian soldiers
C. Simply to participate in the reception party
D. None of the above

19. The country which has the distinction of having the two largest circulated newspapers in the world is
A. Great Britain B. The United States
C. Japan D. China

20. The chronological order of non-verbal communication is
A. Signs, symbols, codes, colours
B. Symbols, codes, signs, colours
C. Colours, signs, codes, symbols
D. Codes, colours, symbols, signs

21. Which of the following statements is not connected with communication ?
A. Medium is the message.
B. The world is an electronic cocoon.
C. Information is power.
D. Telepathy is technological.

22. Communication becomes circular when
A. the decoder becomes an encoder
B. the feedback is absent
C. the source is credible
D. the channel is clear

23. The site that played a major role during the terrorist attack on Mumbai (26/11) in 2008 was
A. Orkut B. Facebook
C. Amazon.com D. Twitter

24. **Assertion (A):** For an effective classroom communication at times it is desirable to use the projection technology.
Reason (R): Using the projection technology facilitates extensive coverage of course contents.
A. Both A. and (R) are true, and (R) is the correct explanation.
B. Both A. and (R) are true, but (R) is not the correct explanation.
C. A. is true, but (R) is false.
D. A. is false, but (R) is true.

25. January 1, 1995 was a Sunday. What day of the week lies on January 1, 1996 ?
A. Sunday B. Monday
C. Wednesday D. Saturday

26. When an error of 1% is made in the length and breadth of a rectangle, the percentage error (%) in the area of a rectangle will be
A. 0 B. 1
C. 2 D. 4

27. The next number in the series 2, 5, 9, 19, 37, ? will be
A. 74 B. 75
C. 76 D. None of the above

28. There are 10 true-false questions in an examination. Then these questions can be answered in
A. 20 ways B. 100 ways
C. 240 ways D. 1024 ways

29. What will be the next term in the following? DCXW, FEVU, HGTS, ?
A. AKPO B. ABYZ
C. JIRQ D. LMRS

30. Three individuals X, Y, Z hired a car on a sharing basis and paid Rs. 1,040. They used it for 7, 8, 11 hours, respectively. What are the charges paid by Y ?
A. Rs. 290 B. Rs. 320
C. Rs. 360 D. Rs. 440

31. Deductive argument involves
A. sufficient evidence
B. critical thinking
C. seeing logical relations
D. repeated observation

32. Inductive reasoning is based on or presupposes
A. uniformity of nature
B. God created the world
C. unity of nature
D. laws of nature

33. To be critical, thinking must be
A. practical
B. socially relevant
C. individually satisfying
D. analytical

34. Which of the following is an analogous statement ?

A. Man is like God
B. God is great
C. Gandhiji is the Father of the Nation
D. Man is a rational being.

Questions from 35 - 36 are based on the following diagram in which there are three intersecting circles. H representing The Hindu, I representing Indian Express and T representing The Times of India. A total of 50 persons were surveyed and the number in the Venn diagram indicates the number of persons reading the newspapers.

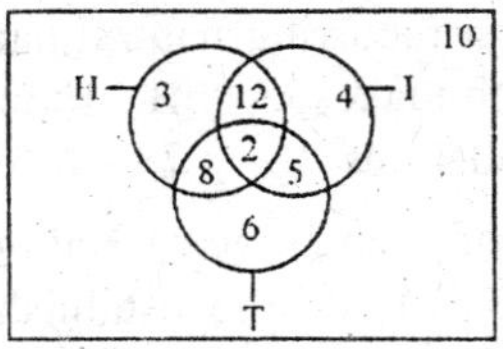

35. How many persons would be reading at least two newspapers ?

A. 23 B. 25
C. 27 D. 29

36. How many persons would be reading almost two newspapers ?

A. 23 B. 25
C. 27 D. 48

37. Which of the following graphs does not represent regular (periodic) behaviour of the variable f(t) ?

1. 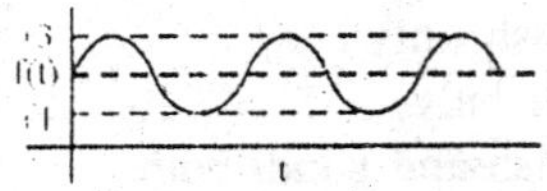

2. 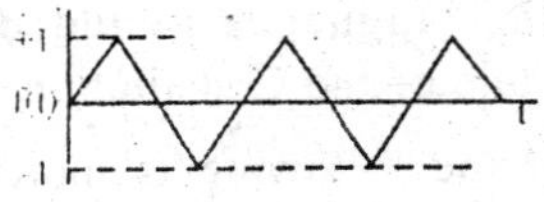

3. 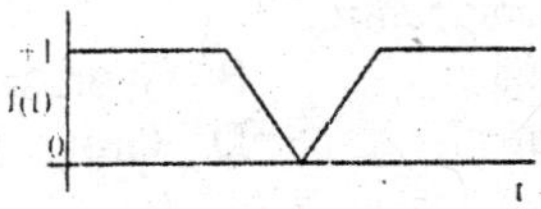

4. 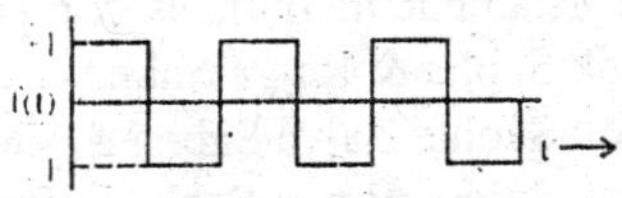

A. 1 B. 2
C. 3 D. 4

Study the following graph and answer the questions 38 to 40.

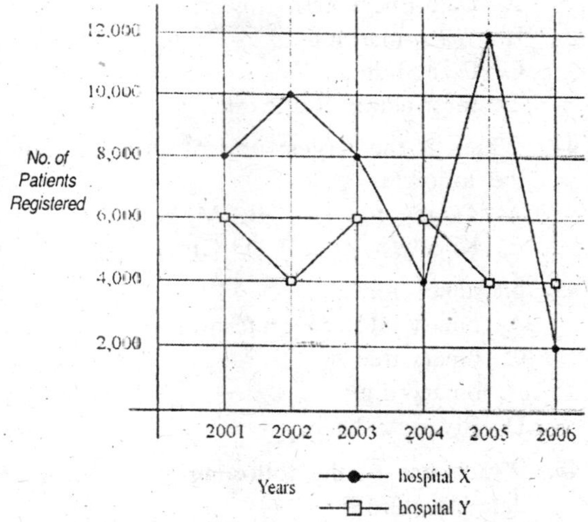

38. In which year total number of patients registered in hospital X and hospital Y was the maximum ?

A. 2003 C. 2005
B. 2004 D. 2006

39. What is the maximum dispersion in the registration of patients in the two hospitals in a year?

A. 8000 C. 4000
B. 6000 D. 2000

40. In which year there was maximum decrease in registration of patients in hospital X ?

A. 2003 B. 2004
C. 2005 D. 2006

41. Which of the following sources of data is not based on primary data collection ?

A. Census of India
B. National Sample Survey
C. Statistical Abstracts of India
D. National Family Health Survey

42. Which of the four data sets have more dispersion ?

A.	88	91	90	92	89	91
B.	0	1	1	0	−1	−2
C.	3	5	2	4	1	5
D.	0	5	8	10	−2	−8

43. Which of the following is not related to information security on the Internet ?
A. Data Encryption
B. Water marking
C. Data Hiding
D. Information Retrieval

44. Which is the largest unit of storage among the following ?
A. Terabyte B. Megabyte
C. Kilobyte D. Gigabyte

45. bit stands for
A. binary information term
C. binary tree
B. binary digit
D. Bivariate Theory

46. Which one of the following is not a linear data structure ?
A. Array B. Binary Tree
C. Queue D. Stack

47. Which one of the following is not a network device ?
A. Router B. Switch
C. Hub D. CPU

48. A compiler is used to convert the following to object code which can be executed
A. High-level language
B. Low-level language
C. Assembly language
D. Natural language

49. The great Indian Bustard bird is found in
A. Thar Desert of Rajasthan
B. Malabar Coast
C. Coastal regions of India
D. Delta regions

50. The Sagarmanthan National Park has been established to preserve the eco-system of which mountain peak ?
A. Kanchenjunga B. Mount Everest
C. Annapurna D. Dhaulavira

51. Maximum soot is released from
A. Petrol vehicles
B. CNG vehicles
C. Diesel vehicles
D. Thermal Power Plants

52. Surface Ozone is produced from
A. Transport sector
B. Cement plants
C. Textile industry
D. Chemical industry

53. Which one of the following non-conventional energy sources can be exploited most economically ?
A. Solar
B. Wind
C. Geo-thermal
D. Ocean Thermal Energy Conversion (OTEC)

54. The most recurring natural hazard in India is
A. Earthquakes B. Floods
C. Landslides D. Volcanoes

55. The recommendation of National Knowledge Commission for the establishment of 1500 Universities is to
A. create more teaching jobs
B. ensure increase in student enrolment in higher education
C. replace or substitute the privately managed higher education institutions by public institutions
D. enable increased movement of students from rural areas to urban areas

56. According to Article 120 of the Constitution of India, the business in Parliament shall be transacted in
A. English only
B. Hindi only
C. English and Hindi both
D. All the languages included in Eighth Schedule of the Constitution

57. Which of the following is more interactive and student centric ?
A. Seminar B. Workshop
C. Lecture D. Group Discussion

58. The Parliament in India is composed of
A. Lok Sabha & Rajya Sabha
B. Lok Sabha, Rajya Sabha & Vice President
C. Lok Sabha, Rajya Sabha & President
D. Lok Sabha, Rajya Sabha with their Secretariats

59. The enrolment in higher education in India is contributed both by Formal System of Education and by System of Distance Education. Distance education contributes

A. 50% of formal system

B. 25% of formal system

C. 10% of the formal system

D. Distance education system's contribution is not taken into account while considering the figures of enrolment in higher education

60. **Assertion A :** The U.G.C. Academic Staff Colleges came into existence to improve the quality of teachers.

Reason (R) : University and college teachers have to undergo both orientation and refresher courses.

A. Both A. and (R) are true and (R) is the correct explanation.

B. Both A. and (R) are correct but (R) is not the correct explanation of A..

C. A. is correct and (R) is false.

D. A. is false and (R) is correct.

ANSWERS

1	2	3	4	5	6	7	8	9	10
D	C	B	C	B	C	A	B	B	B
11	**12**	**13**	**14**	**15**	**16**	**17**	**18**	**19**	**20**
C	B	C	A	D	D	B	A	C	A
21	**22**	**23**	**24**	**25**	**26**	**27**	**28**	**29**	**30**
D	A	A	A	B	C	B	D	C	B
31	**32**	**33**	**34**	**35**	**36**	**37**	**38**	**39**	**40**
C	A	B	A	C	D	C	C	A	D
41	**42**	**43**	**44**	**45**	**46**	**47**	**48**	**49**	**50**
C	D	D	A	B	B	D	A	A	B
51	**52**	**53**	**54**	**55**	**56**	**57**	**58**	**59**	**60**
D	A	A	B	B	C	D	C	B	A

SOME SELECTED EXPLANATORY ANSWERS

27. 2 5 9 19 37 [75]

2×2+1 5×2−1 9×2+1 19×2−1 37×2+1

44. Kilobyte < Megabyte < Gigabyte < Terabyte

49. The great Indian Bustard bird is found in Thar Desert.

58. The Parliament in India is composed of Lok Sabha, Rajya Sabha & President.

Previous Paper (Solved)

UGC-NET (JRF) EXAM JUNE, 2008

PAPER–I

Note : This paper contains **fifty** (50) multiple-choice questions, each question carrying **two** (2) marks. Attempt **all** of them.

1. The teacher has been glorified by the phrase "Friend, philosopher and guide" because :

A. He has to play all vital roles in the context of society

B. He transmits the high value of humanity to students

C. He is the great reformer of the society

D. He is a great patriot

2. The most important cause of failure for teacher lies in the area of :

A. inter personal relationship

B. lack of command over the knowledge of the subject

C. verbal ability

D. strict handling of the students

3. A teacher can establish rapport with his students by :

A. becoming a figure of authority

B. impressing students with knowledge and skill

C. playing the role of a guide

D. becoming a friend to the students

4. Education is a powerful instrument of :

A. Social transformation

B. Personal transformation

C. Cultural transformation

D. All the above

5. A teacher's major contribution towards the maximum self-realization of the student is affected through :

A. Constant fulfilment of the students' needs

B. Strict control of class-room activities

C. Sensitivity to students' needs, goals and purposes

D. Strict reinforcement of academic standards

6. Research problem is selected from the stand point of :

A. Researcher's interest

B. Financial support

C. Social relevance

D. Availability of relevant literature

7. Which one is called non-probability sampling?

A. Cluster sampling

B. Quota sampling

C. Systematic sampling

D. Stratified random sampling

8. Formulation of hypothesis may NOT be required in :

A. Survey method

B. Historical studies

C. Experimental studies

D. Normative studies

9. Field-work based research is classified as :

A. Empirical B. Historical

C. Experimental D. Biographical

10. Which of the following sampling method is appropriate to study the prevalence of AIDS amongst male and female in India in 1976, 1986, 1996 and 2006 ?

A. Cluster sampling
B. Systematic sampling
C. Quota sampling
D. Stratified random sampling

Read the following passage and answer the questions 11 to 15 :

The fundamental principle is that Article 14 forbids class legislation but permits reasonable classification for the purpose of legislation which classification must satisfy the twin tests of classification being founded on an intelligible differentia which distinguishes persons or things that are grouped together from those that are left out of the group and that differentia must have a rational nexus to the object sought to be achieved by the Statute in question. The thrust of Article 14 is that the citizen is entitled to equality before law and equal protection of laws. In the very nature of things the society being composed of unequals a welfare State will have to strive by both executive and legislative action to help the less fortunate in society to ameliorate their condition so that the social and economic inequality in the society may be bridged. This would necessitate a legislative application to a group of citizens otherwise unequal and amelioration of whose lot is the object of state affirmative action. In the absence of the doctrine of classification such legislation is likely to flounder on the bed rock of equality enshrined in Article 14. The Court realistically appraising the social and economic inequality and keeping in view the guidelines on which the State action must move as constitutionally laid down in Part IV of the Constitution evolved the doctrine of classification. The doctrine was evolved to sustain a legislation or State action designed to help weaker sections of the society or some such segments of the society in need of succour. Legislative and executive action may accordingly be sustained if it satisfies the twin tests of reasonable classification and the rational principle correlated to the object sought to be achieved.

The concept of equality before the law does not involve the idea of absolute equality among human beings which is a physical impossibility. All that Article 14 guarantees is a similarity of treatment contra-distinguished from identical treatment. Equality before law means that among equals the law should be equal and should be equally administered and that the likes should be treated alike. Equality before the law does not mean that things which are different shall be as though they are the same. It ofcourse means denial of any special privilege by reason of birth, creed or the like. The legislation as well as the executive government, while dealing with diverse problems arising out of an infinite variety of human relations must of necessity have the power of making special laws, to attain any particular object and to achieve that object it must have the power of selection or classification of persons and things upon which such laws are to operate.

11. Right to equality, one of the fundamental rights, is enunciated in the constitution under Part III, Article :

A. 12 B. 13
C. 14 D. 15

12. The main thrust of Right to equality is that it permits :

A. class legislation
B. equality before law and equal protection under the law
C. absolute equality
D. special privilege by reason of birth

13. The social and economic inequality in the society can be bridged by :

A. executive and legislative action
B. universal suffrage
C. identical treatment
D. none of the above

14. The doctrine of classification is evolved to :

A. Help weaker sections of the society
B. Provide absolute equality
C. Provide identical treatment
D. None of the above

15. While dealing with diverse problems arising out of an infinite variety of human relations, the government :

A. must have the power of making special laws

B. must not have any power to make special laws
C. must have power to withdraw equal rights
D. none of the above

16. Communication with oneself is known as :
A. Group communication
B. Grapevine communication
C. Interpersonal communication
D. Intrapersonal communication

17. Which broadcasting system for TV is followed in India ?
A. NTSE B. PAL
C. SECAM D. NTCS

18. All India Radio before 1936 was known as :
A. Indian Radio Broadcasting
B. Broadcasting Service of India
C. Indian State Broadcasting Service
D. All India Broadcasting Service

19. The biggest news agency of India is :
A. PTI B. UNI
C. NANAP D. Samachar Bharati

20. Prasar Bharati was launched in the year :
A. 1995 B. 1997
C. 1999 D. 2001

21. A statistical measure based upon the entire population is called parameter while measure based upon a sample is known as :
A. Sample parameter
B. Inference
C. Statistics
D. None of these

22. The importance of the correlation co-efficient lies in the fact that :
A. There is a linear relationship between the correlated variables.
B. It is one of the most valid measure of statistics.
C. It allows one to determine the degree or strength of the association between two variables.
D. It is a non-parametric method of statistical analysis.

23. The F-test:
A. is essentially a two tailed test.
B. is essentially a one tailed test.
C. can be one tailed as well as two tailed depending on the hypothesis.
D. can never be a one tailed test.

24. What will be the next letter in the following series : DCXW, FEVU, HGTS, _____
A. AKPO B. JBYZ
C. JIRQ D. LMRS

25. The following question is based on the diagram given below. If the two small circles represent formal class-room education and distance education and the big circle stands for university system of education, which figure represents the university systems.

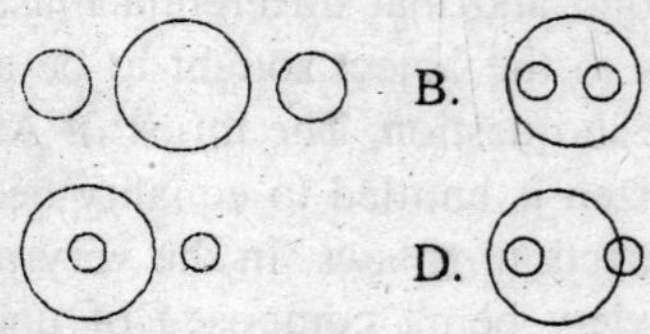

A. B.
C. D.

26. The statement, *'To be non-violent is good'* is a :
A. Moral judgement
B. Factual judgement
C. Religious judgement
D. Value judgement

27. **Assertion (A):** Man is a rational being.
Reason (R): Man is a social being.
A. Both A. and **(R)** are true and **(R)** is the correct explanation of A.
B. Both A. and **(R)** are true but **(R)** is not the correct explanation of A.
C. A. is true but **(R)** is false
D. A. is false but **(R)** is true

28. Value Judgements are :
A. Factual Judgements
B. Ordinary Judgements
C. Normative Judgements
D. Expression of public opinion

29. Deductive reasoning proceeds from :
A. general to particular
B. particular to general
C. one general conclusion to another general conclusion
D. one particular conclusion to another particular conclusion

30. AGARTALA is written in code as 14168171, the code for AGRA is :
A. 1641 B. 1416
C. 1441 D. 1461

31. Which one of the following is the most comprehensive source of population data ?
A. National Family Health Surveys
B. National Sample Surveys
C. Census
D. Demographic Health Surveys

32. Which one of the following principles is *not* applicable to sampling ?
A. Sample units must be clearly defined
B. Sample units must be dependent on each other
C. Same units of sample should be used throughout the study
D. Sample units must be chosen in a systematic and objective manner

33. If January 1st, 2007 is Monday, what was the day on 1st January 1995 ?
A. Sunday B. Monday
C. Friday D. Saturday

34. Insert the missing number in the following series :
4 16 8 64 ? 256
A. 16 B. 24
C. 32 D. 20

35. If an article is sold for Rs. 178 at a loss of 11%; what would be its selling price in order to earn a profit of 11% ?
A. Rs. 222.50 B. Rs. 267
C. Rs. 222 D. Rs. 220

36. WYSIWYG - describes the display of a document on screen as it will actually print
A. What you state is what you get
B. What you see is what you get
C. What you save is what you get
D. What you suggest is what you get

37. Which of the following is *not a* Computer language ?
A. PASCAL B. UNIX
C. FORTRAN D. COBOL

38. A key-board has at least :
A. 91 keys B. 101 keys
C. 111 keys D. 121 keys

39. An E-mail address is composed of
A. two parts B. three parts
C. four parts D. five parts

40. Corel Draw is a popular :
A. Illustration programme
B. Programming language
C. Text programme
D. None of the above

41. Human ear is most sensitive to noise in which of the following ranges :
A. 1-2 KHz B. 100 - 500 Hz
C. 10 - 12 KHz D. 13 - 16 KHz

42. Which one of the following units is used to measure intensity of noise ?
A. decible B. Hz
C. Phon D. Watts/m^2

43. If the population growth follows a logistic curve, the maximum sustainable yield :
A. is equal to half the carrying capacity.
B. is equal to the carrying capacity.
C. depends on growth rates.
D. depends on the initial population.

44. Chemical weathering of rocks is largely dependent upon :
A. high temperature
B. strong wind action
C. heavy rainfall
D. glaciation

45. Structure of earth's system consists of the following :

Match *List-I* with *List-II* and give the correct answer.

List-I *(Zone)*	List-II *(Chemical Character)*
(a) Atmosphere	(i) Inert gases
(b) Biosphere	(ii) Salt, fresh water, snow and ice
(c) Hydrosphere	(iii) Organic substances, skeleton matter
(d) Lithosphere	(iv) Light silicates

Codes :

	(a)	(b)	(c)	(d)
A.	(ii)	(iii)	(i)	(iv)
B.	(i)	(iii)	(ii)	(iv)
C.	(ii)	(i)	(iii)	(iv)
D.	(i)	(i)	(ii)	(iv)

46. NAAC is an autonomous institution under the aegis of :

A. ICSSR B. CSIR

C. AICTE D. UGC

47. National Council for Women's Education was established in :

A. 1958 B. 1976

C. 1989 D. 2000

48. Which one of the following is *not* situated in New Delhi ?

A. Indian Council of Cultural Relations

B. Indian Council of Scientific Research

C. National Council of Educational Research and Training

D. Indian Institute of Advanced Studies

49. Autonomy in higher education implies freedom in :

A. Administration

B. Policy-making

C. Finance

D. Curriculum development

50. Match *List-I* with *List-II* and select the correct answer from the code given below

List-I (Institutions)

(a) Dr. Hari Singh Gour University

(b) S.N.D.T. University

(c) M.S. University

(d) J.N. Vyas University *Codes :*

List-II (Locations)

(i) Mumbai (ii) Baroda

(iii) Jodhpur (iv) Sagar

	(a)	*(b)*	*(c)*	*(d)*
A.	(iv)	(i)	(ii)	(iii)
B.	(i)	(ii)	(iii)	(iv)
C.	(iii)	(i)	(ii)	(iv)
D.	(ii)	(iv)	(i)	(iii)

ANSWERS

1	**2**	**3**	**4**	**5**	**6**	**7**	**8**	**9**	**10**
B	B	B	D	C	C	B	B	A	D
11	**12**	**13**	**14**	**15**	**16**	**17**	**18**	**19**	**20**
C	B	A	A	A	D	B	C	A	B
21	**22**	**23**	**24**	**25**	**26**	**27**	**28**	**29**	**30**
A	C	C	C	B	A	B	C	A	D
31	**32**	**33**	**34**	**35**	**36**	**37**	**38**	**39**	**40**
C	B	D	A	C	B	B	B	A	A
41	**42**	**43**	**44**	**45**	**46**	**47**	**48**	**49**	**50**
B	A	A	C	B	D	A	D	C	A

SOME SELECTED EXPLANATORY ANSWERS

24. D → C (−1), X → W (−1)

F → E (−1), V → U (−1)

H → G (−1), T → S (−1)

∴ J → I (−1), R → Q (−1)

30. Since,

A	G	A	R	T	A	L	A
↓	↓	↓	↓	↓	↓	↓	↓
1	4	1	6	8	1	7	1

Therefore

A	G	R	A
↓	↓	↓	↓
1	4	6	1

34. 4 16 8 64 [16] 256

(16 ×4 → 64, 64 ×4 → 256; 4 ×2 → 8, 8 ×2 → 16)

35. S.P. = 89% of C.P.

$$\Rightarrow 178 = \text{C.P.} \times \frac{89}{100}$$

$$\Rightarrow \text{C.P.} = \frac{100 \times 178}{89} = 200$$

$\therefore$ For 11% Profit, the selling price will be

$$\text{S.P.} = 200 \times \frac{111}{100} = \text{Rs. } 222$$

Previous Paper (Solved)

UGC-NET (JRF) EXAM
DECEMBER, 2008

PAPER–I

Note : This paper contains **fifty** (50) multiple-choice questions, each question carrying **two** (2) marks. Attempt **all** of them.

1. According to Swami Vivekananda, teacher's success depends on:

A. His renunciation of personal gain and service to others .

B. His professional training and creativity

C. His concentration on his work and duties with a spirit of obedience to God

D. His mastery on the subject and capacity in controlling the students

2. Which of the following teacher, will be liked most:

A. A teacher of high idealistic attitude

B. A loving teacher

C. A teacher who is disciplined

D. A teacher who often amuses his students

3. A teacher's most important challenge is:

A. To make students do their home work

B. To make teaching-learning process enjoyable

C. To maintain discipline in the class room

D. To prepare the question paper

4. Value-education stands for:

A. making a student healthy

B. making a student to get a job

C. inculcation of virtues

D. all-round development of personality

5. When a normal student behaves in an erratic manner in the class, you would:

A. pull up the student then and there

B. talk to the student after the class

C. ask the student to leave the class

D. ignore the student

6. The research is always—

A. verifying the old knowledge

B. exploring new knowledge

C. filling the gap between knowledge

D. all of these

7. The research that applies the laws at the time of field study to draw more and more clear ideas about the problem is:

A. Applied research

B. Action research

C. Experimental research

D. None of these

8. When a research problem is related to heterogeneous population, the most suitable sampling method is:

A. Cluster Sampling

B. Stratified Sampling

C. Convenient Sampling

D. Lottery Method

9. The process not needed in experimental research is:

A. Observation

B. Manipulation and replication

C. Controlling

D. Reference collection

10. A research problem is not feasible only when:

A. it is researchable

B. it is new and adds something to knowledge
C. it consists of independent and dependent variables
D. it has utility and relevance

Read the following passage carefully and answer the questions 11 to 15 :

Radically changing monsoon patterns, reduction in the winter rice harvest and a quantum increase in respiratory diseases all part of the environmental doomsday scenario which is reportedly playing out in South Asia. According to a United Nations Environment Programme report, a deadly three-kilometer deep blanket of pollution comprising a fearsome, cocktail of ash, acids, aerosols and other particles has enveloped in this region. For India, already struggling to cope with a drought, the implication of this are devastating and further crop failure will amount to a life and death question for many Indians. The increase in premature deaths will have adverse social and economic consequences and a rise in morbidities will place an unbearable burden on our crumbling health system. And there is no one to blame but ourselves. Both official and corporate India has always been allergic to any mention of clean technology. Most mechanical two wheelers roll of the assembly line without proper pollution control system. Little effort is made for R&D on simple technologies, which could make a vital difference to people's lives and the environment.

However, while there is no denying that South Asia must clean up its act, skeptics might question the timing of the haze report. The Kyoto meet on climate change is just two weeks away and the stage is set for the usual battle between the developing world and the West, particularly the Unites States of America. President Mr. Bush has adamantly refused to sign any protocol, which would mean a change in American consumption level. U.N. environment report will likely find a place in the U.S. arsenal as it plants an accusing finger towards controls like India and China. Yet the U.S.A. can hardly deny its own dubious role in the matter of erasing trading quotas.

Richer countries can simply buy up excess credits from poorer countries and continue to pollute. Rather than try to get the better of developing countries, who undoubtedly have taken up environmental shortcuts in their bid to catch up with the West, the USA should take a look at the environmental profigacy, which is going on within. From opening up virgin territories for oil exploration to relaxing the standards for drinking water, Mr. Bush's policies are not exactly beneficial, not even to America's interests. We realize that we are all in this together and that pollution anywhere should be a global concern otherwise there will only be more tunnels at the end of the tunnel.

11. Both official and corporate India is allergic to:
A. Failure of Monsoon
B. Poverty and Inequality
C. Slowdown in Industrial Production
D. Mention of Clean Technology

12. If the rate of premature death increases it will:
A. Exert added burden on the crumbling economy
B. Have adverse social and economic consequences
C. Make positive effect on our effort to control population
D. Have less job aspirants in the society

13. According to the passage, the two wheeler industry is not adequately concerned about:
A. Passenger safety on the roads
B. Life cover insurance of the vehicle owner
C. Pollution control system in the vehicle
D. Rising cost of the two wheelers

14. What could be the reason behind timing of the haze report just before the Kyoto meet ?
A. United Nations is working hand-in-glove with U.S.A.
B. Organizers of the forthcoming meet to teach a lesson to the U.S.A.
C. Drawing attention of the world towards devastating effects of environment degradation.
D. U.S.A. wants to use it as a handle against the developing countries in the forthcoming meet

15. Which of the following is the indication of environmental degradation in South Asia ?

A. Social and economic inequality
B. Crumbling health care system
C. Inadequate pollution control system
D. Radically changing monsoon pattern

16. Community Radio is a type of radio service that caters to the interest of :

A. Local audience B. Education
C. Entertainment D. News

17. Orcut is a part of :

A. Intra personal Communication
B. Mass Communication
C. Group Communication
D. Interpersonal Communication

18. Match **List-I** with **List-II** and select the correct answer using the codes given below:

List - I (Artists)	**List - II (Art)**
(a) Amrita Shergill	(i) Flute
(b) T. Swaminathan Pillai	(ii) Classical Song
(c) Bhimsen Joshi	(iii) Painting
(d) Padma Subramaniyam	(iv) Bharat Natyam

Codes :

	(a)	(b)	(c)	(d)
A.	(iii)	(i)	(ii)	(iv)
B.	(ii)	(iii)	(i)	(iv)
C.	(iv)	(ii)	(iii)	(i)
D.	(i)	(iv)	(ii)	(iii)

19. Which is not correct in latest communication award ?

A. Salman Rushdie – Booker's Prize - July 20, 2008
B. Dilip Sanghavi – Business Standard CEO Award July 22, 2008
C. Tapan Sinha – Dada Saheb Falke Award, July 21, 2008
D. Gautam Ghosh – Osians – Lifetime Achievement Award July 11, 2008

20. Firewalls are used to protect a communication network system against:

A. Unauthorized attacks
B. Virus attacks
C. Data-driven attacks
D. Fire-attacks

21. Insert the missing number in the following :

$$\frac{2}{3}, \frac{4}{7}, ?, \frac{11}{21}, \frac{16}{31}$$

A. $\frac{10}{8}$ B. $\frac{6}{10}$
C. $\frac{5}{10}$ D. $\frac{7}{13}$

22. In a certain code, GAMESMAN is written as AGMEMSAN. How would DISCLOSE be written in that code ?

A. IDSCOLSE
B. IDCSOLES
C. IDSCOLES
D. IDSCLOSE

23. The letters in the first set have a certain relationship. On the basis of this relationship mark the right choice for the second set :

AST : BRU : : NQV : ?

A. ORW B. MPU
C. MRW D. OPW

24. On what dates of April 1994 did SUNDAY fall?

A. 2, 9, 16, 23, 30
B. 3, 10, 17, 24
C. 4, 11, 18, 25
D. 1, 8, 15, 22, 29

25. Find out the wrong number in the sequence: 125, 127, 130, 135, 142, 153, 165

A. 130 B. 142
C. 153 D. 165

26. There are five books A, B, C, D and E. The book C lies above D, the book E is below A and B is below E. Which is at the bottom ?

A. E B. B
C. A D. C

27. Logical reasoning is based on:

A. Truth of involved propositions
B. Valid relation among the involved propositions

C. Employment of symbolic language
D. Employment of ordinary language

28. Two propositions with the same subject and predicate terms but different in quality are :
A. Contradictory B. Contrary
C. Subaltern D. Identical

29. The premises of a valid deductive argument:
A. Provide some evidence for its conclusion
B. Provide no evidence for its conclusion
C. Are irrelevant for its conclusion
D. Provide conclusive evidence for its conclusion

30. Syllogistic reasoning is :
A. Deductive
B. Inductive
C. Experimental
D. Hypothetical

Study the following Venn diagram and answer questions nos. 31 to 33.

Three circles representing GRADUATES, CLERKS and GOVERNMENT EMPLOYEES are intersecting. The intersections are marked A, B, C, e, f, g and h. Which part best represents the statements in questions 31 to 33 ?

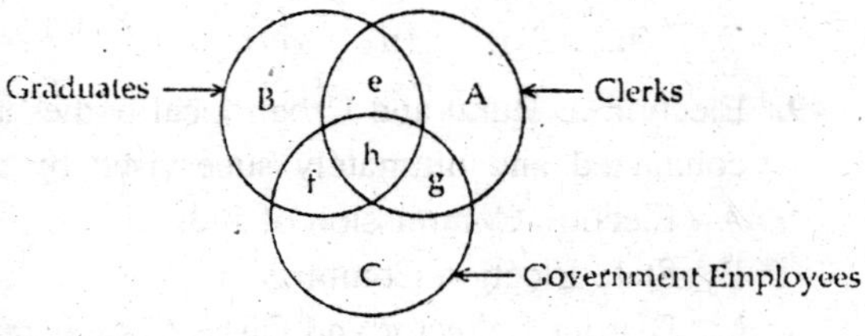

31. Some Graduates are Government employees but not as Clerks.
A. h B. g
C. f D. e

32. Clerks who are graduates as well as government employees :
A. e B. f
C. g D. h

33. Some graduates are Clerks but not Government employees.
A. f B. g
C. h D. e

Study the following graph and answer questions numbered from 34 to 35

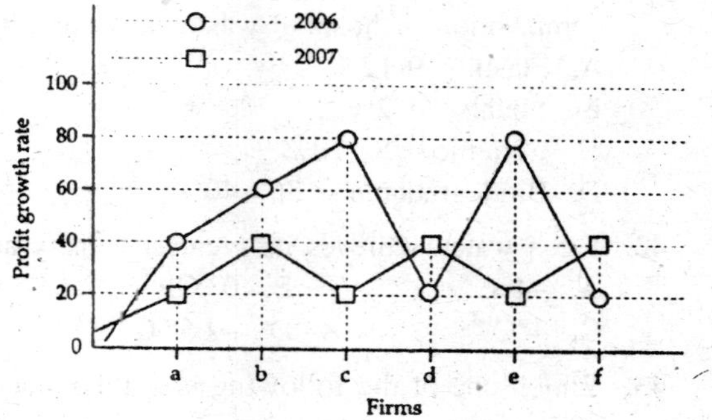

34. Which of the firms got maximum profit growth rate in the year 2006.
A. ab B. ce
C. cd D. ef

35. Which of the firms got maximum profit growth rate in the year 2007.
A. bdf B. acf
C. bed D. ace

36. The accounting software 'Tally' was developed by :
A. HCL B. TCS
C. Infosys D. Wipro

37. Errors in computer programmes are called :
A. Follies B. Mistakes
C. Bugs D. Spam

38. HTML is basically used to design :
A. Web-page
B. Web-site
C. Graphics
D. Tables and Frames

39. 'Micro Processing' is made for :
A. Computer
B. Digital System
C. Calculator
D. Electronic Goods

40. Information, a combination of graphics, text, sound, video and animation is called :
A. Multiprogramme
B. Multifacet

C. Multimedia
D. Multiprocess

41. Which of the following pairs regarding typical composition of hospital wastes is incorrect ?
A. Plastic- 9-12%
B. Metals- 1-2%
C. Ceramic - 8 10%
D. Biodegradable - 35 - 40%

42. Fresh water achieves its greatest density at :
A. –4°C B. 0° C
C. 4°C D. –2.5° C

43. Which one of the following is not associated with earthquakes ?
A. Focus B. Epicenter
C. Seismograph D. Swells

44. The tallest trees in the world are found in the region :
A. Equatorial region
B. Temperate region
C. Monsoon region
D. Mediterranean region

45. Match **List-I** with **List-II** and select the correct answer from the codes given below :

List - I (National Parks)	List - II (States)
(a) Periyar	(i) Orissa
(b) Nandan Kanan	(ii) Kerala
(c) Corbett National Park	(iii) Rajasthan
(d) Sariska Tiger Reserve	(iv) Uttarakhand

Codes :

	(a)	(b)	(c)	(d)
A.	(ii)	(i)	(iv)	(iii)
B.	(i)	(ii)	(iv)	(iii)
C.	(iii)	(ii)	(i)	(iv)
D.	(i)	(ii)	(iii)	(iv)

46. According to Radhakrishnan Commission, the aim of Higher Education is :
A. To develop the democratic values, peace and harmony
B. To develop great personalities who can give their contributions in politics, administration, industry and commerce
C. Both A. and B.
D. None of these

47. The National Museum at New Delhi is attached to:
A. Delhi University
B. a Deemed University
C. a Subordinate Office of the JNU
D. Part of Ministry of Tourism and Culture

48. Match **List-I** with **List-II** and select the correct answer from the code given below :

List - I (Institutions)	List - II (Locations)
(a) National Law Institute	(i) Shimla
(b) Indian Institute of Advanced Studies	(ii) Bhopal
(c) National Judicial Academy	(iii) Hyderabad
(d) National Savings Institute	(iv) Nagpur

Codes :

	(a)	(b)	(c)	(d)
A.	(iii)	(ii)	(iv)	(i)
B.	(i)	(ii)	(iii)	(iv)
C.	(iv)	(iii)	(i)	(ii)
D.	(iii)	(i)	(ii)	(iv)

49. Election of Rural and Urban local bodies are conducted and ultimately supervised by :
A. Election Commission of India
B. State Election Commission
C. District Collector and District Magistrate
D. Concerned Returning Officer

50. Which opinion is not correct ?
A. Education is a subject of concurrent list of VII schedule of Constitution of India
B. University Grants Commission is a statutory body
C. Patent, inventions, design, copyright and trade marks are the subject of concurrent list
D. Indian Council of Social Science Research is a statutory body related to research in social sciences

ANSWERS

1	2	3	4	5	6	7	8	9	10
D	C	B	C	B	D	A	B	D	B
11	**12**	**13**	**14**	**15**	**16**	**17**	**18**	**19**	**20**
D	B	C	C	D	A	D	A	B	A
21	**22**	**23**	**24**	**25**	**26**	**27**	**28**	**29**	**30**
D	A	D	B	D	B	B	A	D	A
31	**32**	**33**	**34**	**35**	**36**	**37**	**38**	**39**	**40**
C	D	D	B	A	B	C	A	A	C
41	**42**	**43**	**44**	**45**	**46**	**47**	**48**	**49**	**50**
D	C	D	B	A	C	D	D	B	C

SOME SELECTED EXPLANATORY ANSWERS

21. Since, $\frac{2}{3}=\frac{2}{2\times2-1}$

$\frac{4}{7}=\frac{4}{4\times2-1}$

$\frac{11}{21}=\frac{11}{11\times2-1}$

and $\frac{16}{31}=\frac{16}{16\times2-1}$

Therefore $\frac{7}{13}=\frac{7}{7\times2-1}$

22. Since,

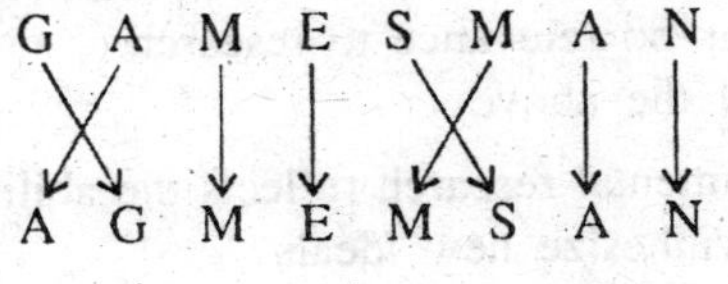

Therefore,

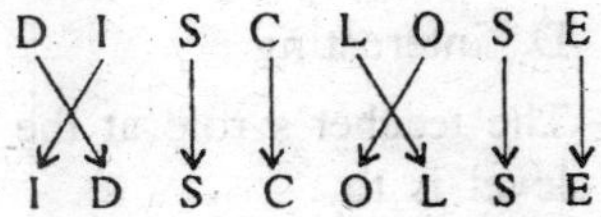

23. Since,

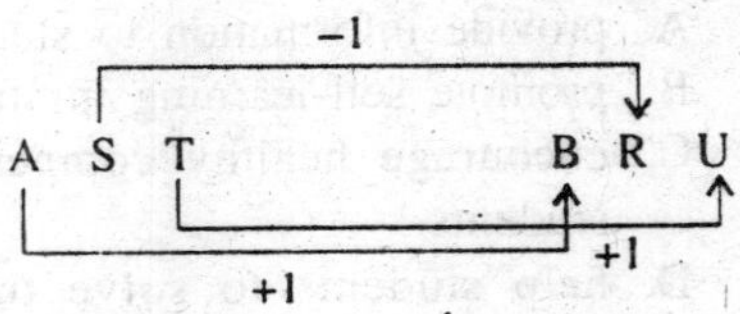

Therefore,

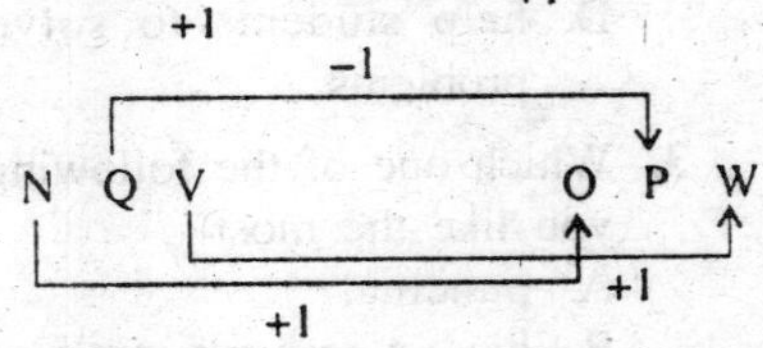

25.

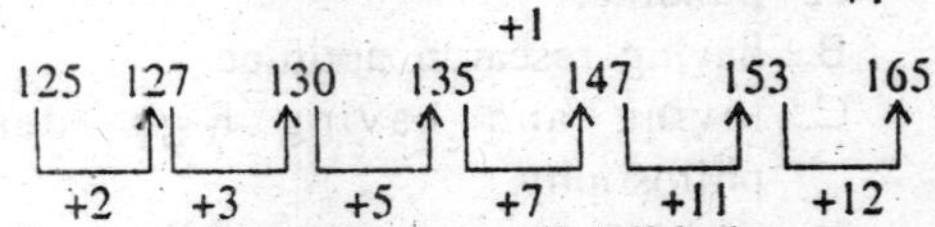

Except 12, rest are not divisible by any numbers.

IIIIIIIII

Previous Paper (Solved)

UGC-NET (JRF) EXAM
JUNE, 2007

PAPER–I

Note : This paper contains **fifty** (50) multiple-choice questions, each question carrying **two** (2) marks. Attempt **all** of them.

1. Teacher uses visual-aids to make learning:
A. simple
B. more knowledgeable
C. quicker
D. interesting

2. The teacher's role at the higher educational level is to :
A. provide information to students
B. promote self-learning in students
C. encourage healthy competition among students
D. help students to solve their personal problems

3. Which one of the following teachers would you like the most
A. punctual
B. having research aptitude
C. loving and having high idealistic philosophy
D. who often amuses his students

4. Micro teaching is most effective for the student-teacher :
A. during the practice-teaching
B. after the practice-teaching
C. before the practice-teaching
D. none of the above

5. Which is the least important factor in teaching?
A. punishing the students
B. maintaining discipline in the class
C. lecturing in impressive way
D. drawing sketches and diagrams on the black-board

6. To test null hypothesis, a researcher uses :
A. t test
B. ANOVA
C. x^2
D. factorial analysis

7. A research problem is feasible only when :
A. it has utility and relevance
B. it is researchable
C. it is new and adds something to knowledge
D. all the above

8. Bibliography given in a research report :
A. shows vast knowledge of the researcher
B. helps those interested in further research
C. has no relevance to research
D. all the above

9. Fundamental research reflects the ability to :
A. Synthesize new ideals
B. Expound new principles
C. Evaluate the existing material concerning research
D. Study the existing literature regarding various topics

10. The study in which the investigators attempt to trace an effect is known as
A. Survey Research

B. 'Ex-post Facto' Research
C. Historical Research
D. Summative Research

Read the following passage and answer the questions 11 to 15 :

All political systems need to mediate the relationship between private wealth and public power. Those that fail risk a dysfunctional government captured by wealthy interests. Corruption is one symptom of such failure with private willingness-to-pay trumping public goals. Private individuals and business firms pay to get routine services and to get to the head of the bureaucratic queue. They pay to limit their taxes, avoid costly regulations, obtain contracts at inflated prices and get concessions and privatised firms at low prices. If corruption is endemic, public officials - both bureaucrats and elected officials - may redesign programmes and propose public projects with few public benefits and many opportunities for private profit. Ofcourse, corruption, in the sense of bribes, pay-offs and kickbacks, is only one type of government failure. Efforts to promote 'good governance' must be broader than anti-corruption campaigns. Governments may be honest but inefficient because no one has an incentive to work productively, and narrow elites may capture the state and exert excess influence on policy. Bribery may induce the lazy to work hard and permit those not in the inner circle of cronies to obtain benefits. However, even in such cases, corruption cannot be confined to 'functional' areas. It will be a temptation whenever private benefits are positive. It may be a reasonable response to a harsh reality but, over time, it can facilitate a spiral into an even worse situation.

11. The governments which fail to focus on the relationship between private wealth and public power are likely to become :
A. Functional
B. Dysfunctional
C. Normal functioning
D. Good governance

12. One important symptom of bad governance is :
A. Corruption
B. High taxes
C. Complicated rules and regulations
D. High prices

13. When corruption is rampant, public officials always aim at many opportunities for :
A. Public benefits B. Public profit
C. Private profit D. Corporate gains

14. Productivity linked incentives to public/private officials is one of the indicatives for:
A. Efficient government
B. Bad governance
C. Inefficient government
D. Corruption

15. The spiralling corruption can only be contained by promoting :
A. Private profit
B. Anti-corruption campaign
C. Good governance
D. Pay-offs and kick backs

16. Press Council of India is located at :
A. Chennai B. Mumbai
C. Kolkata D. Delhi

17. Adjusting the photo for publication by cutting is technically known as :
A. Photo cutting
B. Photo bleeding
C. Photo cropping
D. Photo adjustment

18. Feed-back of a message comes from :
A. Satellite B. Media
C. Audience D. Communicator

19. Collection of information in advance before designing communication strategy is known as :
A. Feed-back B. Feed-forward
C. Research study D. Opinion poll

20. The aspect ratio of TV screen is :
A. 4 : 3 B. 4 : 2
C. 3 : 5 D. 2 : 3

21. Which is the number that comes next in the sequence ?
9, 8, 8, 8, 7, 8, 6, ___
A. 5 B. 6
C. 8 D. 4

22. If in a certain language PUNCTUAL is coded as 16598623, how would ACTUPULN be coded?

A. 8 3 4 5 3 6 B. 2 9 8 6 1 6 3 5
C. 8 3 4 5 3 0 D. 8 3 4 5 3 9

23. The question to be answered by factorial analysis of the quantitative data does not explain one of the following :

A. Is 'X' related to 'Y' ?
B. How is 'X' related to 'Y' ?
C. How does 'X' affect the dependent variable 'Y' at different levels of another independent variable 'K' or 'M' ?
D. How is 'X' by 'K' related to 'M' ?

24. January 12, 1980 was Saturday, what day was January 12, 1979 :

A. Saturday B. Friday
C. Sunday D. Thursday

25. How many Mondays are there in a particular month of a particular year, if the month ends on Wednesday ?

A. 5 B. 4
C. 3 D. None of the above

26. From the given four statements, select the two which cannot be true but yet both can be false. Choose the right pair :

(i) All men are mortal
(ii) Some men are mortal
(iii) No man is mortal
(iv) Some men are not mortal

A. (i) and (ii) B. (iii) and (iv)
C. (i) and (iii) D. (ii) and (iv)

27. A Syllogism must have :

A. Three terms B. Four terms
C. Six terms D. Five terms

28. Copula is that part of proposition which denotes the relationship between :

A. Subject and predicate
B. Known and unknown
C. Major premise and minor premise
D. Subject and object

29. "E" denotes :

A. Universal Negative Proposition
B. Particular Affirmative Proposition
C. Universal Affirmative Proposition
D. Particular Negative Proposition

30. 'A' is the father of 'C', and 'D' is the son of 'B'. 'E' is the brother of 'A'. If 'C' is the sister of 'D', how is 'B' related to 'E' ?

A. daughter B. husband
C. sister-in-law D. brother-in-law

31. Which of the following methods will you choose to prepare choropleth map of India showing urban density of population :

A. Quartiles B. Quintiles
C. Mean and SD D. Break - point

32. Which of the following methods is best suited to show on a map the types of crops being grown in a region :

A. Choropleth B. Chorochromatic
C. Choroschematic D. Isopleth

33. A ratio represents the relation between :

A. Part and Part
B. Part and Whole
C. Whole and Whole
D. All of the above

34. Out of four numbers, the average of the first three numbers is thrice the fourth number. If the average of the four numbers is 5, the fourth number is :

A. 4.5 B. 5
C. 2 D. 4

35. Circle graphs are used to show :

A. How various sections share in the whole
B. How various parts are related to the whole
C. How one whole is related to other wholes
D. How one part is related to other parts

36. On the keyboard of computer each character has an "ASCII" value which stands for :

A. American Stock Code for Information Interchange
B. American Standard Code for Information Interchange
C. African Standard Code for Information Interchange
D. Adaptable Standard Code for Information Change

37. Which part of the Central Processing Unit (CPU) performs calculation and makes decisions :

A. Arithematic Logic Unit
B. Alternating Logic Unit
C. Alternate Local Unit
D. American Logic Unit

38. "Dpi" stands for :

A. Dots per inch
B. Digits per unit
C. Dots pixel inch
D. Diagrams per inch

39. The process of laying out a document with text, graphics, headlines and photographs is involved in:

A. Deck Top Publishing
B. Desk Top Printing
C. Desk Top Publishing
D. Deck Top Printing

40. Transfer of data from one application to another line is known as :

A. Dynamic Disk Exchange
B. Dodgy Data Exchange
C. Dogmatic Data Exchange
D. Dynamic Data Exchange

41. Tsunami occurs due to :

A. Mild earthquakes and landslides in the oceans
B. Strong earthquakes and landslides in the oceans
C. Strong earthquakes and landslides in mountains
D. Strong earthquakes and landslides in deserts

42. Which of the natural hazards have big effect on Indian people each year ?

A. Cyclones B. Floods
C. Earthquakes D. Landslides

43. Comparative Environment Impact Assessment study is to be conducted for :

A. the whole year
B. three seasons excluding monsoon
C. any three seasons
D. the worst season

44. Sea level rise results primarily due to :

A. Heavy rainfall
B. Melting of glaciers
C. Submarine volcanism
D. Seafloor spreading

45. The plume rise in a coal based power plant depends on :

(i) Buoyancy
(ii) Atmospheric stability
(iii) Momentum of exhaust gases Identify the correct code :

A. (i) and (ii) only
B. (ii) and (iii) only
C. (i) and (iii) only
D. (i), (ii) and (iii)

46. Value education makes a student :

A. Good citizen
B. Successful businessman
C. Popular teacher
D. Efficient manager

47. Networking of libraries through electronic media is known as

A. Inflibnet B. Libinfnet
C. Internet D. HTML

48. The University which telecasts interactive educational programmes through its own channel is :

A. B. R. Ambedkar Open University, Hyderabad
B. I. G. N. O. U.
C. University of Pune
D. Annamalai University

49. The Government established the University Grants Commission by an Act of Parliament in the year :

A. 1980 B. 1948
C. 1950 D. 1956

50. Universities having central campus for imparting education are called :

A. Central Universities
B. Deemed Universities
C. Residential Universities
D. Open Universities

ANSWERS

1	2	3	4	5	6	7	8	9	10
D	A	A	B	A	C	D	B	B	B
11	**12**	**13**	**14**	**15**	**16**	**17**	**18**	**19**	**20**
B	A	C	A	C	D	C	C	D	A
21	**22**	**23**	**24**	**25**	**26**	**27**	**28**	**29**	**30**
C	B	C	B	D	B	A	B	A	D
31	**32**	**33**	**34**	**35**	**36**	**37**	**38**	**39**	**40**
B	C	B	C	A	A	A	A	C	D
41	**42**	**43**	**44**	**45**	**46**	**47**	**48**	**49**	**50**
B	B	A	B	D	A	A	B	D	B

SOME SELECTED EXPLANATORY ANSWERS

22. Since,

P U N C T U A L
↓ ↓ ↓ ↓ ↓ ↓ ↓ ↓
1 6 5 9 8 6 2 3

Similarly,

A C T U P U L N
↓ ↓ ↓ ↓ ↓ ↓ ↓ ↓
2 9 8 6 1 6 3 5

30. Hints:

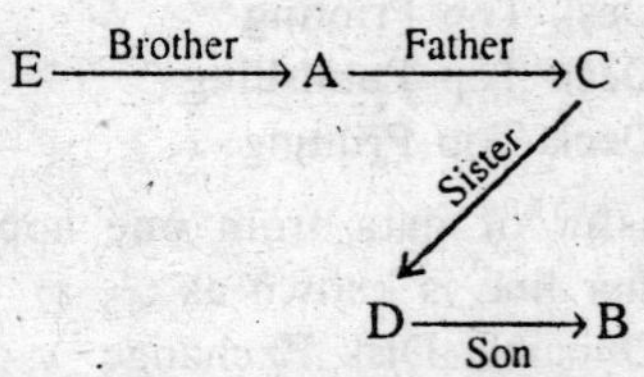

It is clear from the above figure 'E', is the Brother-in-law of 'B'.

34. Let 4th number be $3x$

$\therefore$ Average of first three numbers = $3x$

and Average of all four numbers = 5

From question

$$5 \times 4 = 3 \times 3x + x$$

$$\Rightarrow \quad 20 = 9x + x$$

$$\Rightarrow \quad x = 2$$

IIIIIIIII

Previous Paper (Solved)

UGC-NET (JRF) EXAM
DECEMBER, 2007

PAPER–I

Note : This paper contains **fifty** (50) multiple-choice questions, each question carrying **two** (2) marks. Attempt **all** of them.

1. Verbal guidance is least effective i the learning of:

A. Aptitudes B. Skills
C. Attitudes D. Relationship

2. Which is the most important aspect of the teacher's rle in learning?

A. The development of insight inrto what consititutes an adequate performance
B. The development of insigh into what consititutes the pitfalls and dangers to be avoided
C. The provision of encouragement and moral support
D. Te provision of continuous diagnostic and remedial help

3. The most appropriate purpose of learning is:

A. personal adjustment
B. modification of behaviour
C. social and political awarness
D. preparing oneself for employment

4. The students who keep on asking questions in the class should be :

A. encouraged to find answer independently
B. advised to meet the teacher after the class
C. encouraged to continue questioning
D. advised not to disturb during the lecture

5. Maximum participation of students is possible in teaching through :

A. discussion method
B. lecture method
C. audio-visual aids
D. text book method

6. Generalised conclusion on the basis of a sample is technically known as :

A. Data analysis and interpretation
B. Parameter inference
C. Statistical inference
D. All of the above

7. The experimental study is based on :

A. The manipulation of variables
B. Conceptual parameters
C. Replication of research
D. Survey of literature

8. The main characteristic of scientific research is :

A. empirical B. theoretical
C. experimental D. all of the above

9. Authenticity of a research finding is its :

A. Originality B. Validity
C. Objectivity D. All of the above

10. Which technique is generally followed when the population is finite?

A. Area Sampling Technique
B. Purposive Sampling Technique
C. Systematic Sampling Technique
D. None of the above

Read the following passage and answer the questions 11 to 15 :

Gandhi's overall social and environmental philosophy is based on what human beings need rather than what they want. His early introduction to the teachings of Jains, Theosophists. Christian sermons, Ruskin and Tolstoy, and most significantly the *Bhagavad Gita,* were to have profound impact on the development of Gandhi's holistic thinking on humanity, nature and their ecological interrelation. His deep concern for the disadvantaged, the poor and rural population created an ambience for an alternative social thinking that was at once far-sighted, local and immediate. For Gandhi was acutely aware that the demands generated by the need to feed and sustain human life, compounded by the growing industrialization of India, far outstripped the finite resources of nature. This might nowadays appear naive or commonplace, but such pronouncements were as rare as they were heretical a century ago. Gandhi was also concerned about the destruction, under colonial and modernist designs, of the existing infrastructures which had more potential for keeping a community flourishing within ecologically-sensitive traditional patterns of subsistence, especially in the rural areas, than did the incoming Western alternatives based on nature-blind technology and the enslavement of human spirit and energies.

Perhaps the moral principle for which Gandhi is best known is that of active non-violence, derived from the traditional moral restraint of not injuring another being. The most refined expression of this value is in the great epic of the *Mahabharata, (c.* 100 BCE to 200 CE), where moral development proceeds through placing constraints on the liberties, desires and acquisitiveness endemic to human life. One's action is judged in terms of consequences and the impact it is likely to have on another. Jainas had generalized this principle to include all sentient creatures and biocommunities alike. Advanced Jaina monks and nuns will sweep their path to avoid harming insects and even bacteria. Non-injury is a non-negotiable universal prescription.

11. Which one of the following have a profound impact on the development of Gandhi's holistic thinking on humanity, nature and their ecological interrelations?

A. Jain teachings B. Christian sermons
C. Bhagavad Gita D. Ruskin and Tolstoy

12. Gandhi's overall social and environmental philosophy is based on human beings' :

A. need B. desire
C. wealth D. welfare

13. Gandhiji's deep concern for the disadvantaged, the poor and rural population created an ambience for an alternative :

A. rural policy B. social thinking
C. urban policy D. economic thinking

14. Colonial policy and modernisation led to the destruction of :

A. major industrial infrastructure
B. irrigation infrastructure
C. urban infrastructure
D. rural infrastructure

15. Gandhi's active non-violence is derived from :

A. Moral restraint of not injuring another being
B. Having liberties, desires and acquisitiveness
C. Freedom of action
D. Nature-blind technology and enslavement of human spirit and energies

16. DTH service was started in the year :

A. 2000 B. 2002
C. 2004 D. 2006

17. National Press day is celebrated on :

A. 16th November B. 19th November
C. 21st November D. 30th November

18. The total number of members in the Press Council of India are

A. 28 B. 14
C. 17 D. 20

19. The right to impart and receive information is guaranteed in the Constitution of India by Article :

A. 19 (2) (a) B. 19 (16)
C. 19 (2) D. 19 (1) (a)

20. Use of radio for higher education is based on the presumption of :

A. Enriching curriculum based instruction

B. Replacing teacher in the long run
C. Everybody having access to a radio set
D. Other means of instruction getting outdated

21. Find out the number which should come at the place of question mark which will complete the following series :
5, 4, 9, 17, 35, ? = 139
A. 149 B. 79
C. 49 D. 69

Questions 22 to 24 are based on the following diagram in which there are three interlocking circles I, S and P, where circle I stands for Indians, circle S for Scientists and circle P for Politicians. Different regions in the figure are lettered from a to f.

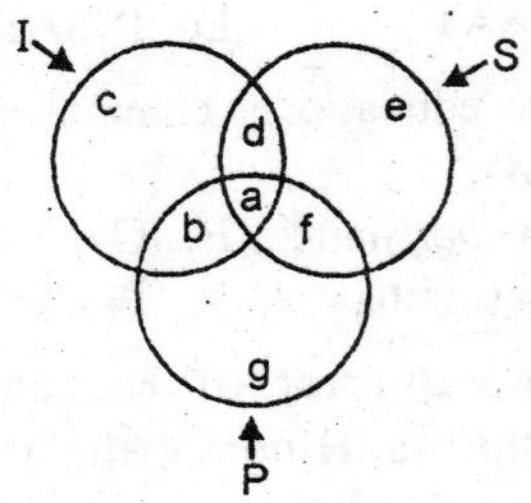

22. The region which represents Non-Indian Scientists who are Politicians :
A. f B. d
C. a D. c

23. The region which represents Indians who are neither Scientists nor Politicians
A. g B. c
C. f D. a

24. The region which represents Politicians who are Indians as well as Scientists :
A. b B. c
C. a D. d

25. Which number is missing in the following series ? 2, 5, 10, 17, 26, 37, 50,?
A. 63 B. 65
C. 67 D. 69

26. The function of measurement includes :
A. Prognosis B. Diagnosis
C. Prediction D. All of the above

27. Logical arguments are based on :
A. Scientific reasoning
B. Customary reasoning
C. Mathematical reasoning
D. Syllogistic reasoning

28. Insert the missing number 4 : 17 : : 7 : ?
A. 48 C. 50
B. 49 D. 51

29. Choose the odd worde
A. Nun C. Monk
B. Knight D. Priest

30. Choose the number which is different from others in the group
A. 49 B. 63
C. 77 D. 81

31. Probability sampling implies :
A. Stratified Random Sampling
B. Systematic Random Sampling
C. Simple Random Sampling
D. All of the above

32. Insert the missing number

$\frac{36}{62}, \frac{39}{63}, \frac{43}{61}, \frac{48}{64}, ?$

A. $\frac{51}{65}$ B. $\frac{56}{60}$

C. $\frac{54}{65}$ D. $\frac{33}{60}$

33. At what time between 3 and 4 O'clock will the hands of a watch point in opposite directions ?
A. 40 minutes past three
B. 45 minutes past three
C. 50 minutes past three
D. 55 minutes past three

34. Mary has three children. What is the probability that none of the three children is a boy?

A. $\frac{1}{2}$ B. $\frac{1}{3}$

C. $\frac{3}{4}$ D. 1

35. If the radius of a circle is increased by 50 per cent. Its area is increased by

A. 125 per cent B. 100 per cent
C. 75 per cent D. 50 per cent

36. CD ROM stands for :

A. Computer Disk Read Only Memory
B. Compact Disk Read Over Memory
C. Compact Disk Read Only Memory
D. Computer Disk Read Over Memory

37. The 'brain' of a computer which keeps peripherals under its control is called

A. Common Power Unit
B. Common Processing Unit
C. Central Power Unit
D. Central Processing Unit

38. Data can be saved on backing storage medium known as :

A. Compact Disk Recordable
B. Computer Disk Rewritable
C. Compact Disk Rewritable
D. Computer Data Rewritable

39. RAM means :

A. Random Access Memory
B. Rigid Access Memory
C. Rapid Access Memory
D. Revolving Access Memory

40. www represents :

A. who what and where
B. weird wide web
C. word wide web
D. world wide web

41. Deforestation during the recent decades has led to :

A. Soil erosion
B. Landslides
C. Loss of bio-diversity
D. All the above

42. Which one of the following natural hazards is responsible for causing highest human disaster ?

A. Earthquakes B. Volcanic eruptions
C. Snow-storms D. Tsunami

43. Which one of the following is appropriate for natural hazard mitigation?

A. International AID
B. Timely Warning System
C. Rehabilitation
D. Community Participation

44. Slums in metro-city are the result of :

A. Rural to urban migration
B. Poverty of the city-scape
C. Lack of urban infrastructure
D. Urban-governance

45. The great Indian Bustard bird is found in :

A. Thar Desert of India
B. Coastal regions of India
C. Temperate Forests in the Himalaya
D. Tarai zones of the Himalayan Foot

46. The first Indian Satellite for serving the educational sector is known as :

A. SATEDU B. INSAT - B
C. EDUSAT D. INSAT-C

47. Exclusive educational channel of IGNOU is known as :

A. Cyan Darshan B. Cyan Vani
C. Door Darshan D. Prasar Bharati

48. The head quarter of Mahatma Gandhi Antarrashtriya Hindi Vishwavidyalaya is situated in :

A. Sevagram B. New Delhi
C. Wardha D. Ahmedabad

49. Match List-I with List-II and select the correct answer using the codes given below

List-I *(Institutes)*	**List-II** *(Locations)*
(a) Central Institute of English and Foreign Languages	(i) Chitrakoot
(b) Gramodaya Vishwavidyalaya	(ii) Hyderabad
(c) Central Institute of Higher Tibetan Studies	(iii) New Delhi
(d) IGNOU	(iv) Dharmasala

Codes :

	(a)	(b)	(c)	(d)
A.	(ii)	(i)	(iv)	(iii)
B.	(iv)	(iii)	(ii)	(i)

C. (iii) (iv) (i) (ii)
D. (i) (ii) (iv) (iii)

50. The aim of vocationalization of education is :

A. preparing students for a vocation along with knowledge

B. converting liberal education into vocational education

C. giving more importance to vocational than general education

D. making liberal education job-oriented

ANSWERS

1	**2**	**3**	**4**	**5**	**6**	**7**	**8**	**9**	**10**
B	A	B	A	A	C	C	C	D	C
11	**12**	**13**	**14**	**15**	**16**	**17**	**18**	**19**	**20**
C	A	B	C	A	D	A	A	D	B
21	**22**	**23**	**24**	**25**	**26**	**27**	**28**	**29**	**30**
D	A	B	D	B	D	D	C	B	C
31	**32**	**33**	**34**	**35**	**36**	**37**	**38**	**39**	**40**
D	C	C	D	A	C	D	C	A	D
41	**42**	**43**	**44**	**45**	**46**	**47**	**48**	**49**	**50**
D	A	B	A	A	C	A	C	A	D

SOME SELECTED EXPLANATORY ANSWERS

21. $4 \times 2 = 8 + 1 = 9$

$9 \times 2 = 18 - 1 = 17$

$17 \times 2 = 34 + 1 = 35$

$35 \times 2 = 70 - 1 = 69$

$69 \times 2 = 138 + 1 = 139$

25. 2 5 10 17 26 37 50 65

+3 +5 +7 +9 +11 +13 +15

28. Since, 4 → 17 ($4^2 + 1$)

Similarly, 7 → 50 ($7^2 + 1$)

30. $49 = 4 + 9 = 13 = 1 + 3 = 4 = 2^2$
$63 = 6 + 3 = 9 = 3^2$
$77 = 7 + 7 = 14 = 4 + 1 = 5$
$81 = 8 + 1 = 9 = 3^2$

Previous Paper (Solved)

UGC-NET (JRF) EXAM JUNE, 2006

PAPER–I

Note : This paper contains **fifty** (50) multiple-choice questions, each question carrying **two** (2) marks. Attempt **all** of them.

1. Which of the following comprise teaching skill :

A. Black Board writing

B. Questioning

C. Explaining

D. All the above

2. Which of the following statements is most appropriate?

A. Teachers can teach.

B. Teachers help can create in a student a desire to learn.

C. Lecture Method can be used for developing thinking.

D. Teachers are born.

3. The first Indian chronicler of Indian history was :

A. Megasthanese B. Fahiyan

C. Huan Tsang D. Kalhan

4. Which of the following statements is correct?

A. Syllabus is a part of curriculum.

B. Syllabus is an annexure to curriculum.

C. Curriculum is the same in all educational institutions affiliated to a particular university.

D. Syllabus is not the same in all educational institutions affiliated to a particular university.

5. Which of the two given options is of the level of understanding?

(I) Define noun.

(II) Define noun in your own words.

A. Only I B. Only II

C. Both I and II D. Neither I nor II

6. Which of the following options are the main tasks of research in modern society ?

(I) to keep pace with the advancement in knowledge.

(II) to discover new things.

(III) to write a critique on the earlier writings.

(IV) to systematically examine and critically analyse the investigations/sources with objectivity.

A. IV, II and I B. I, II and III

C. I and III D. II, III and IV

7. Match List-I (Interviews) with List-II (Meaning) and select the correct answer from the code given below :

List - I (Interviews)

(a) structured interviews

(b) Unstructured interviews

(c) Focussed interviews

(d) Clinical interviews

List - II (Meaning)

(i) greater flexibility approach

(ii) attention on the questions to be answered

(iii) individual life experience

(iv) Pre determined question

(v) non-directive

Code:

	(a)	*(b)*	*(c)*	*(d)*
A.	(iv)	(i)	(ii)	(iii)
B.	(ii)	(iv)	(i)	(iii)
C.	(v)	(ii)	(iv)	(i)
D.	(i)	(iii)	(v)	(iv)

8. What do you consider as the main aim of inter disciplinary research ?

A. To bring out holistic approach to research.

B. To reduce the emphasis of single subject in research domain.

C. To over simplify the problem of research.

D. To create a new trend in research methodology.

9. One of the aims of the scientific method in research is to :

A. improve data interpretation

B. eliminate spurious relations

C. confirm triangulation

D. introduce new variables

10. The depth of any research can be judged by:

A. title of the research.

B. objectives of the research.

C. total expenditure on the research.

D. duration of the research.

Read the following passage and answer the questions 11 to 15 :

The superintendence, direction and control of preparation of electoral rolls for, and the conduct of, elections to Parliament and State Legislatures and elections to the offices of the President and the Vice - President of India are vested in the Election Commission of India. It is an independent constitutional authority.

Independence of the Election Commission and its insulation from executive interference is ensured by a specific provision under Article 324 (5) of the constitution that the chief Election Commissioner shall not be removed from his office except in like manner and on like grounds as a Judge of the Supreme Court and conditions of his service shall not be varied to his disadvantage after his appointment.

In C.W.P. No. 4912 of 1998 (Kushra Bharat Vs. Union of India and others), the Delhi High Court directed that information relating to Government dues owed by the candidates to the departments dealing with Government accommodation, electricity, water, telephone and transport etc. and any other dues should be furnished by the candidates and this information should be published by the election authorities under the commission.

11. The text of the passage reflects or raises certain questions :

A. The authority of the commission can not be challenged.

B. This would help in stopping the criminalization of Indian politics.

C. This would reduce substantially the number of contesting candidates.

D. This would ensure fair and free elections.

12. According to the passage, the Election Commission is an independent constitutional authority. This is under Article No. :

A. 324 B. 356

C. 246 D. 161

13. Independence of the Commission means :

A. have a constitutional status.

B. have legislative powers.

C. have judicial powers.

D. have political powers.

14. Fair and free election means :

A. transparency

B. to maintain law and order

C. regional considerations

D. role for pressure groups

15. The Chief Election Commissioner can be removed from his office under Article :

A. 125 B. 352

C. 226 D. 324

16. The function of mass communication of supplying information regarding the processes, issues, events and societal developments is known as :

A. content supply B. surveillance

C. gratification D. correlation

17. The science of the study of feedback systems in humans, animals and machines is known as :

A. cybernetics
B. reverse communication
C. selectivity study
D. response analysis

18. Networked media exist in inter-connected :
A. social environments
B. economic environments
C. political environments
D. technological environments

19. The combination of computing, telecommunications and media in a digital atmosphere is referred to as :
A. online communication
B. integrated media
C. digital combine
D. convergence

20. A dialogue between a human-being and a computer programme that occurs simultaneously in various forms is described as :
A. man-machine speak B. binary chat
C. digital talk D. interactivity

21. Insert the missing number :

$\frac{16}{32}, \frac{15}{33}, \frac{17}{31}, \frac{14}{34}, ?$

A. $\frac{19}{35}$ B. $\frac{19}{30}$
C. $\frac{18}{35}$ D. $\frac{18}{30}$

22. Monday falls on 20th March 1995. What was the day on 3rd November 1994 ?
A. Thursday B. Sunday
C. Tuesday D. Saturday

23. The average of four consecutive even numbers is 27. The largest of these numbers is
A. 36 B. 32
C. 30 D. 28

24. In a certain code, FHQK means GIRL. How will WOMEN be written in the same code?
A. VNLDM B. FHQKN
C. XPNFO D. VLNDM

25. At what time between 4 and 5 O'Clock will the hands of a watch point in opposite directions?
A. 45 min. past 4 C. 50— min. past 4
B. $40\frac{4}{11}$ min. past 4 D. $54\frac{6}{11}$ min. past 4

26. Which of the following conclusions is logically valid based on statement given below ?

Statement : Most teachers are hard working.

Conclusions :
(I) Some teachers are hard working.
(II) Some teachers are not hard working.
A. Only (I) is implied
B. Only (II) is implied
C. Both (I) and (II) are implied
D. Neither (I) nor (II) is implied

27. Who among the following can be asked to make a statement in Indian Parliament ?
A. Any MLA
B. Chief of Army Staff
C. Solicitor General of India
D. Mayor of Delhi

28. Which of the following conclusions is logically valid based on statement given below?

Statement : Most of the Indian states existed before independence.

Conclusions :
(I) Some Indian States existed before independence.
(II) All Indian States did not exist before independence.
A. only (I) is implied
B. only (II) is implied
C. Both (I) and (II) are implied
D. Neither (I) nor (II) is implied

29. Water is always involved with landslides. This is because it :
A. reduces the shear strength of rocks
B. increases the weight of the overburden
C. enhances chemical weathering
D. is a universal solvent

30. Direction for this question :
Given below are two statements (A) and (B) followed by two conclusions (i) and (ii).

Considering the statements to be true, indicate which of the following conclusions logically follow from the given statements by selecting one of the four response alternatives given below the conclusion :

Statements :

1. all businessmen are wealthy.
2. all wealthy people are hard working.

Conclusions :

(i) All businessmen are hard working.
(ii) All hardly working people are not wealthy

A. Only (i) follows
B. Only (ii) follows
C. Only (i) and (ii) follows
D. Neither (i) nor (ii) follows

31. Using websites to pour out one's grievances is called :

A. cyberventing B. cyber ranting
C. web hate D. web plea

32. In web search, finding a large number of documents with very little relevant information is termed :

A. poor recall
B. web crawl
C. poor precision rate
D. poor web response

33. The concept of connect intelligence is derived from :

A. virtual reality
B. fuzzy logic
C. bluetooth technology
D. value added networks

34. Use of an ordinary telephone as an Internet applicance is called :

A. voicenet B. voice telephone
C. voice line D. voice portal

35. Video transmission over the Internet that looks like delayed livecasting is called :

A. virtual video
B. direct broadcast
C. video shift
D. real-time video

36. Which is the smallest North-east State in India?

A. Tripura B. Meghalaya
C. Mizoram D. Manipur

37. Tamilnadu coastal belt has drinking water shortage due to :

A. high evaporation
B. sea water flooding due to tsunami
C. over exploitation of ground water by tubewells
D. seepage of sea water

38. While all rivers of Peninsular India flow into the Bay of Bengal, Narmada and Tapti flow into the Arabian Sea because these two rivers:

A. Follow the slope of these rift valleys
B. The general slope of the Indian peninsula is from east to west
C. The Indian peninsula north of the Satpura ranges, is tilted towards the west
D. The Indian peninsula south of the satpura ranges is tilted towards east

39. Soils in the Mahanadi delta are less fertile than those in the Godavari delta because of:

A. erosion of top soils by annual floods
B. inundation of land by sea water
C. traditional agriculture practices
D. the derivation of alluvial soil from red-soil hinterland

40. Which of the following institutions in the field of education is set up by the MHRD Government of India ?

A. Indian council of world Affair, New Delhi
B. Mythic Society, Bangalore
C. National Bal Bhawn, New Delhi
D. India International Centre, New Delhi

41. **Assertion (A)** : Aerosols have potential for modifying climate

Reason (R) : Aerosols interact with both short waves and radiation

A. Both A. and **(R)** are true, and **(R)** is the correct explanation of A.
B. Both A. and **(R)** are true, but **(R)** is not the correct explanation of A.
C. A. is true, but **(R)** is false
D. A. is false, but **(R)** is true

42. 'SITE' stands for :

A. System for International technology and Engineering
B. Satellite Instructional Television Experiment
C. South Indian Trade Estate
D. State Institute of Technology and Engineering

43. What is the name of the Research station established by the Indian Government for 'Conducting Research at Antarctic?

A. Dakshin Gangotri
B: Yamunotri
C. Uttari Gangotri
D. None of the above

44. Ministry of Human Resource Development (HRD) includes :

A. Department of Elementary Education and Literacy
B. Department of Secondary Education and Higher Education
C. Department of Women and Child Development
D. All the above

45. Parliament can legislate on matters listed in the State list :

A. With the prior permission of the President.
B. Only after the constitution is amended suitably.
C. In case of inconsistency among State legislatures.
D. At the request of two or more States.

The following pie chart indicates the expenditure of a country on various sports during a particular year. Study the pie chart and answer it Question Number 46 to 50.

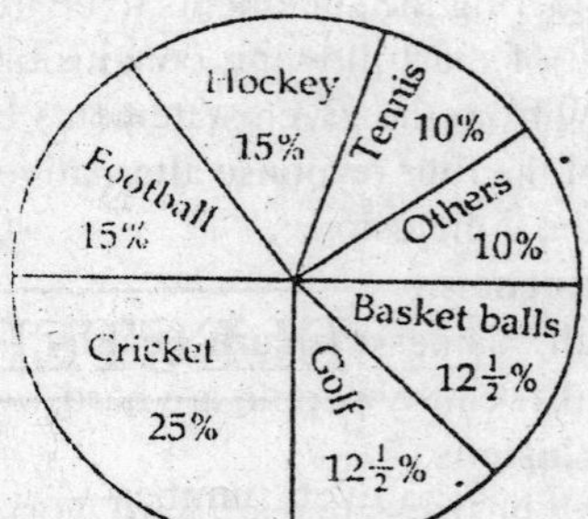

46. The ratio of the total expenditure on football to that of expenditure on hockey is:

A. 1 : 15 B. 1 : 1
C. 15 : 1 D. 3 : 20

47. If the total. expenditure on sports during the year was Rs. 1,20,000,00 how much was spent on basket ball?

A. Rs. 9,50,000 C. Rs. 12,00,000
B. Rs. 10,00,000 D. Rs. 15,00,000

48. The chart shows that the most popular game of the country is :

A. Hockey B. Football
C. Cricket D. Tennis

49. Out of the following country's expenditure is the same on :

A. Hockey and Tennis
B. Golf and Basket ball
C. Cricket and Football
D. Hockey and Golf

50. If the total expenditure on sport during the year was Rs. 1,50,00,000 the expenditure on cricket and hockey together was :

A. Rs. 60,00,000 C. Rs. 37,50,000
B. Rs. 50,00,000 D. Rs. 25,00,000

ANSWERS

1	2	3	4	5	6	7	8	9	10
D	B	D	A	B	A	A	A	B	B
11	**12**	**13**	**14**	**15**	**16**	**17**	**18**	**19**	**20**
D	A	A	B	D	A	A	D	D	D
21	**22**	**23**	**24**	**25**	**26**	**27**	**28**	**29**	**30**
D	A	C	C	D	C	C	B	B	A

31	32	33	34	35	36	37	38	39	40
A	A	D	C	D	C	D	A	A	C
41	**42**	**43**	**44**	**45**	**46**	**47**	**48**	**49**	**50**
A	B	A	D	D	B	A	C	B	A

SOME SELECTED EXPLANATORY ANSWERS

23. Four consecutive even number—

$= x, x + 2, x + 4, x + 6$

According to question,

$$\frac{x+x+2+x+4+x+6}{4} = 27$$

$$= \frac{4x+12}{4} = 27 = 4x = 108 - 12 \Rightarrow 96$$

$$x = \frac{96}{4} = 24$$

Hence, The largest number $= x + 4$

$= 24 + 6 = 30$

24.

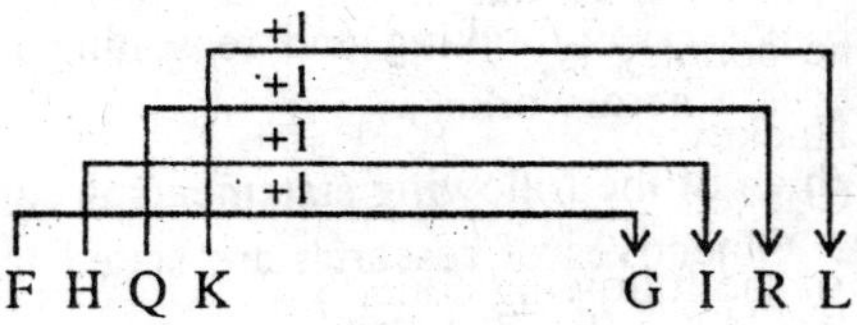

Therefore,

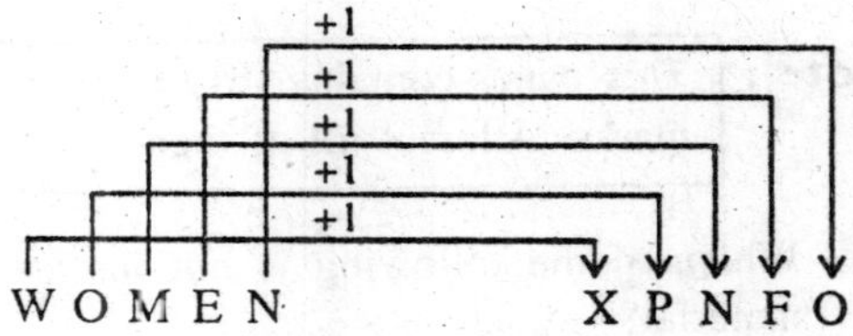

36. Area of the following states are:

Tripura	–	10,491,69
Meghalaya	–	22,429
Manipur	–	22,327
Mizoram	–	21,087

Previous Paper (Solved)

UGC-NET (JRF) EXAM
DECEMBER, 2006

PAPER–I

Note : This paper contains **fifty** (50) multiple-choice questions, each question carrying **two** (2) marks. Attempt **all** of them.

1. Which of the following is **not** instructional material?

A. Over Head Projector
B. Audio Casset
C. Printed Material
D. Transparency

2. Which of the following statements is **not** correct?

A. Lecture Method can develop reasoning
B. Lecture Method can develop knowledge
C. Lecture Method is one way process
D. During Lecture Method students are passive

3. The main objective of teaching at Higher Education Level is:

A. To prepare students to pass examination
B. To develop the capacity to take decisions
C. To give new information
D. To motivate students to ask quètions during leçture

4. Which of the following statement is correct?

A. Reliability ensures validity
B. Validity ensures reliability
C. Reliability and validity are independent of each other
D. Reliability does not depend on objectivity

5. Which of the following indicates evaluation?

A. Ram got 45 marks out of 200
B. Mohan got 38 percent marks in English
C. Shyam got First Division in final examination
D. All the above

6. Research can be conducted by a person who :

A. has studied research methodology
B. holds a postgraduate degree
C. possesses thinking and reasoning ability
D. is a hard worker

7. Which of the following statements is correct?

A. Objectives of research are stated in first chapter of the thesis
B. Researcher must possess analytical ability
C. Variability is the source of problem
D. All the above

8. Which of the following is ***not*** the Method of Research?

A. Observation B. Historical
C. Survey D. Philosophical

9. Research can be classified as :

A. Basic, Applied and Action Research
B. Quantitative and Qualitative Research
C. Philosophical, Historical, Survey and Experimental Research
D. All the above

10. The first step of research is :

A. Selecting a problem
B. Searching a problem
C. Finding a problem
D. Identifying a problem

Read the following passage and answer the question nos. 11 to 15 :

After almost three decades of contemplating Swarovski-encrusted navels on increasing flat abs, the Mumbai film industry is on a discovery of India and itself. With budgets of over 30 crore each, four soon to be released movies by premier directors are exploring the idea of who we are and redefining who the other is. It is a fundamental question which the bling-bling, glam-sham and disham-disham tends to avoid. It is also a question which binds an audience when the lights go dim and the projector rolls : as a nation, who are we ? As a people, where are we going?

The Germans coined a word for it, Zeitgeist, which perhaps Yash Chopra would not care to pronounce. But at 72, he remains the person who can best capture it. After being the first to project the diasporic Indian on screen in Lamhe in 1991, he has returned to his roots in a new movie. Veer Zaara, set in 1986, where Pakistan, the traditional other, the part that got away, is the lover and the saviour. In Subhas Ghai's Kisna, set in 1947, the other is the English woman. She is not a memsahib, but a mehbooba. In Ketan Mehta's The Rising, the East India Englishman is not the evil oppressor of countless cardboard characterisations, which span the spectrum from Jewel in the Crown to Kranti, but an honourable friend.

This is Manoj Kumar's Desh Ki dharti with a difference : there is culture, not contentious politics; balle balle, not bombs : no dooriyan (distance), only nazdeekiyan (closeness).

All four films are heralding a new hero and heroine. The new hero is fallible and vulnerable, committed to his dharma, but also not afraid of failure - less of a boy and more of a man. He even has a grown up name : Veer Pratap Singh in Veer-Zaara and Mohan Bhargav in Swades. The new heroine is not a babe, but often a bebe, dressed in traditional Punjabi clothes, often with the stereotypical body type as well, as in Bride and Prejudice of Gurinder Chadha.

11. Which word Yash Chopra would not be able to pronounce?

A. Bling + bling B. Zeitgeist
C. Montaz D. Dooriyan

12. Who made Lamhe in 1991?

A. Subhash Ghai B. Yash Chopra
C. Aditya Chopra D. Sakti Samanta

13. Which movie is associated with Manoj Kumar?

A. Jewel in the Crown
B. Kisna
C. Zaara
D. Desh Ki dharti

14. Which is the latest film by Yash Chopra?

A. Deewar
B. Kabhi Kabhi
C. Dilwale Dulhaniya Le Jayenge
D. Veer *Zaara*

15. Which is the dress of the heroine in Veer-Zaara?

A. Traditional Gujarati Clothes
B. Traditional Bengali Clothes
C. Traditional Punjabi Clothes
D. Traditional Madrasi Clothes

16. Which one of the following can be termed as verbal communication?

A. Prof. Sharma delivered the lecture in the class room.
B. Signal at the cross-road changed from green to orange.
C. The child was crying to attract the attention of the mother.
D. Dipak wrote a letter for leave application.

17. Which is the 24 hours English Business news channel in India?

A. Zee News B. NDTV 24 × 7
C. CNBC D. India News

18. Consider the following statements in communication :

(i) Hema Malini is the Chairperson of the Children's Film Society, India.
(ii) Yash Chopra is the Chairman of the Central Board of Film Certification of India.
(iii) Sharmila Tagore is the Chairperson of National Film Development Corporation.

(iv) Dilip Kumar. Raj Kapoor and Preeti Zinta have all been recipients of Dada Saheb Phalke Award.

Which of the statements given above is/are correct?

A. (i) and (iii) B. (ii) and (iii)
C. (iv) only D. (iii) only

19. Which of the following pair is *not* correctly matched?

A. N. Ram : The Hindu
B. Barkha Dutt : Zee News
C. Pranay Roy : NDTV 24 × 7
D. Prabhu Chawla : Aaj taak

20. "Because you deserve to know" is the punchline used by :

A. The Times of India
B. The Hindu
C. Indian Express
D. Hindustan Times

21. In the sequence of numbers 8, 24, 12, X, 18, 54 the missing number X is :

A. 26 B. 24
C. 36 D. 32

22. If A stands for 5, B for 6, C for 7, D for 8 and so on, then the following numbers stand for 17, 19, 20, 9 and 8 :

A. PLANE B. MOPED
C. MOTOR D. TONGA

23. The letters in the first set have certain relationship. On the basis of this relationship what is the right choice for the second set ? AST : BRU : : NQV : ?

A. ORW B. MPU
C. MRW D. OPW

24. In a certain code, PAN is written as 31 and PAR as 35. In this code PAT is written as:

A. 30 B. 37
C. 38 D. 39

25. The sides of a triangle are in the ratio of $\frac{1}{2}:\frac{1}{3}:\frac{1}{4}$. If its perimeter is 52 cm, the length of the smallest side is :

A. 9 cm B. 10 cm
C. 11 cm D. 12 cm

26. Which one of the following statements is **completely non-sensical**?

A. He was a bachelor, but he married recently.
B. He is a bachelor, but he married recently.
C. When he married, he was not a bachelor.
D. When he was a bachelor, he was not married.

27. Which of the following statements are **mutually contradictory**?

(i) All flowers are not fragrant,
(ii) Most flowers are not fragrant,
(iii) None of the flowers is fragrant,
(iv) Most flowers are fragrant.

Choose the correct answer from the code given below :

Code:

A. (i) and (ii) B. (i) and (iii)
C. (ii) and (iii) D. (iii) and (iv)

28. Which of the following statements **say the same thing**?

(i) "I am a teacher" (said by Arvind)
(ii) "I am a teacher" (said by Binod)
(iii) "My son is a teacher" (said by Binod's father)
(iv) "My brother is a teacher" (said by Binod's sister)
(v) "My brother is a teacher" (said by Binod's only sister)
(vi) "My sole enemy is a teacher" (said by Binod's only enemy) Choose the correct answer from the code given below :

Code :

A. (i) and (ii) B. (ii), (iii), (iv) and (v)
C. (ii) and (vi) D. (v) and (vi)

29. Which of the following are **correct ways of arguing**?

(i) There can be no second husband without a second wife.
(ii) Anil is a friend of Bob, Bob is a friend of Raj, hence Anil is a friend of Raj.
(iii) A is equal to B, B is equal to C, hence A is equal to C.
(iv) If everyone is a liar, then we cannot prove it.

Choose the correct answer from the code given below :

Code :

A. (iii) and (iv) B. (i), (iii) and (iv)
C. (ii), (iii) and (iv) D. (i), (ii), (iii) and (iv)

30. Which of the following statement/s are ALWAYS FALSE?

(i) The sun will not rise in the East some day.
(ii) A wooden table is not a table,
(iii) Delhi city will be drowned under water,
(iv) Cars run on water as fuel.

Choose the correct answer from the code given below :

Code :

A. (i), (iii) and (iv) B. Only (iii)
C. (i), (ii) and (iii) D. (ii) alone

Study the following graph and answer question numbers 31 to 33 :

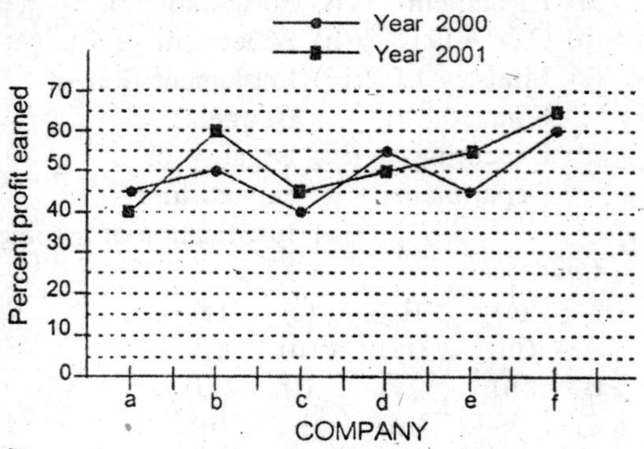

31. In the year 2000, which of the following Companies earned maximum percent profit?

A. a B. b
C. d D. f

32. In the year 2001, which of the following Companies earned minimum percent profit ?

A. a B. c
C. d D. e

33. In the years 2000 and 2001, which of the following Companies earned maximum average percent profit?

A. f B. e
C. d D. b

34. Human Development Report for 'each' of the year at global level has been published by :

A. UNDP B. WTO
C. IMF D. World Bank

35. The number of students in four classes A, B, C, D and their respective mean marks obtained by each of the class are given below :

	Class A	Class B	Class C	Class D
Number of students	10	40	30	20
Arithmetic mean	20	30	50	15

The combined mean of the marks of four classes together will be :

A. 32 B. 50
C. 20 D. 15

36. LAN stands for :

A. Local And National
B. Local Area Network
C. Large Area Network
D. Live Area Network

37. Which of the following statement is correct?

A. Modem is a software
B. Modem helps in stabilizing the voltage
C. Modem is the operating system
D. Modem converts the analog signal into digital signal and vice-versa

38. Which of the following is the appropriate definition of a computer?

A. Computer is a machine that can process information.
B. Computer is an electronic device that can store, retrieve and process both qualitative and quantitative data quickly and accurately.
C. Computer is an electronic device that can store, retrieve and quickly process only quantitative data.
D. Computer is a machine that can store, retrieve and process quickly and accurately only qualitative information

39. Information and Communication Technology includes :

A. On line learning
B. Learning through the use of EDUSAT
C. Web Based Learning
D. All the above

40. Which of the following is the appropriate format of URL of e-mail?

A. www_mail.com
B. www@mail.com
C. WWW@mail.com
D. www.mail.com

41. The most significant impact of volcanic erruption has been felt in the form of :

A. change in weather
B. sinking of islands
C. loss of vegetation
D. extinction of animals

42. With absorption and decomposition of CO_2 in ocean water beyond desired level, there will be :

A. decrease in temperature
B. increase in salinity
C. growth of phyto plankton
D. rise in sea level

43. Arrange column II in proper sequence so as to match it with column I and choose the correct answer from the code given below :

Column I *Water Quality*	*Column II* *pH Value*
(a) Neutral	(i) 5
(b) Moderately acidic	(ii) 7
(c) Alkaline	(iii) 4
(d) Injurious	(iv) 8

Code :

	(a)	(b)	(c)	(d)
A.	(ii)	(iii)	(i)	(iv)
B.	(i)	(iii)	(ii)	(iv)
C.	(ii)	(i)	(iv)	(iii)
D.	(iv)	(ii)	(iii)	(i)

44. The maximum emission of pollutants from fuel sources in India is caused by :

A. Coal
B. Firewood
C. Refuse burning
D. Vegetable waste product

45. The urbanisation process accounts for the wind in the urban centres during nights to remain :

A. faster than that in rural areas
B. slower than that in rural areas
C. the same as that in rural areas
D. cooler than that in rural areas

46. The University Grants Commission was constituted on the recommendation of :

A. Dr. Sarvapalli Radhakrishnan Commission
B. Mudaliar Commission
C. Sargent Commission
D. Kothari Commission

47. Which one of the following Articles of the Constitution of India safeguards the rights of Minorities to establish and run educational institutions of their own liking?

A. Article 19 B. Article 29
C. Article 30 D. Article 31

48. Match List-I (Institutions) with List-II (Functions) and select the correct answer by using the code given below :

List - I ***(Institutions)***	**List - II** ***(Functions)***
(a) Parliament	(i) Formulation of Budget
(b) C & A.G.	(ii) Enactment of Budget
(c) Ministry of Finance	(iii) Implementation of Budget
(d) Executing Departments	(iv) Legality of expenditure
	(v) Justification of Income

Code :

	(a)	(b)	(c)	(d)
A.	(iii)	(iv)	(ii)	(i)
B.	(ii)	(iv)	(i)	(iii)
C.	(v)	(iii)	(iv)	(ii)
D.	(iv)	(ii)	(iii)	(v)

49. Foundation training to the newly recruited IAS (Probationers) is imparted by :

A. Indian Institute of Public Administration
B. Administrative Staff College of India
C. L.B.S. National Academy of Administration
D. Centre for Advanced Studies

50. Electoral disputes arising out of Presidential and Vice-Presidential Elections are settled by:

A. Election Commission of India
B. Joint Committee of Parliament
C. Supreme Court of India
D. Central Election Tribunal

ANSWERS

1	2	3	4	5	6	7	8	9	10
D	A	B	B	D	C	D	B	D	D
11	**12**	**13**	**14**	**15**	**16**	**17**	**18**	**19**	**20**
B	B	D	D	C	C	C	D	B	D
21	**22**	**23**	**24**	**25**	**26**	**27**	**28**	**29**	**30**
C	B	D	B	D	B	B	B	A	D
31	**32**	**33**	**34**	**35**	**36**	**37**	**38**	**39**	**40**
D	A	A	A	A	B	D	B	D	B
41	**42**	**43**	**44**	**45**	**46**	**47**	**48**	**49**	**50**
A	C	C	C	B	A	C	B	C	C

SOME SELECTED EXPLANATORY ANSWERS

21. 8 → 24 (×3), 12 → **36** (×3), 18 → 54 (×3)

8 24 12 [36] 18 54

22. Since,

A	B	C	D	E	F	G	H
↓	↓	↓	↓	↓	↓	↓	↓
5	6	7	8	9	10	11	12
I	J	K	L	M	N	O	P
↓	↓	↓	↓	↓	↓	↓	↓
13	14	15	16	17	18	19	20
Q	R	S	T	U	V		
↓	↓	↓	↓	↓	↓		
21	22	23	24	25	26		

Therefore,

17	19	20	9	8
↓	↓	↓	↓	↓
M	O	P	E	D

23. Since,

A S T → B R U

(A → B: +1; S → R: −1; T → U: +1)

Therefore,

N Q V → O P W

(N → O: +1; Q → P: −1; V → W: +1)

24. Since,

P A N $\Rightarrow$ 16 + 1 + 14 (Sum of the position in English Alphabet)

$\Rightarrow$ 31

and P A R $\Rightarrow$ 16 + 1 + 18

$\Rightarrow$ 35

Therefore

P A T $\Rightarrow$ 16 + 1 + 20

$\Rightarrow$ 37

25. Let the sides of the triangle are $\frac{1}{2}x, \frac{1}{3}x$ and $\frac{1}{4}x$

$$\therefore 52 = \frac{1}{2}x + \frac{1}{3}x + \frac{1}{4}x$$

$$= x\left[\frac{1}{2} + \frac{1}{3} = \frac{1}{4}\right] = \frac{13x}{12}$$

$$\Rightarrow 52 = \frac{13x}{12} \Rightarrow x = 48$$

$\therefore$ First side of the triangel $= 48 \times \frac{1}{2} = 24$

Second side of the triangle $= 48 \times \frac{1}{3} = 16$

Third side of the triangle $= 48 \times \frac{1}{4} = 12$

(Smalles + side)

Previous Paper (Solved)

UGC-NET (JRF) EXAM DECEMBER, 2005

PAPER–I

Note : This paper contains **fifty** (50) multiple-choice questions, each question carrying **two** (2) marks. Attempt **all** of them.

1. Team teaching has the potential to develop:
A. Competitive spirit
B. Cooperation
C. The habit of supplementing the teaching of each other
D. Highlighting the gaps in each other's teaching

2. Which of the following is the most important characteristic of Open Book Examination system?
A. Students become serious.
B. It improves attendance in the classroom.
C. It reduces examination anxiety amongst students.
D. In compels students to think.

3. Which of the following methods of teaching encourages the use of maximum senses?
A. Problem-solving method
B. Laboratory method
C. Self-study method
D. Team teaching method

4. Which of the following statement is correct ?
A. Communicator should have fine senses
B. Communicator should have tolerance power
C. Communicator should be soft spoken
D. Communicator should have good personality

5. An effective teacher is one who can :
A. control the class
B. give more information in less time
C. motivate students to learn
D. correct the assignments carefully

6. One of the following is **not** a quality of researcher :
A. Unison with that of which he is in search
B. He must be of alert mind
C. Keenness in enquiry
D. His assertion to outstrip the evidence

7. A satisfactory statistical quantitative method should **not** possess one of the following qualities :
A. Appropriateness B. Measurability
C. Comparability D. Flexibility

8. Books and records are the primary sources of data in :
A. historical research
B. participatory research
C. clinical research
D. laboratory research

9. Which of the following statement is correct?
A. objectives should be pin-pointed
B. objectives can be written in statement or question form
C. another word for problem is variable
D. all the above

10. The important pre-requisites of a researcher in sciences, social sciences and humanities are :

A. laboratory skills, records, supervisor, topic
B. Supervisor, topic, critical analysis, patience
C. archives, supervisor, topic, flexibility in thinking
D. topic, supervisor, good temperament, preconceived notions

Read the following passage and answer the questions 11 to 15 :

Knowledge creation in many cases requires creativity and idea generation. This is especially important in generating alternative decision support solutions. Some people believe that an individual's creative ability stems primarily from personality traits such as inventiveness, independence, individuality, enthusiasm, and flexibility. However, several studies have found that creativity is not so much a function of individual traits as was once believed, and that individual creativity can be learned and improved. This understanding has led innovative companies to recognise that the key to fostering creativity may be the development of an idea-nurturing work environment. Idea-generation methods and techniques, to be used by individuals or in groups, are consequently being developed. Manual methods for supporting idea generation, such as brainstorming in a group, can be very successful in certain situations. However, in other situations, such an approach is either not economically feasible or not possible. For example, manual methods in group creativity sessions will not work or will not be effective when : (1) there is no time to conduct a proper idea-generation session; (2) there is a poor facilitator (or no facilitator at all); (3) it is too expensive to conduct an idea-generation session; (4) the subject matter is too sensitive for a face-to-face session; or (5) there are not enough participants, the mix of participants is not optimal, or there is no climate for idea generation. In such cases, computerised idea-generation methods have been tried, with frequent success.

Idea-generation software is designed to help stimulate a single user or a group to produce new ideas, options and choices. The user does all the work, but the software encourages and pushes, something like a personal trainer. Although idea-generation software is still relatively new, there are several packages on the market. Various approaches are used by idea-generating software to increase the flow of ideas to the user. Idea Fisher, for example, has an associate lexicon of the English language that cross-references words and phrases. These associative links, based on analogies and metaphors, make it easy for the user to be fed words related to a given theme. Some software packages use questions to prompt the user towards new, unexplored patterns of thought. This helps users to break out of cyclical thinking patterns, conquer mental blocks, or deal with bouts of procrastination.

11. The author, in this passage has focussed on
A. knowledge creation
B. idea-generation
C. creativity
D. individual traits

12. Fostering creativity needs an environment of
A. decision support systems
B. idea-nurturing
C. decision support solutions
D. alternative individual factors

13. Manual methods for the support of idea-generation, in certain occasions,
A. are alternatively effective
B. can be less expensive
C. do not need a facilitator
D. require a mix of optimal participants

14. Idea-generation software works as if it is a :
A. stimulant
B. knowledge package
C. user-friendly trainer
D. climate creator

15. Mental blocks, bouts of procrastination and cyclical thinking patterns can be won when :
A. innovative companies employ electronic thinking methods
B. idea-generation software prompts questions
C. manual methods are removed
D. individuals acquire a neutral attitude towards the software

16. Level C of the effectiveness of communication is defined as :

A. channel noise
B. semantic noise
C. psychological noise
D. source noise

17. Recording a television programme on a VCR is an example of :
A. time-shifting
B. content reference
C. mechanical clarity
D. media synchronisation

18. A good communicator is the one who offers to his audience :
A. plentiful of information
B. a good amount of statistics
C. concise proof
D. repetition of facts

19. The largest number of newspapers in India is published from the state of :
A. Kerala B. Maharashtra
C. West Bengal D. Uttar Pradesh

20. Insert the missing number :
8 24 12 ? 18 54
A. 26 B. 24
C. 36 D. 32

21. January 1, 1995 was Sunday. What day of the week lies on January 1, 1996?
A. Sunday B. Monday
C. Saturday D. None of these

22. The sum of a positive number and its reciprocal is twice the difference of the number and its reciprocal. The number is :

A. $\sqrt{2}$ B. $\frac{1}{\sqrt{2}}$

C. $\sqrt{3}$ D. $\frac{1}{\sqrt{3}}$

23. In a certain code, ROUNDS is written as RONUDS. How will PLEASE will be written in the same code :
A. L P A E S E B. P L A E S E
C. L P A E E S D. P L A S E E

24. At what time between 5.30 and 6.00 will the hands of an clock be at right angles ?

A. $43\frac{5}{11}$ min. past 5

B. $43\frac{7}{11}$ min. past 5

C. 40 min. past 5
D. 45 min past 5

25. Statements : I. All students are ambitious
II. All ambitious persons are hard working
Conclusions :(i) All students are hard-working
(ii) All hardly working people are not ambitious Which of the following is correct ?
A. Only (i) is correct
B. Only (ii) is correct
C. Both (i) and (ii) are correct
D. Neither (i) nor (ii) is correct

26. Statement : Most students are intelligent
Conclusions : (i) Some students are intelligent
(ii) All students are not intelligent
Which of the following is implied?
A. Only (i) is implied
B. Only (ii) is implied
C. Both (i) and (ii) are implied
D. Neither (i) nor (ii) is implied

27. Statement : Most labourers are poor
Conclusions : (i) Some labourers are poor
(ii) All labourers are not poor Which of the following is implied ?
A. Only (i) is implied
B. Only (ii) is implied
C. Both (i) and (ii) are implied
D. Neither (i) nor (ii) is implied

28. Line access and avoidance of collision are the main functions of :
A. the CPU
B. the monitor
C. network protocols
D. wide area networks

29. In the hypermedia database, information bits are stored in the form of :
A. signals B. cubes
C. nodes D. symbols

30. Communications bandwidth that has the highest capacity and is used by microwave, cable and fibre optics lines is known as :

A. hyper-link B. broadband
C. bus width D. carrier wave

31. An electronic bill board that has a short text or graphical advertising message is referred to as :

A. bulletin B. strap
C. bridge line D. banner

32. Which of the following is not the characteristic of a computer ?

A. computer is an electrical machine
B. computer cannot think at its own
C. computer processes information error free
D. computer can hold data for any length of time

33. Bitumen is obtained from :

A. Forests and Plants
B. Kerosene oil
C. Crude oil
D. underground mines

34. Malaria is caused by :

A. bacterial infection
B. viral infection
C. parasitic infection
D. fungal infection

35. The cloudy nights are warmer compared to clear nights (without clouds) during winter days. This is because :

A. clouds radiate heat towards the earth
B. clouds prevent cold wave from the sky, descend on earth
C. clouds prevent escaping of the heat radiation from the earth
D. clouds being at great heights from earth absorb heat from the sun and send towards the earth

36. Largest soil group of India is :

A. Red soil C. Sandy soil
B. Black soil D. Mountain soil

37. Main pollutant of the Indian coastal water is :

A. oil spill
B. municipal sewage
C. industrial effluents
D. aerosols

38. Human ear is most sensitive to noise in the following frequency ranges

A. 1-2 KHz B. 100-500 Hz
C. 10-12 KHz D. None of these

39. Which species of chromium is toxic in water :

A. Cr + 2
B. Cr + 3
C. Cr + 6
D. Cr is non-toxic element

40. Match List - I (Dams) with List - II (River) in the following

List -1 (Dams)	List - II (River)
(a) Bhakra	(i) Krishna
(b) Nagarjunasagar	(ii) Damodar
(c) Panchet	(iii) Sutlej
(d) Hirakud	(iv) Bhagirathi
(e) Tehri	(v) Mahanadi

Code:

	(a)	(b)	(c)	(d)	(e)
A.	(v)	(iii)	(iv)	(ii)	(i)
B.	(iii)	(i)	(ii)	(v)	(iv)
C.	(i)	(ii)	(iv)	(iii)	(v)
D.	(ii)	(iii)	(iv)	(i)	(v)

41. A negative reaction to a mediated communication is described as :

A. flak
B. fragmented feedback
C. passive response
D. non-conformity

42. The launch of satellite channel by IGNOU on 26th January 2003 for technological education for the growth and development of distance education is :

A. Eklavya channel
B. Gyandarshan channel
C. Rajrishi channel
D. None of these

43. Match List - I with List-II and select the correct answer from the code given below :

List -1 (Institutions)

(a) The Indian Council of Historical Reasearch (ICHR)

(b) The Indian Institute of Advanced Studies (HAS)
(c) The Indian Council of Philosophical Research
(d) The Central Institute of Coastal Engineering for fisheries

List - II (Locations)
(i) Shimla
(ii) New Delhi
(iii) Banglore Research (ICPR)
(iv) Lucknow

	a	b	c	d
A.	(ii)	(i)	(iv)	(iii)
B.	(i)	(ii)	(iii)	(iv)
C.	(ii)	(iv)	(i)	(iii)
D.	(iv)	(iii)	(ii)	(i)

44. Which of the following is not a Fundamental Right ?
A. Right to equality
B. Right against exploitation
C. Right to freedom of speech and expression
D. Right of free compulsory education of all children upto the age of 14

45. The Lok - Sabha can be dissolved before the expiry of its normal five year term by
A. The Prime Minister
B. The Speaker of Lok Sabha
C. The President on the recommendation of the Prime Minister
D. None of the above

Study the following graph carefully and answer Q.No. 46 to 50 given below it :

EXPORT OF TINS

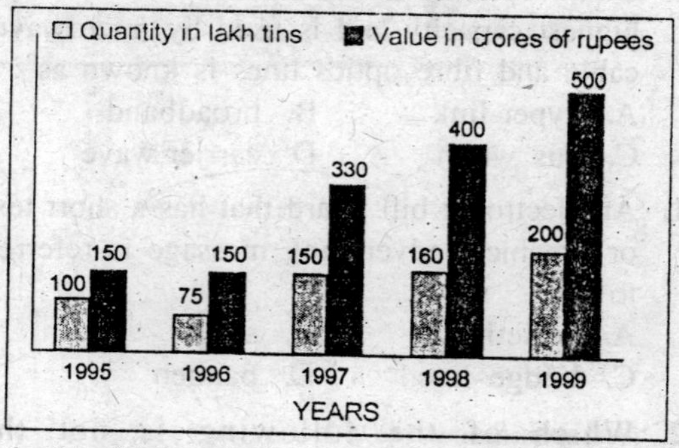

46. In which year the value per tin was minimum?
A. 1995 B. 1996
C. 1998 D. 1999

47. What was the difference between the tins exported in 1997 and 1998?
A. 10 B. 1000
C. 100000 D. 1000000

48. What was the approximate percentage increase in export value from 1995 to 1999?
A. 350 B. 330.3
C. 433.3 D. None of these

49. What was the percentage drop in export quantity from 1995 to 1996 ?
A. 75 B. 50
C. 25 D. None of these

50. If in 1998, the tins were exported at the same rate per tin as that in 1997, what would be the value (in crores of rupees) of export in 1998?
A. 400 B. 375
C. 352 D. 330

ANSWERS

1	2	3	4	5	6	7	8	9	10
C	D	B	A	C	D	D	A	A	B
11	**12**	**13**	**14**	**15**	**16**	**17**	**18**	**19**	**20**
A	B	A	A	B	A	D	A	D	C
21	**22**	**23**	**24**	**25**	**26**	**27**	**28**	**29**	**30**
B	D	B	B	C	B	B	C	A	B
31	**32**	**33**	**34**	**35**	**36**	**37**	**38**	**39**	**40**
B	A	D	C	C	A	C	D	C	B
41	**42**	**43**	**44**	**45**	**46**	**47**	**48**	**49**	**50**
C	A	A	D	C	A	A	D	C	C

SOME SELECTED EXPLANATORY ANSWERS

20. 8, 24, 12, [36], 18, 54

8 → 24 (+4); 12 → 18 (+6); 24 → 36 (+12); 36 → 54 (+18)

$\therefore$ Required number = 24 + 12 = 36

21. $\because$ 1st January 1995 → Sunday

$\therefore$ 31st December 1995 → Sunday

($\because$ 1995 was not a leap year)

$\therefore$ 1st January 1996 = Monday

22. $x + \frac{1}{x} = 2\left(x - \frac{1}{x}\right)$

$\Rightarrow \frac{x^2+1}{x} = 2\left(\frac{x^2-1}{x}\right)$

$\Rightarrow x^2 + 1 = 2x^2 - 2$

$\Rightarrow x^2 = 3$

$\therefore \quad x = \sqrt{3}$

23. Since,

1 2 3 4 5 6   1 2 4 3 5 6

R O U N D S → R O N U D S

Therefore,

1 2 3 4 5 6   1 2 4 3 5 6

P L E A S E → P L A E S E

IIIIIIIII

Previous Paper (Solved)

UGC-NET (JRF) EXAM DECEMBER, 2004

PAPER–I

Note : This paper contains **fifty** (50) multiple-choice questions, each question carrying **two** (2) marks. Attempt **all** of them.

1. Discussion Method can be used when:
   A. The topic is very difficult
   B. The topic is easy
   C. The topic is difficult
   D. All the above

2. Which of the following is a teaching aid?
   A. Working Model of Wind Mill
   B. Tape Recorder
   C. 16 mm Film Projector
   D. All the above

3. The main aim of teaching is:
   A. To develop only reasoning
   B. To develop only thinking
   C. Both (A) and (B)
   D. To give information

4. The quality of teaching is reflected :
   A. By the attendance of students in the class
   B. By the pass percentage of students
   C. By the quality of questions asked by students
   D. By the duration of silence maintained in the class

5. The present annual examination system :
   A. promotes rote learning
   B. does not promote good study habits
   C. does not encourage students to be regular in class
   D. All the above

6. A college wants to give training in use of Statistical Package for Social Sciences (SPSS) to researchers. For this the college should organise :
   A. Conference B. Seminar
   C. Workshop D. Lecture

7. Which of the following is NOT the characteristic of a research ?
   A. Research is systematic
   B. Research is not a process
   C. Research is problem oriented
   D. Research is not passive

8. Which of the following statement is correct?
   A. Discoveries are researches
   B. Researches lead to discovery
   C. Invention and Research are related
   D. None of the above

9. Which of the following statement is correct ?
   A. In research, objectives can be worded in question form
   B. In research, objectives can be worded in statement form
   C. Objectives are to be stated in Chapter I of the Thesis
   D. All the above

10. Match List A with List B and choose the correct answer from the code given below :
    List A
    (a) Historical Method
    (b) Survey Method
    (c) Philosophical Method
    (d) Experimental Method

List B

(i) Past events
(ii) Vision
(iii) Present events
(iv) Exceptional cases
(v) Future action

Code :

	(a)	(b)	(c)	(d)
A.	(i)	(iii)	(ii)	(v)
B.	(i)	(ii)	(iv)	(v)
C.	(i)	(iv)	(ii)	(v)
D.	(i)	(ii)	(iii)	(iv)

Read the following passage and answer the question numbers 11 to 15.

Each day at the Shantiniketan School starts with the Saraswati Vandana. When painting competitions are held in the school, images of Hindu gods and goddesses are most common. Sanskrit is a favourite subject of many a student. Nothing new about it except that the 1,200 - odd students studying in the Hindu - run school are Muslims.

In 1983, when Ranchodbhai Kiri started Shantiniketan in the all - Muslim Juhapura area of Ahmedabad in Gujarat, only 20 percent of the students were Muslims. But when riots involving the Muslims of Juhapura and the Hindus of nearby Jivrajpark -Vejalpur affected the locality, Hindus started migrating. Today, all the students are Muslims and the school is an unparalled example of harmony. In the 2002, when a section of inflamed Muslims wanted the school closed, the parents of the students stood like a wall behind it.

Shantiniketan's principal says, "We never thought of moving the school out of the area because of the love and affection of the local Muslims. Indeed they value the high standard of education which we have set." Such is the reputation of the school that some of the local Muslim strongmen accused of involvement in communal riots are willing to protect the school during the riots.

The parents of Shantiniketan's students believe that it's the best school when it comes to the quality of the teaching. A large number of students have gone for both graduation and post graduation studies. Significantly, the only Muslim teacher in the 40 - member teaching staff, Husena Mansuri, teaches Sanskrit. Infact, she is so happy at the school that she recently declined the principalship of another Muslim - run school.

Some of the students' entries in a recent school painting competition mere truly moving. One drew a pciture of Bharat Mata with a mosque and temple, while another portrayed a boy tying rakhi to his sister. Trully, Shantiniketan is a beacon of hope that, despite the provocations from both communities, Hindus and Muslims can live side-by-side with mutual respect.

11. How the Shantiniketan school starts the day?
A. National anthem
B. Prayer
C. Saraswati Vandana
D. Puja

12. Write the subject which is preferred by most of the students
A. Hindi B. English
C. Sanskrit D. Gujarati

13. Who protects the school during the riot times?
A. Local Muslims B. Hindus
C. Politicians D. Christians

14. Who is the teacher of Sanskrit?
A. Ranchodbhai Kiri
C. Husena Mansuri
B. Manisha Vakil
D. Husena Khatoon

15. What is the hope despite the communal riots?
A. Hindus and Muslims cannot live side by side
B. Hindus and Muslims can live side by side
C. Only Hindus can live
D. Only Muslims can live

16. Match List I with List II and choose the correct answer using the codes given below

List I *(Distinguished Ladies)*	List II *(Area of work)*
(a) Jhumpa Lahiri	(i) Journalist
(b) Barkha Dutt	(ii) Novel Writing
(c) Aparna Sen	(iii) Film Actress
(d) Smita Patil	(iv) Film Director

Code :

	(a)	(b)	(c)	(d)
A.	(iv)	(iii)	(ii)	(i)
B.	(ii)	(i)	(iv)	(iii)
C.	(iv)	(i)	(iii)	(ii)
D.	(ii)	(iii)	(iv)	(i)

17. Which of the following pair is not correctly matched ?

A. Aajtaak - 24 hours news channel
B. P.M. Stations - Radio
C. National Geography channel - Television
D. Vir Sanghvi - India Today

18. Which is the oldest soap opera telecasted in India?

A. Kahani Ghar Ghar Ke
B. Buniad
C. Humlog
D. Saas bhi Kabhi Bahu Thee

19. Which satellite channel uses the adline, "Knowing is everything"?

A. BBC World　　B. Star
C. Sony　　D. Zee

20. Which is the "First made in India" Kids channel of television ?

A. Cartoon Network
B. Walt Disney
C. United Home Entertainment's Hungama TV
D. Nick Jr.

21. The letters in the first set have certain relationships. On the basis of the relationship which is the right choice for the second set?

BF : GK : : LP : ?

A. JK　　B. QU
C. VW　　D. RQ

22. If the BLOOD is coded as 24113 and BRUST as 20678, then code for ROBUST is :

A. 620781　　B. 012678
C. 678102　　D. 610732

23. A bag contains an equal number of one rupee, 50 paise and 25 paise coins. If the total amount in the bag is Rs. 35, how many coins of each type are there?

A. 15　　B. 18
C. 20　　D. 25

24. In the sequence of numbers

$\frac{2}{3}, \frac{4}{7}, X, \frac{11}{21}, \frac{16}{31}$

the missing number X is :

A. $\frac{8}{10}$　　B. $\frac{6}{10}$
C. $\frac{5}{10}$　　D. $\frac{7}{10}$

25. If A stands for 5 , B for 6, C for 7, D for 8, and so on, what do the following numbers stand for :

22, 25, 8, 22 and 5 ?

A. PRIYA　　B. NEEMA
C. MEENA　　D. RUDRA

26. Which of the following statements are always true ?

(a) A wooden table is a table
(b) Now, it is raining or not raining
(c) The sun rises in the East every day
(d) A chicken comes out of a hen's egg

Choose the correct answer from the code given below :

Code :

A. (a) and (c)
B. (a), (c) and (d)
C. (a) and (b)
D. (b) and (c)

27. Which of the following statements are mutually inconsistent?

(a) Mostly poets are not egoistic
(b) Mostly poets are humble
(c) Some poets are egoistic
(d) Some poets are not non - egoistic

Choose the correct answer from the code given below :

Code :

A. (a) and (d)　　B. (b) and (c)
C. (a) and (c)　　D. (c) and (d)

28. Which of the following statements is/are absolutely impossible?

(a) A woman giving birth to her own grandchild
(b) A man attending his own funeral
(c) The Sun not rising in the East some day
(d) Cars running without petrol

Choose the correct answer from the code given below :

Code :

A. (a) and (b) B. (c) and (d)
C. (b) D. (a)

29. Which of the following are incorrect ways of arguing?

(a) If horses are cows, and if cows are sheep, then all horses must be sheep.
(b) If top actors are famous, and Shah Rukh Khan is famous, then Shah Rukh Khan is a top actor
(c) Lata is the second sister of Raju, hence Raju is the second brother of Lata
(d) A is not equal to B, but B is equal to C, hence A is equal to C. Choose the correct answer from the code given below :

Code :

A. (a), (b) and (c)
B. (a), (c) and (d)
C. (b), (c) and (d)
D. (a), (b) and (d)

30. Which of the following statements say the same thing?

(a) "I am clever" (said by Rama)
(b) "I am clever" (said by Raju)
(c) "My son is clever" (said by Rama's father)
(d) "My brother is clever" (said by Rama's sister)
(e) "My brother is clever" (said by Rama's only sister)
(f) "My sole enemy is clever" (said by Rama's only enemy) Choose the correct answer from the code given below :

Code :

A. (a), (c), (d), (e) and (f)
B. (a) and (b)
C. (d) and (e)
D. (a) and (f)

Study the following graph and answer Question Numbers 31 to 33:

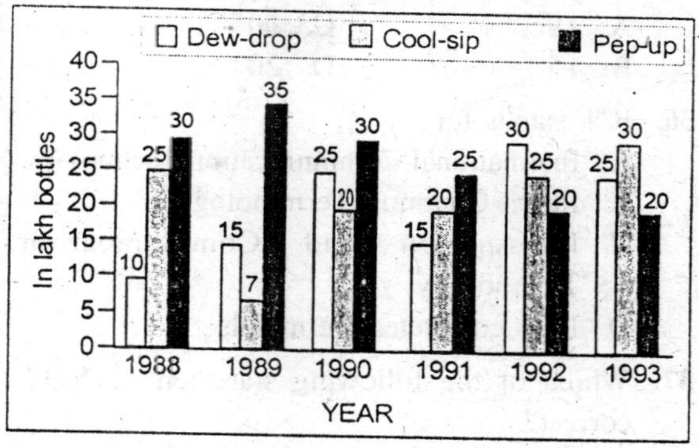

31. In which year was the sale of 'Pep - up' the maximum?

A. 1990 B. 1992
C. 1993 D. None of the above

32. In the case of which soft drink was the average annual sale maximum during the period 1988 -1993.

A. Pep - up only
B. Cool - sip only
C. Cool - sip and Dew - drop
D. Pep - up and Dew - drop

33. What was the approximate percent drop in the sale of Pep - up in 1990 over its sale in 1989?

A. 5 B. 12
C. 14 D. 20

34. The "Report on Currency and Finance" for each of the financial year in India is published by:

A. Reserve Bank of India
B. Ministry of Finance
C. Planning Commission
D. Central Statistical Organisation

35. The number of students in two classes A and B and the respective "mean" of the marks obtained by each of the class are given in the following table :

	Class A	Class B
Number of Students	20	80
Arithmatic Mean	10	20

The combined "mean" of the marks of the two classes will be :

A. 18 C. 10
B. 15 D. 20

36. ICT stands for :
A. International Communication Technology
B. Intera Common Terminology
C. Information and Communication Technology
D. Inter connected Terminals

37. Which of the following statement is **NOT** correct?
A. Computer is capable of processing only digital signal
B. Computer is capable of analysing both quantitative and qualitative data
C. Appropriate software is required for processing the data
D. Computer is capable of processing digital as well as analog signals

38. Which of the following is the appropriate definition of Information Technology?
A. Information Technology refers to the use of hardware and software for processing information
B. Information Technology refers to the use of hardware and software for distribution of useful information
C. Information Technology refers to the use of hardware and software for storage, retrieval, processing and distributing information of many kinds.
D. Information Technology refers to the use of principles of Physical sciences and Social sciences for processing of information of many kinds.

39. Which of the following statement is correct ?
A. Virus improves the speed of processing information through computer
B. Internet does not allow the virus to spread
C. Virus is a part of software
D. Virus is an operating system

40. Which of the following is correct statement?
A. Computers can be used for diagnosing the difficulty of a student in learning a subject
B. Psychological testing can be done with the help of computer provided a software is available
C. A set of instructions is called a programme
D. All the above

41. Global warning during winter becomes more pronounced at the :
A. Equator
B. Poles
C. Tropic of Cancer
D. Tropic of Capricorn

42. In the study of man - environment interaction, the statement of Miss Semple that "the humans are solely the product of their environment", is :
A. An opinion
B. A prejudice
C. A fact
D. A widely accepted phenomenon

43. In analysis of man - environment relationship Pragmatic Possibilism implies that :
A. There is no limit for man to exploit resources of earth
B. There are limited possibilities to explore earth's resources
C. The man has to watch and assess the situation and then go ahead with resource utilization
D. The man has to keep in mind only his basic needs while planning to harness the potential of resourceful earth

44. Arrange Column II in proper sequence so as to match it with Column I and choose the correct answer from the code given below :

Column I *(Activity)*	Column II *(Noise level)*
(a) Hearing	(i) 30 dB
(b) Whispering	(ii) 1 dB
(c) Interference with sleep	(iii) 60 dB
(d) Normal talk	(iv) 30 - 50 dB

Code :

	(a)	(b)	(c)	(d)
A.	(i)	(ii)	(iii)	(iv)
B.	(ii)	(i)	(iv)	(iii)
C.	(iv)	(ii)	(iii)	(i)
D.	(iii)	(i)	(ii)	(iv)

45. The maximum loss of forest lands in India is caused by :

A. River valley projects
B. Industries
C. Means of transportation
D. Agriculture

46. In which year the University Grants Commission was established?

A. 1948 B. 1944
C. 1953 D. 1960

47. Another name of Basic Education or Nai Talim is :

A. Compulsory Education
B. New Education Policy
C. Wardha Education Plan
D. Sarva Shikshya Abhiyan

48. The Idea of 'Democratic Decentralisation' in India was popularised by :

A. A.D. Gorwala Committee, 1951
B. Paul H. Appleby Committee, 1953
C. B.R. Mehta Committee, 1957
D. Ashok Mehta Committee, 1978

49. In India, a political party is recognised as a National or Regional Party by the :

A. President of India
B. Election Commission of India
C. Law ministry in consultation with the Law Commission of India
D. Union Parliament in consultation with the State Legislatures

50. Which of the following factors is/are responsible for the increase of the role of Government in Developing Countries ?

(a) Economic Planning
(b) Rising expectation of People
(c) Privatisation
(d) Emergence of the concept of Welfare State

Select the most appropriate answer from the code given below :

Code :

A. (a) and (d) B. (a), (b) and (d)
C. Only (c) D. Only (d)

ANSWERS

1	2	3	4	5	6	7	8	9	10
A	D	C	C	D	C	B	B	D	A
11	**12**	**13**	**14**	**15**	**16**	**17**	**18**	**19**	**20**
C	C	A	C	B	B	D	C	A	C
21	**22**	**23**	**24**	**25**	**26**	**27**	**28**	**29**	**30**
B	B	C	D	D	B	A	C	C	A
31	**32**	**33**	**34**	**35**	**36**	**37**	**38**	**39**	**40**
D	A	C	A	A	C	D	C	C	D
41	**42**	**43**	**44**	**45**	**46**	**47**	**48**	**49**	**50**
B	A	C	A	D	C	C	C	B	B

SOME SELECTED EXPLANATORY ANSWERS

22. Since,

D	B	L	O	R	U	S	T
↓	↓	↓	↓	↓	↓	↓	↓
3	2	4	1	0	6	7	8

Therefore,

R	O	B	U	S	T
↓	↓	↓	↓	↓	↓
0	1	2	6	7	8

23. Let the total number of each type of coins is x.

∴ From question

$$100x + 50x + 25x = 3500$$

$$\Rightarrow 175x = 3500$$

$$\Rightarrow x = \frac{3500}{175} = 20$$

U.G.C. (NET/JRF)

TEST PAPERS

(SOLVED)

Note: Each test paper contains **sixty (60)** questions, each question carrying **two (2)** marks. Candidate is expected to answer any **fifty (50)** questions.

UGC-NET / JRF Exam

TEST PAPER-I

1. Why should a student not be punished severely?
A. He may quarrel with a teacher.
B. He may leave the school and join another.
C. His parent may quarrel with the teacher.
D. The student may develop a negative attitude towards his studies, teacher and school.

2. A teacher exploits students in your school. In this situation, what you will do?
A. Report the matter to the principal.
B. not interfere in this matter.
C. Guide the teacher please stop this activity.
D. Go on Satyagraha against the teacher.

3. How will you demonstrate your impartial behaviour?
A. By maintaining high self esteem and egoistic behaviour.
B. By making own behaviour more balanced and fair.
C. By assaulting a teacher.
D. By criticising the teacher community.

4. It is popularly said that any two students are not alike. This means
A. each and every student differs in his physical and mental set up.
B. they are different in their mental strength.
C. they differ in their familiar and social status.
D. All of these

5. Which of the following is a product of learning?
A. Maturation B. Intelligence
C. Skills D. Forgetness

6. Below are listed some qualities
(i) Keenness of observation (ii) Persistence (iii) Industry (iv) Faith (v) Logical Reasoning
Which of the following represent the essential qualities of a researcher?
A. (i), (ii), (iii) and (iv)
B. (ii), (iii), (iv) and (v)
C. (i), (ii), (iii) and (v)
D. (i), (iii), (iv) and (v)

7. A good researcher
A. should collect data consistent from his objectives.
B. should always collect data to fit in his purpose.
C. should keep collecting varieties of information until hypothesis are found correct.
D. should collect huge amount of data.

8. A good piece of research is a product of
A. collective scholarship
B. good research library
C. penetrating and analytical mind
D. touch of genius

9. UNO has fixed the target for 'Education for All' till the year
A. 2014 B. 2012
C. 2015 D. 2013

10. On matter of academics (knowledge) a researcher should consider himself as
A. entirely dependent on the teacher
B. open minded and radical
C. a status quo maintainer
D. fairly knowledgeable

Directions (Qs. 11-15) : *Read the following passage and answer the questions.*

PASSAGE

What is the future which awaits our children? The underlying assumption of the question that Indian children have a common future is itself dubious. It can legitimately be asked whether a student who is well fed, attending a boarding school in the salubrious climate of the hills, and learning to use computers has any future in common with a malnourished child who goes to a school with no black boards, if needed he does go to school. The latter may have no worthwhile to analyse the significance of this marginalisation of more than 75% of the children in this country.

The failure to provide an infrastructure for primary education in the villages of India more than 40 years after independence is in sharp contrast with the sophisticated institutions, for technical institutes of higher education are funded by government, which essentially means that the money to support them comes from taxes. And since indirect taxation forms a substantial part of the taxes collected by the government, the financial burden is borne by all the people. L.K. Jha put it graphically when he observed that 25 paise of every rupee spent on educating an 11+ student comes from the pockets of men and women whose children may never enter a proper classroom.

11. The author is trying to highlight which of the following?

A. Need of sophisticated education for rural poor.

B. Faulty system of direct taxes.

C. The greatness of L.K. Jha.

D. Need to have common future for Indian children.

12. What seems to be likely answer of the author to the question posed by him in the first sentence of the passage?

I. There is no common future for the Indian children.

II. The future is worthwhile for majority of Indian children.

III. The majority may never enter a proper classroom.

A. Only I B. Only II

C. Only III D. Both I and II

13. Which of the following pairs have been termed as 'sharp contrast' by the author?

I. Infrastructure for technical education.

II. Lack of infrastructure for rural primary schools.

III. 25 paise of every rupee earned by government is spent on education.

IV. The financial burden of higher technical education is borne by all people.

V. 75% of children have limited opportunities.

A. III and IV B. I and II

C. II and IV D. II and V

14. According to the author, who among the following doesn't have a hopeful and prosperous future?

A. All students from technical institutes.

B. All students financially supported by Government.

C. Both A. and B.

D. None of these

15. Which of the following statements are not correct with reference to the passage?

I. The author welcomes Government's initiative on primary education.

II. 75% of children are of bright future.

III. 25% cost of educating a technocrat comes from poor people.

A. Only I and II B. Only II and III

C. Only I and III D. All I, II and III

16. Communicator is the person who

A. initiates the communication process

B. completes the communication

C. controls the communication process

D. avoids the communication process

17. A channel is

A. medium, which carries the message

B. an agent which reacts on the behalf of receiver

C. an agent who encoded/decoded the message

D. all of the above

18. Which of the following mediums is most mechanical?

A. Public meeting B. Radio

C. Cinema D. Newspaper

19. How many IITs will be set up in the 11th Five Years Plan?

A. 6 B. 8
C. 7 D. 9

20. The reach of different modes of media is known as

A. Media reach B. Media access
C. Media exposure D. Media effects

21. ?, 19, 37, 61, 91, 127, 169.

A. 8 B. 7
C. 9 D. 11

22. BYW, DUX, FQY, ...?

A. HZM B. HCZ
C. HMZ D. None of these

23. 17 : 19 : : 47 : ?

A. 53 B. 59
C. 41 D. 34

Directions (Qs. 24-25) : *Study the following codes and their meaning in a code language and then answer the following questions*

134 means good and tasty
478 means see good picture
729 means picture are faint.

24. Which number here has been used for faint?

A. 9 B. 2
C. Data inadequate D. 7

25. Which number is used for good?

A. 1 B. 3
C. 4 D. 7

26. Which one of the following is different from the others?

Gold, Silver, Tin, Mercury, Iron, Platinum.

A. Silver B. Tin
C. Mercury D. Iron

27. Which of the following represents the relation between gold, diamond, metal.

A. 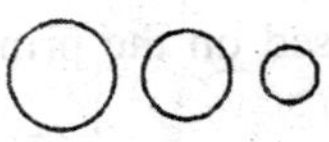 B. 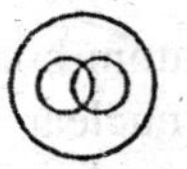

C. 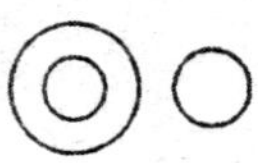 D. 

28. In this question, there are two statements followed by several conclusions. Choose the best after applying logical reasoning.

(i) Water is liquid
(ii) Ice is water

A. Ice is liquid B. Ice is not liquid
C. No ice is liquid D. None of these

29. Statements :

I. If footballs are made of iron cricket bats are made of woods.
II. Cricket bats are not made of wood.

Conclusions :

I. Footballs are not made of iron.
II. Footballs are made of iron.

A. Conclusion I follows
B. Conclusion II follows
C. Both I and II follow
D. Neither I or II follows

30. Statements :

I. My son is not old enough to vote.
II. My son has handsome personality.

Inference : My son is a boy under age of 18 years.

A. Inference is definitely true.
B. Inference is definitely false.
C. Inference is probably false or true.
D. Inference cannot be drawn.

Directions (Qs. 31-35) : *The questions are based on the table, graph and the information given below:*

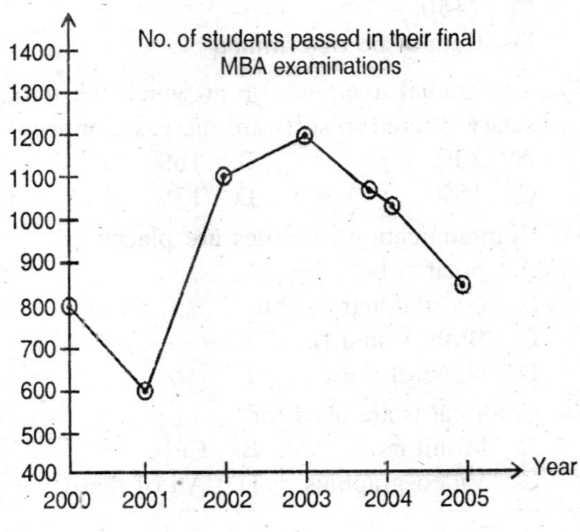

The table gives the percentage of students in the class of MBA who sought employment in the area of Finances, Marketing and Software with the average starting salary.

Year	Finance		Marketing		Software		Others
	% of students	Start salary	% of students	Start salary	%	S.	%
2000	22	5450	36	5170	19	5290	23
2001	17	6380	48	6390	23	6440	12
2002	23	7550	43	7630	21	7050	13
2003	19	8920	37	8960	16	7760	28
2004	32	9810	32	10,220	20	8640	16

31. The number of students who got job in finance is less than the number of students getting marketing jobs, in the five years by :

A. 734 B. 650
C. 725 D. 548

32. In 2002, students seeking job in finance earned Rs. ..... more than those opting for software (in lakhs).

A. 43 B. 33.8
C. 38.4 D. 42

33. What is the percentage increase in the average salary of finance from 2000 to 2004?

A. 78 B. 80
C. 68 D. 70

34. What is the average monthly salary offered to a management graduate in the year 2001?

A. 5170
B. 6334
C. 7150
D. Cannot be determined

35. The annual average rate at which the initial salary offered in software increases approx

A. 20% B. 16%
C. 15% D. 17%

36. Communication satellites are placed in

A. polar orbit
B. geostationary orbit
C. Both A. and B.
D. None of these

37. Color cards are used for

A. Monitors B. CPU
C. Video graphics D. All of these

38. Which of the following is not much required for effective computerisation system in a bank?

A. Effective customer service
B. Effective bank office integration
C. Focus on manual records
D. None of these

39. Data is computerised to

A. meet the business requirement
B. to increase the integrity value of the data
C. to ensure optimal utilization of resources
D. modularity

40. The full form of the abbreviation 'OCR' is

A. Optical Catalog Representation
B. Optical Character Recognition
C. Optical Computer Recorder
D. Optical Compressor and Recorder

41. Which of the following is a cause of Acid Rain?

I. It is a result of Air Pollution.
II. It is caused by presence of oxides of nitrogen and sulphur in the air which forms nitric oxide and sulphuric oxide with rain water.
III. The rain carries sulphuric acid and nitric acid to earth surface.

A. Only II and III B. Only I
C. Only I and II D. All of these

42. Excessive loading with nutrients and algal growth (bloom) causing reduction in O_2 level in water. This phenomenon is known as

A. Retrogenation B. Retrofication
C. Eutrophication D. None of these

43. Which of the following Acts was amended in 1991?

A. Environment (Protection) Act 1986
B. Air Act 1981
C. Wild Life (Protection) Act 1972
D. Motor Vehicle Act, 1938

44. An atom bomb is based on the principle of

A. nuclear fusion
B. nuclear spallation
C. nuclear fission
D. None of these

45. Which of the following place has a thermal Power Plant?

A. Belimela B. Ennore
C. Tarapur D. Salal

46. CSV (Centre for Science in Villages) is under which of the following universities?

A. Pondicherry University
B. Visva Bharati
C. Baba Saheb Bhimrao Ambedkar University, Lucknow
D. Assam University, Dorgakona

47. Freedom of Press as such

A. has been guaranteed by the constitution.
B. has not been expressly guaranteed by the constitution.
C. has been given only to selected institutions.
D. None of these

48. Fundamental Rights of the Indian citizens are contained in .... of the Indian Constitution.

A. Part I B. Part II
C. Part III D. Part IV

49. In which of the following states was the Panchayati Raj first introduced?

A. Rajasthan B. Gujarat
C. U.P. D. Bihar

50. Which of the following is wrongly matched?

A. Indian Institute of Mass Communication—New Delhi
B. Indian Institute of Technology—Poai (Mumbai)
C. Indian Institute of Management—Indore
D. Indian Institute of Chemical Technology — Bangalore

51. India is a:

A. Secular State B. Bilingual State
C. Communist State D. Capitalist State

52. What is the literal meaning of secularism?

A. Freedom to worship any God
B. Death of religion
C. Separation of religion from the state
D. None of these

53. The Tenth Schedule to the Constitution of India relates to:

A. Panchayati Raj Institutions
B. Anti-defection Act
C. List of languages recognised by the Constitution
D. Procedure for amendment to the Constitution

54. The real powers in the Central Government are enjoyed, according to the Constitution of India by the:

A. President of India
B. Vice-President of India
C. Prime Minister of India
D. Council of Ministers

55. The Council of Ministers is responsible to the:

A. President B. Lok Sabha
C. Vice-President D. Supreme Court

56. Central Processing Unit (CPU) -

A. The computer's primary processing hardware which interprets and execute program instructions and manages the function of input, output and storage devices.
B. is considered to be heart of the computer.
C. may reside on a single chip on the computer's motherboard, or on a larger card inserted into a special slot on the motherboard
D. All the above

57. The Arithmetic and Logic Unit (ALU)-

A. is the component of CPU.
B. performs arithmetic and logical operations.
C. Both A and B
D. None of the above

58. Data

A. A a collection of unorganized items that can include letters, numbers, symbols, images and sounds that computer process and organize it into meaningful information.
B. is a set of standards for controlling the transfer of business documents, such as purchase orders and invoices, between computers.
C. Both A and B
D. None of the above

59. E-MAIL
A. stands for electronic mail
B. stores purchase orders and invoices, between computers.
C. Both A and B
D. None of the above

60. EDI
A. stands for Electronic Data Interchange (EDI)
B. is a set of standards for controlling the transfer of business documents, such as purchase orders and invoices, between computers.
C. Both A and B
D. None of the above

ANSWERS

1	2	3	4	5	6	7	8	9	10
D	C	B	A	C	C	A	C	C	B
11	**12**	**13**	**14**	**15**	**16**	**17**	**18**	**19**	**20**
D	A	C	A	A	A	A	C	B	B
21	**22**	**23**	**24**	**25**	**26**	**27**	**28**	**29**	**30**
B	C	A	C	C	C	C	A	A	C
31	**32**	**33**	**34**	**35**	**36**	**37**	**38**	**39**	**40**
A	B	B	D	B	B	A	C	C	B
41	**42**	**43**	**44**	**45**	**46**	**47**	**48**	**49**	**50**
D	C	C	C	B	B	B	C	A	D
51	**52**	**53**	**54**	**55**	**56**	**57**	**58**	**59**	**60**
A	C	B	C	B	D	C	A	A	A

SOME SELECTED EXPLANATORY ANSWERS

21. The difference between seventh and sixth terms is 169 – 127 = 42.
The difference between sixth and fifth terms is 127 – 91 = 36.
The difference between fifth and fourth terms = 91 – 61 = 30 and so on.
This shows that the differences are in arithmetic progression of 12, 18, 24, 30, 36, 42, ...
So the 1st term will be 19 – 12 = 7.

23. 17 and 19 are consecutive prime numbers. Similarly 47 and 53 are consecutive prime numbers.

24. The code for faint can be 2 or 9. It is not clearly given by the codes.

27. Gold is a type of metal whereas diamond is non metallic.

30. The voting age is not given here. So, we can not definitely say about the age of the child.

32. In 2002, students seeking jobs in finance earned in one month = 7550 × 23% × 1100 = 19,10,150
In 2002, students seeking jobs in software earned in one month = 7650 × 21% × 1100 = 16,28,550
∴ Annual difference between the two = (19,10,150 – 16,28,550) × 12% = 33.79 Lakh ≈ 33.8 Lakh.

33. Required percentage increase

$$= \left(\frac{9810 - 5450}{5450}\right) \times 100\% = 80\%.$$

34. The value cannot be determined.

35. Annual growth rate

$$= \left(\frac{8640 - 5290}{5290 \times 4} \times 100\right)\% = 15.83\% \approx 16\%.$$

UGC-NET / JRF Exam

TEST PAPER-II

1. According to Dewry, education is a
A. social need
B. personal need
C. psychological need
D. theoretical need

2. The teacher ought to know the problems prevalent in the field of education. The reason is that
A. only a teacher can do something about solving them
B. he can tell about the same to another teacher
C. teachers can tell the government about it
D. with this knowledge, the teacher can have information about education

3. Of great importance in determining the amount of transference that occurs in learning is the
A. IQ of teacher
B. knowledge of the teacher
C. use of appropriate elements
D. presence of identical elements

4. The education aims at the fullest realisation of all the potentialities of children. It implies that
I. teacher and parents must know what children are capable of and what potentialities they possess.
II. they should provide suitable opportunities and favourable environmental facilities which are conducive to the maximum growth of children.
III. it is necessary that their attitudes are helpful, encouraging and sympathetic.
A. I and II B. II and III
C. I and III D. All of them

5. Why a teacher is called the leader of the class?
A. He masters the art of oratory like a political leader.
B. He is autocratic emperor of his class.
C. He belongs to a recognised teacher's union.
D. He is a maker of the future of his students.

6. Minimum Programme of Guidance includes
A. data collector service
B. occupational information service
C. counselling service
D. all of these

7. To study the relationship of family size with income a researcher classifies his population into different income slabs and then takes a random sample from each slab. Which technique of sampling does he adopt?
A. Random Sampling
B. Stratified Random Sampling
C. Cluster Sampling
D. Systematic Sampling

8. In any research one should
A. know everything in the area without bothering to learn the details of any
B. know more and more about less and less in certain specific sub area
C. not try out anything blindly but wait until a sudden flash appears in his mind
D. none of these

9. A theory is correct because
A. its advocate has written a big volume to establish it.
B. its is supported by a large number of scholars.
C. it has a large number of followers.
D. its derivations match with most observations.

10. A non-fictional literary composition that forms an independent part of a publication, as a newspaper or magazine is known as

A. paper B. article
C. symposium D. none of these

Directions (Qs. 11-15) : *Study the following passage and answer the questions*

PASSAGE

Corduroy is fast establishing itself as this year's fabric. While the ribbed cotton itself provides utilitarian tenacity, texture and warmth, it is the fabric's long held associations that may provide a hint to its current revival as a fabric for all seasons. It is Corduroy's link with good breeding and country living that made it an essential ingredient in the gentleman's Wardrobe along with Wellington boots and a decent woollen. It combines the comfortable non-sense appeal of cotton with the perfectly correct luxury finish of velvet. Corduroy has the ability to appear either supremely sophisticated or rough and ready.

11. According to author, the special quality of Corduroy is that

A. it contains the correct mixture of cotton and velvet.
B. it needs no ironing.
C. it combines the virtues of both cotton and velvet.
D. both the rich and not so rich can afford to buy it.

12. Corduroy is essential in a gentleman's Wardrobe because

A. its current revival gives a taste of the latest fashion.
B. it has its associations with good upbringing and a conservative life style.
C. it goes with Wellington boots.
D. it can be an ideal alternative to woollen cloths.

13. Corduroy is a fabric for all seasons because

A. it can be worn not only in winter but also in summer.
B. gentlemen can wear it on both formal and informal occasions.
C. of its peculiar texture and warmth.
D. it is made popular by catchy advertisements.

14. When the writer refers to Corduroy's 'utilitarian tenacity' he means that

A. it has remained fashionable over several years.
B. it is useful because it is durable.
C. it does not need frequent washing.
D. though expensive, it is economic in long run.

15. Which of the following best describes the passage?

A. It persuades us to buy Corduroy.
B. It makes us understand the everlasting appeal of Corduroy to the young.
C. It tells us about the usefulness of Corduroy.
D. It tells about the virtues of Corduroy.

16. Which of the following media can be used effectively in large group communications?

A. Television
B. Overhead Projector
C. Video
D. Computer

17. Which process of communication is best for controlling noise in a classroom?

A. Saying 'don't talk'.
B. Raising one's voice above students voice.
C. Remaining calm and just looking at student.
D. Continue teaching without caring for noise.

18. Discussion in the class will be more effective if the topic of discussion is

A. not introduced
B. stated before the start of discussion
C. written on the board without introducing it.
D. informed to the student well in advance.

19. The communication which transpires inside a person is known as

A. intrapersonal communication.
B. inter-personal communication.

C. mass communication.
D. group communication.

20. Rhetorics means
A. art of entry
B. source of persuability
C. Both A. and B.
D. None of these

21. What should come in place of the question mark (?) in the following series?
102, 99, 104, 97, 106?
A. 100 B. 95
C. 96 D. 93

22. A D C F
C F E H
O R ? ?
A. LK B. MN
C. ST D. QT

23. In this question, group of letters are given. Three of them are similar. One is different from the rest. Find the odd man out.
A. AbcdE B. IfghO
C. ApqrL D. UlmnE

24. EDITOR : MAGAZINE
Choose the pair from the answer choices (a-d) that best expresses the relationship similar to that expressed by the question pair.
A. Novel : Writer
B. Poem : Poet
C. Chair : Carpenter
D. Director : Film

25. If EFGHIJK is coded as VUTSRQP then LIMIT can be coded as
A. KNRNC B. ORNRG
C. JKOKG D. RSTSG

26. The relationship between Animal, Cows, Dogs can be shown by

A. 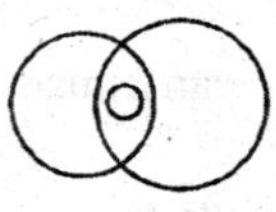 B. 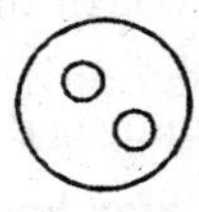

C. 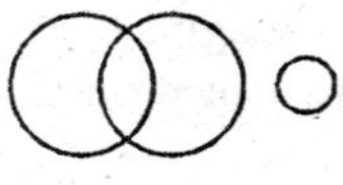 D. 

27. In this question there are two statements followed by four conclusions numbered I, II, III and IV.
Statements :
I. All books are trees.
II. All trees are lions.
Conclusions :
I. All books are lions.
II. All lions are books.
III. All trees are books.
IV. Some lions are books.
A. Only II and III follow.
B. Only I and IV follow.
C. None of conclusions follow.
D. All conclusion follows.

28. Amit is the son of Rahul. Sarika, Rahul's sister has a son Sonu and a daughter Rita. Raja is the maternal uncle of Sonu.
How is Rita related to Raja.
A. Sister
B. Daughter
C. Niece
D. Aunt

29. **Statements :**
I. All pens are daughters.
II. All daughters are clerks.
Conclusions :
I. All pens are clerks.
II. Some clerks are daughters.
A. Only I follows
B. Only II follows
C. Both I and II follow
D. None of these

30. **Statement :** India's economy is depending mainly on forests.
Assumptions :
I. Trees should be preserved to improve Indian economy.
II. India wants only maintenance of forests to improve economic conditions.
A. Only I is implicit
B. Only II is implicit
C. Both I and II are implicit
D. Neither I nor II is implicit

Directions (Qs. 31-35) : *Study the following pie chart and answer the questions based on it.*

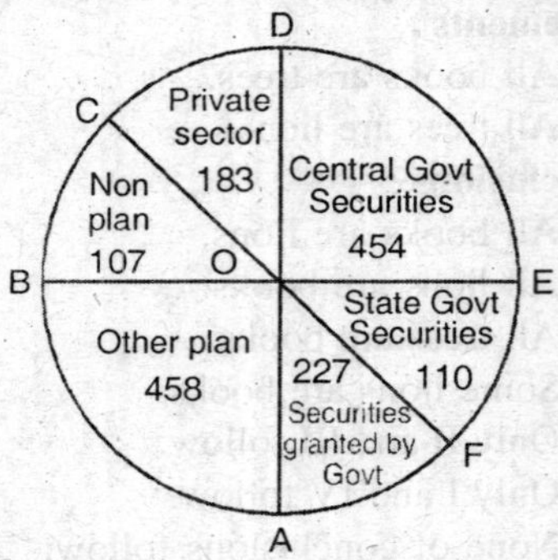

31. The percentage or gross investment in state government securities is nearly

A. 9.2% B. 8.6%
C. 7.8% D. 7.1%

32. The magnitude of ∠AOC is nearly

A. 123° B. 126°
C. 115° D. 132°

33. The investment in plan and non-plan sector together is more or less than the investment in government securities. (Central and State) by ....

A. more, 4 crore B. more, 1 crore
C. more, 111 crore D. less, 106 crore

34. The investment in private sector is nearly what per cent higher than the investment in State Government Security?

A. 66% B. 54%
C. 46% D. 44%

35. The ratio of area of the circle above ∠COF to the area of the circle below it is about

A. 0.92 B. 0.94
C. 0.96 D. 1

36. Communication satellites are placed in

A. Polar Orbit
B. Geostationary Orbit
C. Both A. and B.
D. None of these

37. Network Access Point is

A. a public communication system facility taken care by various internet service providers.
B. a set of protocols governing the exchange of information between two end points.
C. a particular route chosen by the protocol for routing the network traffic.
D. a common network server that controls the routing decisions of all the ISOs.

38. Full form of www is

A. world wide web B. wet world web
C. Both A. and B. D. None of these

39. ATMs are ....

A. stand alone machines
B. networked machines
C. electrical machines
D. electronic mailer machines

40. O.M.R. is

A. Open Mark Reader
B. Option Multiple Report
C. Optical Mark Reader
D. None of these

41. Which of the following statements is/are true about ozone layer?

A. This layer is found in upper atmosphere, which absorbs UV rays.
B. These rays can cause skin cancer and genetic disorder.
C. It is depleting due to human activities.
D. All of these

42. Which of the following is a non point source of water pollution?

A. Lawn B. Coal mines
C. Factories D. None of these

43. Which of the following can be used for Earthquake Prediction?

A. Ground uplift and tilting
B. Foreshocks
C. Animal Behaviours
D. All of these

44. Which of the following can cause explosive volcanic eruption?

A. Low viscosity of magma
B. High viscosity of magma
C. High water content in ground
D. None of these

45. Which of the following power plants is/are situated in Delhi?

A. Pragati Power Station
B. Indraprastha Power Plant
C. Badarpur Thermal Power Plant
D. All of these

46. How many principle level of qualifications within the higher education system in our country exist?

A. 4 B. 6
C. 3 D. 2

47. Which institution brought co-ordination and co-operation between Union and States in the field of education?

A. NCERT (National Council for Educational Research and Training)
B. CABE (Central Advisory Board of Education)
C. CCCE (Council for Co-ordination and Co-operation on Education)
D. None of these

48. The Prime Minister is the chairman of

A. Planning Commission
B. Finance Commission
C. Minorities Commission
D. None of these

49. A person can be a member of Council of Ministers without being a member of Parliament for a maximum period of

A. one year B. 180 days
C. 90 days D. 30 days

50. How many types of emergencies have been envisaged by the constitution?

A. One B. Two
C. Three D. Four

51. The Prime Minister is:

A. nominated by the President
B. elected by the Chief Ministers of States
C. is the leader of the majority party of Lok Sabha
D. is not elected; it is a hereditary post

52. The quorum of the Parliament is fixed at:

A. one-tenth of the membership of the House
B. one-third of the membership of the House
C. one-half of the membership of the House
D. four-fifths of the membership of the House

53. Why are the Fundamental Rights considered fundamental?

A. Necessary for the successful working of democratic institution
B. Basic to the welfare, dignity and happiness of the individual
C. Constitution is based on these
D. All of these
E. Only A and B

54. The judges of the Supreme Court are appointed by the:

A. Prime Minister of India
B. Speaker of the Lok Sabha
C. President of India
D. Ministry of Law & Justice

55. The President's Rule is imposed in a State or in a Union Territory when the:

A. Governor of a State or the Chief Commissioner or a Lt Governor advises the President to do so because the Government in that State/Territory cannot be carried on in accordance with the provisions of the Constitution
B. Chief Minister of a State requests to this effect
C. Chief Justice of the State High Court recommends through the Governor
D. President knows best
E. Elections are being held there

56. Hardware

A. The physical components of a computer
B. includes—processors, memory chips, input/output devices, tapes, disks, cables, modems.
C. Both A and B
D. None of the above

57. Input

A. A data or instruction that you enter into the memory of a computer.

B. hardware components that result in the transfer of data.
C. Both A and B
D. None of the above

58. Four types of Input are
A. data, programs, commands and user responses.
B. hardware components that result in the transfer of data.
C. Both A and B
D. None of the above

59. The input devices are the
A. computer hardware that accepts data and instructions from user.
B. communication between hardware components that result in the transfer of data.
C. Both A and B
D. None of the above

60. Input/Output devices(I/O)
A. Communications between the user and the computer that results in transfer of data
B. Communication between hardware components that result in the transfer of data.
C. Both A and B
D. None of the above

ANSWERS

1	2	3	4	5	6	7	8	9	10
A	A	A	D	B	D	B	B	D	A
11	**12**	**13**	**14**	**15**	**16**	**17**	**18**	**19**	**20**
D	B	A	B	D	B	C	D	A	B
21	**22**	**23**	**24**	**25**	**26**	**27**	**28**	**29**	**30**
B	D	C	D	B	B	A	C	A	A
31	**32**	**33**	**34**	**35**	**36**	**37**	**38**	**39**	**40**
D	D	B	A	B	B	A	A	D	C
41	**42**	**43**	**44**	**45**	**46**	**47**	**48**	**49**	**50**
D	A	D	B	D	C	B	A	B	C
51	**52**	**53**	**54**	**55**	**56**	**57**	**58**	**59**	**60**
C	A	E	C	A	C	A	A	A	C

SOME SELECTED EXPLANATORY ANSWERS

21. 102, 99, 104, 97, 106, [95]

(−2 from 99 to 97; −2 from 97 to 95)

23. Each group of letter consists of two vowels, one each in the beginning and in the end. In between two vowels, three letters in alphabetic sequence are given. In C., there is only one vowel.

31. Total investment = 454 + 110 + 227 + 458 + 107 + 183
= 1539 crore.

Investment in State Govt. securities = 110 crore.

∴ Required percentage

$$= \frac{110}{1539} \times 100 = 7.14\%.$$

33. Investment in Plan and Non-plan sector = 565 crore

Investment in Government securities (Central and State) = 564 crore.

∴ Investment in socially oriented sector is more than government securities by 1 crore.

UGC-NET / JRF Exam

TEST PAPER-III

1. Each child grows in its own unique way. The wide individual differences are caused by
   A. heredity
   B. endowment
   C. environmental enfluences
   D. All of these

2. When you make a mistake while teaching in the class and your students point it out angrily then what will you do?
   A. You will break all limits of anger
   B. You will feel sorry for committing the blunder
   C. You will scold him/her and resist them
   D. You will leave the class for few days

3. What can a teacher do to develop integrated personalities of his pupil?
   A. Children should be encouraged and helped to set themselves well defined goals and objectives which they can hope to achieve
   B. They should be helped to build their self esteem to develop a sense of worthiness and positive ego image
   C. Life in schools should be so planned that children are able to express themselves fully
   D. All of these

4. In the guidance of learning a teacher has many important roles. Which one of the following is the least important aspect of the teachers role in the guidance of learning?
   A. The provision of continuous diagnostic and remedial help
   B. The forestalling of habits
   C. The provision of encouragement and morale support
   D. The development of insight into what constitute the pitfalls and danger to be avoided.

5. Our modern day schools are oriented towards the development on the part of its students of
   A. socially acceptable behaviour
   B. personnel adequacy and independence
   C. a sound system of ethical values
   D. adequate behaviour

6. Ordinarily a good piece of research follows four phases. They are given below.
   (*i*) Planning to observe
   (*ii*) Interpreting the findings
   (*iii*) Setting objectives
   (*iv*) Analysing the observations
   Which of the following orders for these phase is correct?
   A. (*iii*), (*i*), (*iv*) and (*ii*)
   B. (*i*), (*iii*), (*ii*) and (*iv*)
   C. (*i*), (*ii*), (*iii*) and (*iv*)
   D. (*i*), (*iv*), (*iii*) and (*i*)

7. Which of the following is not correct? A belief becomes a scientific truth when it
   A. is established experimentally
   B. is arrived logically
   C. is accepted by many people
   D. can be replicated

8. A statistical measure based on the entire population is called parameter while measure based upon a sample is known as
   A. sample parameter
   B. inference
   C. statistic
   D. all of these

9. Collective psychology of the whole period is a theory which
   A. can explain all phases of historical development
   B. means the psychology of the whole society

C. means psychological approach of data collection

D. all of these

10. Which of the following is/are characteristics of hypothesis?

I. It should be amendable to testing within a reasonable time.

II. It must consist of known facts

III. It must be clear in its concept

A. only I and III

B. only II and III

C. only I and II

D. all of these I, II and III

Directions (Qs. 11-15): *Study the following passage and the answer the questions given below.*

PASSAGE

Reading may be pursued for different purposes. Some read for pleasure, some for distinction and some for applying knowledge to practical necessities of life. Those who read for pleasure find the company of poets and thinkers more stimulating than that of men of flesh and blood. Those who seek fineness of perception and subtley in reasoning are naturally driven to the company of those who weigh their words and use them with precision and caution. Lastly, those whose pursuit is more practical, read books in so far as the knowledge gained through them may be applied to the necessities of work-a-day life. Those who read for pleasure are fond of retiring from the din of daily life to the warm contact of personalities who have left behind their account to how they reacted to the life around. Since there is no bond between us and the men of past excepting one of sympathy and understanding the reader can easily surrender himself to a companionship which is purely imaginary. Those who read for acquiring mental distinction are interested in philosophical thought, the formulation of system of thinking. Lastly, those who follow intellectual pursuits for knowledge of facts and their relations to one another are readers whose interest is chiefly scientific.

11. It is practical to

A. do better things than reading

B. apply knowledge to day-to-day life

C. use bombastic words

D. ignore those fond of reading

12. Reading is desirable

A. for a variety of aims

B. only when we are seeking pleasure

C. for getting a degree

D. for theoretical knowledge only

13. Philosophy is associated with

A. system of thinking

B. knowledge of facts

C. a flight of imagination

D. a surrender to evil

14. Poets and thinkers enthuse

A. men of flesh and blood

B. those with no vacation

C. skinny and weird persons

D. those reading for pleasure

15. The relationship between us and those who are no more

A. can never be fruitful

B. can lead to real friendship

C. calls for sympathy and understanding

D. can be dangerous for all.

16. Feed back is

A. immediate reaction of receiver

B. response of receiver to communicator's message

C. analysis done by the receiver of the communicator's message

D. none of these

17. The communication, which involves interaction with mass audience is known as

A. intrapersonal

B. interpersonal communication

C. mass communication

D. group communication

18. Which of the following is not true about communication?

A. Communication is systematic

B. Communication is process

C. Communicating message must have a meaning

D. All are true.

19. According to Crowlay which of the following can be the result of social isolation?

A. Stress
B. Disease
C. Early death
D. All of these

20. Which of the following decipher correct sequences?

A. Message - channel - receiver - encoder-decoder
B. Encoder - message - channel - decoder - feedback
C. Encoder - channel - message - decoder - system
D. None of these

21. M P K R I T?

A. U B. V
C. W D. G

22. 10, 18, 34, ?? 130, 254, 258

A. 32 B. 60
C. 68 D. 66

23. Which one of the following is different from the rest three?

A. Liquid petroleum gas
B. Compressed natural gas
C. Petrol
D. Nitrogen

24. If LIMIT is coded as ORNRG and SOUR is coded as HLFI, then HIGH can be coded as,

A. STRS B. SRTS
C. RSTR D. GLOG

25. In this question a related pair of words in capital letter is followed by four pair of words. Select that lettered pair that expresses the relationship that is most similar to that of the capitalised pair. TRIOLOGY : NOVEL

A. Serial : Episode
B. Rice : Husk
C. Involve : Crime
D. Gun : Cartridge

26. Which of the following figures represents the relationship between smokers, lawyers and non-smokers?

A. 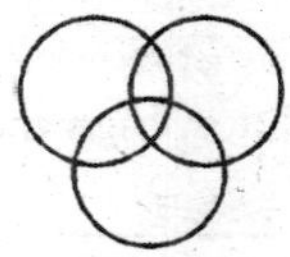
B. 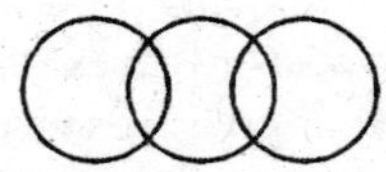
C. 
D. 

27. Statements : All girls are beautiful.
Vidya is a girl.

Conclusion : I. Vidya is beautiful.
II. Vidya in not beautiful.

A. only conclusion I follows
B. only conclusion II follows
C. either I or II follows
D. None of these

28. Statement: All student are not lazy.
Conclusion: No student is lazy.

A. the conclusion is true
B. conclusion is false
C. conclusion is doubtful
D. conclusion is irrelevant

29. Statement: Should higher education be restricted to the most deserving students?
Arguments: I. Yes, only deserving people are entitled to this luxury.
II. No, it is against the principles of equality of educational opportunity.

A. only Arg I is strong
B. only Arg II is strong
C. Both the arguments are strong
D. Neither I nor II is strong

30. Statement : Of all the newspapers published in India. The Times of India has the largest number of readers.

Assumptions

I. The volume of readership of all newspapers in India is known
II. No newspaper in India other than 'The Times of India' has a large readership.

A. only assumption I is implicit
B. only assumption II is implicit
C. both I and II are implicit
D. neither of them is implicit

Directions (Qs. 31-35): *Answer the questions based on the following information.*

A company produces five types of shirts A, B, C, D, and E using cloth of three qualities, high, medium and low, using dyes of three qualities, high medium and low. One shirt requires 1.5m of cloth. The following table gives respectively.

Shirt	Numbers in thousand	Distribution of cloth (%)			Distribution of dye (%)		
		High	Medium	Low	High	Medium	Low
A	20	80	20	–	70	15	15
B	30	30	40	30	20	50	30
C	30	–	70	30	–	60	40
D	10	–	60	40	–	40	60
E	10	–	10	90	–	20	80

The number of shirts (of each category) produced in thousands.

31. What is the total requirement of cloth?
A. 1,50,000 m B. 2,00,000 m
C. 2,25,000 m D. 2,50,00 m

32. How many metres of low quality cloth is consumed?
A. 22,500 m B. 46,500 m
C. 60,00 m D. 40, 000 m

33. How many metres of high quality cloth is consumed by A-type shirts?
A. 8000 m B. 1,12,000 m
C. 24,000 m D. 30,000 m

34. What is the radio of three qualities of dyes in high quality cloth?
A. 2 : 3 : 5
B. 1 : 2 : 5
C. 7 : 9 : 10
D. Cannot be determined

35. What is the ratio of low-quality dye used for type shirts to that used for D-type shirts?
A. 3 : 2 B. 2 : 1
C. 1 : 2 D. 2 : 3

36. Indian satellite launching station is situated at
A. Thumba B. Chilka lake
C. Sri Harikota D. Hasan

37. What is the full form of SITE?
A. Satellite Instructional Television Experiment
B. Satellite Institutional Television Experience
C. Student Incorporation in Telecommunication
D. None of these

38. FTP is better than HTTP because
A. it uses separate channels for data transmission and flow control
B. it transfers data from the web server
C. it transfers data from the life sever
D. it copies file to the user's hard disk in the destination specified by the user

39. Which of the following is wrong about water based extinguishing system used in computer labs?
A. Water cools the equipment relatively quickly
B. Release of water can be controlled
C. Water and halon gas systems cann't co-exit
D. All are true

40. Which of the following materials is suitable for water purification?
A. Zeolites B. Quartz
C. Silicones D. Asbestos

41. Which of the following is true about the step of questionable development.
A. The forest should be conserved
B. The wild animals should be conserved
C. Sanctuary and national park should be well maintained
D. All of these

42. Which of the following is an adverse effect of over exploitation of natural and Industrial development?

A. It has led to large scale consumption of fossil fuel

B. It has led to large scale mining of ores

C. It has led to construction of large dams.

D. All of these

43. Tides in ocean are caused by

A. Gravitational pull of the moon on the earth's surface including sea water

B. Gravitational pull of the sun on the earth's surface only and not on the sea water

C. Gravitational pull of the moon and the sun on the earth's surface including sea water

D. None of these

44. Match List-I and List-II and select the correct answer using the codes given below the lists.

List-I (Storm)	**List-(II) (Place/country)**
1. Cyclone	A. China
2. Hurricane	B. Australia
3. Typhoon	C. India
4. Willy-Willy	D. USA

Codes :

A. 3 4 2 1 B. 4 3 2 1

C. 3 4 1 2 D. 4 3 1 2

45. Tehri Dam Project is located in which of the following states?

A. Madhya Pradesh B. Rajasthan

C. Haryana D. Uttrakhand

46. Which of the following is responsible for all matters within higher education sector other than funding?

A. Association of Indian Universities (AIU)

B. University Grants Commission (UGC)

C. AJCTE

D. None of these

47. Which of the following does not come under vocational courses?

A. Agro based food Industry (Crop based)

B. Sericulture

C. Vegetable seed production

D. None of these

48. Administrative law means

A. a law passed by Union

B. law or rules made by executive

C. law relating to administration of non governmental Institutions

D. all of these

49. Which one of the following is the range of frequency used in optical communication?

A. $10^8 - 10^9$ Hz

B. $10^{16} - 10^{17}$ Hz

C. $10^3 - 10^4$ Hz

D. $10^{13} - 10^{14}$ Hz

50. Indian Institute of Foreign Trade is situated in

A. Lucknow B. Dehradun

C. New Delhi D. Mumbai

51. The Directive Principles:

A. aim at establishing welfare state of Gandhian conception

B. aim at giving ideals to be incorporated at a later stage

C. aim at giving support to the Fundamental Rights

D. A and B only

52. Agriculture, including research and education, falls in:

A. State List B. Union List

C. Concurrent List D. None of the above

53. Which of the following are the ideals set forth in the Preamble?

A. Social, economic and political Justice

B. Equality of status and of opportunity

C. Liberty of thought, expression, belief, faith and worship

D. All of these

54. Fundamental Rights of the citizens are:

A. non-justiciable

B. justiciable

C. justiciable if the highest court feels it should be

D. Some rights are justiciable while others are not

55. In India the executive is responsible directly to the:

A. Legislature B. President
C. Judiciary D. People

56. Microsoft office

A. is a suite of Microsoft primary application for window and Macintosh.
B. includes some combination of word, Excel, Powerpoint, Access and schedule along with a host of internet and other utilities.
C. Both A and B
D. None of the above

57. Modem:

A. Abbreviation for modulator/demodulator.
B. It is an Input/Output device that allows computer to communicate through telephone lines.
C. converts outgoing digital data into analog signals that can be transmitted over phone lines and converts incoming audio signals into digital data that can be processed by the computer.
D. All the above

58. Multimedia

A. refers to the integration of multiple media such as visual imagery, text, video, sound, and animation
B. often associated with the information superhighway, or with interactive T.V—that can produce videos (informaion on demand) or with hypermedia .
C. is a combination of software and hardware, both.
D. All the above

59. Multimedia

A. is a very powerful form of communicating ideas, searching for information and experiencing new concepts of common media.
B. enhance business presentations
C. Both A and B
D. None of the above

60. Motherboard

A. is the main circuit board, also called system board, in an electronic device which consists of sockets that accepts additional boards.
B. is a very powerful form of comm-unicating ideas
C. The interactive feature of network
D. None of the above

ANSWERS

1	2	3	4	5	6	7	8	9	10
D	B	D	D	D	B	A	C	A	D
11	**12**	**13**	**14**	**15**	**16**	**17**	**18**	**19**	**20**
B	A	A	D	C	B	C	D	D	B
21	**22**	**23**	**24**	**25**	**26**	**27**	**28**	**29**	**30**
D	D	D	B	A	B	A	B	D	A
31	**32**	**33**	**34**	**35**	**36**	**37**	**38**	**39**	**40**
A	B	C	D	B	C	A	A	C	A
41	**42**	**43**	**44**	**45**	**46**	**47**	**48**	**49**	**50**
D	D	C	C	D	A	D	B	D	C
51	**52**	**53**	**54**	**55**	**56**	**57**	**58**	**59**	**60**
D	A	D	B	A	C	D	D	C	A

SOME SELECTED EXPLANATORY ANSWERS

21. The sequence is in Alphabetical progression where each letter is separated from the following one by 2, 4, 6, 8, 10 and 12 letters, alternately forward and backward.
M (NO) P (ONML) K (LMNOPQ) R (QPONMLKJ) I (JKLMNOPQRS) T (SRQPONMKLJIH) G and so.

22. Double number and subtract 2 each time.
$10 \times 2 - 2 = 18,$ $18 \times 2 - 2 = 34,$
$34 \times 2 - 2 = 66$ $66 \times 2 - 2 = 130$
So the required number is 66.

25. A triology is a work consisting of three novels, a serial is a work consisting of a number of series (instalments) there is a whole and part relationship

29. Equality of educational opportunity does not mean that everyone must be given the chance of getting education irrespective of his talents. It simply means that any citizen of India will not be discriminated on the basis of his caste, creed, colour or profession. Higher education entails higher costs so scrutiny is a must here.

31. Total cloth requirement = Number of shirts × cloth required per shirt.
= (20 + 30 + 30 + 10 + 10) × 10,00 × 1.5
= 1,50,000 m

32. Total low quality cloth consumed
= 1.5 (30,000 × 30% + 30,000 × 30% + 110,000 × 40% + 10,000 × 90%)
= 46,500 m

33. Quantity used for A-type shirt made of high cloth = 20,000 × 80% × 1.5 = 24,000 m

34. No relationship between type of shirt and cloth used and type of shirt and dye used, hence no relationship between type of cloth and dye used can be found.

35. Low quality dye used for C-type shirt
= 30,000 × 40%
= 12,000 unit
Low quality dye used for D type shirt
= (10,000 × 60%)
= 6,000 unit

Hence, required ratio = $\frac{12,000}{6,000} = 2:1.$

UGC-NET / JRF Exam

TEST PAPER-IV

1. A teacher can help adolescent to over come his special problems, and help him to adjust to the environment. Which of the following attitude, he should not made?
   A. He should impart right information about sex.
   B. He should redirect the energies of the adolescent to fruitful channels through sports and other constructive activities
   C. He should have unsympathetic attitude towards others
   D. He should have right information about sex

2. In our present society where values are deteriorating, the excellent education will be which
   A. enables one to earn in an easy manner
   B. exaggerates the competition in the society
   C. works for establishment of human and cultural value
   D. deaccelerates the social change in society

3. A backward child is a slow learner. He does not respond satisfactorily to the ordinary school curriculum and to the usual methods. The causes of this phenomena are
   A. poor intellectual ability and low intelligence
   B. physical defects and diseases
   C. emotional disturbance
   D. all of the above

4. Catharsis means discharge of emotions. A teacher can let off pent up energy of his disciple through
   A. picnic/excursions
   B. mock-parliament
   C. celebration of festivals
   D. all of these

5. If back benchers are always talking in the classroom a teacher should
   A. let them do what they are doing
   B. punish them
   C. ask them to sit on the front benches
   D. none of the above

6. The process not needed in experimental research is
   A. observation
   B. controlling
   C. manipulation and replication
   D. reference collection

7. While writing a research report a researcher
   A. must not use the numerical figures in numbers in the beginning of sentences
   B. must arrange it in logical, topical and chronological order
   C. must compare his result with those of other studies
   D. All of the above

8. The other name of independent variable for an experimental research is/are
   A. treatment variable
   B. experimental variable
   C. manipulated variable
   D. all of these

9. Area (cluster) sampling technique is used when
   A. Population is scattered and large size of the sample is to be drawn
   B. population is heterogeneous
   C. long survey is needed
   D. A. and C..

10. An example of scientific knowledge is
    A. authority of Prophet or great man
    B. social tradition and customs
    C. religious scriptures
    D. laboratory and field experiments.

Directions (Qs. 11-15) : *Study the following passage and give answers on the basis of passage.*

PASSAGE

There was a marked difference of quality between the personages who haunted the near bridge of brick of brick and the personages who haunted the far one of stone. Those of lowest character preferred the former, adjoining the town; they did not mind the glare of the public eye. They had been of no account during their successes and though they might feel dispirited, they had no sense of shame in their ruin. Instead of sighing at their adversaries they spat, and instead of saying the iron had entered into their luck. The miserables who would pause on the remoter bridge were of a politer stamp persons who did not know how to get rid of the weary time. The eyes of this species were mostly directed over the parapet upon the running water below. While one on the town ward bridge did not mind who saw him so, and kept his back to the parapet to survey the passer by, one on this never faced the road, never turned his head at coming foot-steps, but sensitive to his own condition, watched the current whenever a stranger approached, as if some strange fish interested him, though every finned thing had been poached out of the river years before.

11. The two bridges were known for
- A. attaching dejected people to them
- B. being equidistant from town
- C. being haunted place
- D. their similar design

12. People belonging to the lower strata, in their moments of distress
- A. felt ashamed of their failures
- B. dressed shabbily to earn sympathy
- C. visited the brick-made bridge
- D. remembered their days of glory

13. The bridge of stone was frequented by
- A. all the sections of society
- B. the sophisticated but luckless
- C. those fond of fishing
- D. none of above

14. The attitude of the lowly and genteel towards strangers was.
- A. virtulently hostile
- B. completely indifferent
- C. entirely different
- D. virtually the same.

15. In this passage, the author is trying to
- A. explain the variety of ways in which strongers can be treated
- B. describe how people of different classes behaved when unhappy
- C. explain the way different sections of people like to dress
- D. explain the difference between the construction of two bridges.

16. Major limitation of mass communication is
- A. it is very costly
- B. the feedback system is weak
- C. more time is required to produce the message
- D. the success largely depends upon the producer

17. Which of the following is not 'essential' for communication in research work?
- A. Command over language
- B. Statement of objectives
- C. Conclusions drawn
- D. Procedure followed

18. The most powerful barrier of communication in the classroom is:
- A. noise in classroom
- B. confusion on the part of teacher
- C. more outside disturbance in the classroom
- D. lack of teaching air.

19. Effective communication will make the receivers?
- A. enjoy it
- B. accept it
- C. pass it on others
- D. think about it

20. Communication will be effective
- A. if it is delivered slowly and clearly
- B. if it is delivered in a calm situation
- C. if it reaches the receiver completely
- D. if it reaches the receiver as intended by sender

21. In this question, four words have been given, out of which three are alike in some manner and fourth one is different. Choose the odd one out.

A. Kennel B. House
C. Stable D. Aviary

22. Find the missing term/terms in the following letter series.
W, V, T, S, Q, P, N, M, ? ?

A. I, J B. J, I
C. K, J D. J, K

23. In the following series find the wrong number 2, 3, 8, 27, 112, 575, 3396.

A. 3 B. 27
C. 575 D. 112

24. In a certain code SUBSTITUTION is written as. ITSBUSNOITUT. How is DISTRIBUTION is written in that code?

A. IRTSIDNOITUB B. IRTSIDNOIBUT
C. IRTDISNOITUB D. IRTDISNOIUTB

25. Land is related to cape in the same way as water is, related to ....

A. strait B. lagoon
C. bay D. island

26. Which of the following figures represent the relation between factory, machinery, product

A. 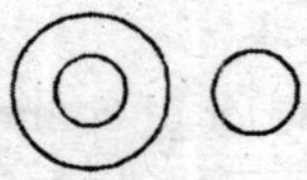 B. 

C. 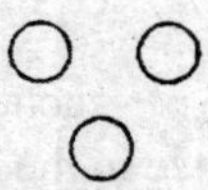 D. 

27. Assertion X : Carbohydrates provide energy to body

Reason Y : Obesity is caused by excessive intake of carbohydrates.

A. Both X and Y are true and Y is correct explanation of A
B. Both X and Y are false
C. X is true but Y is false
D. Both X and Y are true but Y is not correct explanation of X.

28. A tree always has which of the following?

A. Branches B. Leaves
C. Fruits D. Roots

29. Statements : All flowers are stems
All stems are roots.

Conclusions :

I. All roots are flowers
II. All stems are flowers

A. only conclusion I follows
B. only conclusion II follows
C. both I and II follow
D. neither I nor II follows

30. Statement : Should there be a complete ban on strike by government employees in India?

Arguments :

I. Yes this is the only way to teach discipline to the employees
II. No, this deprives the citizen their democratic right.

A. only argument I is strong
B. only argument II is strong
C. Both I and II are strong
D. None of them is strong

Directions (Qs. 31-35): *The following pie chart depict the budget of a state. Study it carefully and answer the questions given below it.*

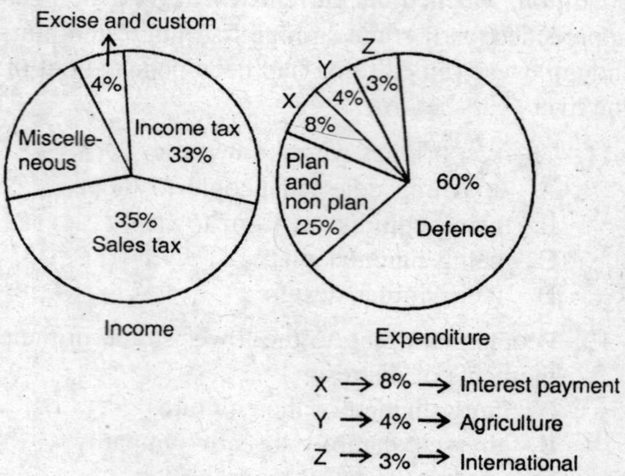

31. In the income section, how many degrees (approx) should there be in central angle of the sector representing income tax?

A. 105° B. 120°
C. 135° D. 150°

32. If an amount of Rs 10 lakh is constituted excise and custom duty how many million constituted state's income (in lakh Rs) for the year?

A. 150 B. 200
C. 250 D. 300

33. If total expenditure of state is Rs. 20 crore in a year, how many crore are spent on international in that year?
A. 0.2 B. 0.4
C. 0.6 D. 0.8

34. What is the ratio of income from sales tax to that from miscellaneous?
A. 1 : 1 B. 5 : 4
C. 4 : 5 D. 1 : 2

35. What is the ratio of combined expenditure for Defence + Agriculture to all other expenditure?
A. 9 : 16
B. 16 : 9
C. 20 : 11
D. 11 : 20

36. What is the full form of APPLE?
A. Advance People Practical Learning Experiment
B. Ariane People Payload Experiment
C. Ariane Passenger Pay Load Experiment
D. Advance Passenger Pay Load Experience

37. Which of the following villages was 1st total computer literate village?
A. Chamravattam (Kerala)
B. Hosur (Karnataka)
C. Kotapully (Tamil Nadu)
D. None of these

38. A picture is stored as JPEG because
A. It is faster to retrieve the images in this format
B. Images in this format takes less memory space
C. Images in this format uses better colour scheme
D. All of these

39. Internet was started as ....
A. TCPI/P experiment
B. Network for defence forces of USA
C. Group of research scientists of Bell lab
D. Contribution was done by all the above Institution

40. Compiler is a/an
A. operating system
B. application software
C. utility
D. none of these

41. Which of the following are non-biodegradable pollutants?
I. DDT II. CFC
III. Insecticides IV. Faecal matter
A. (*i*), (*ii*) and (*iv*)
B. (*i*), (*ii*) and (*iii*)
C. (*ii*), (*iii*) and (*iv*)
D. (*i*), (*ii*) and (*iv*)

42. Water for civil supplies are commonly purified by
A. Chlorination B. Distillation
C. Filtration D. Decantation

43. The non conventional source of energy is
A. sun B. coal
C. petroleum D. diesel

44. Chipko movement is related with
A. soil conservation
B. forest conservation
C. water conservation
D. gene conservation

45. Match List-I with List-II

List-I (National park/Wild life sanctuary)	**List-II (State)**
A. Bondla wildlife sanctuary	1. Orissa
B. Kangerghat national park	2. Assam (Asom)
C. Orang sanctuary	3. Chhattisgarh
D. Ushakothi wildlife sanctuary	4. Goa
	5. Tripura

Codes :

	A	B	C	D
A.	1	2	3	5
B.	4	3	2	1
C.	2	3	5	4
D.	4	1	2	3

46. Which of the following are true?
A. Distance learning is not confined to space and time

B. Distance learning encourages the use of community resources and students creativity to enrich the content offered through the distance learning technology
C. On line courses require a basic but working knowledge of computers and world wide web
D. All of these are true

47. The salary of members of parliament is determined by
A. the President
B. the Union cabinet
C. the Speaker
D. the Parliament

48. The Greenhouse effect gases trap only the feat of following radiations
A. Solar B. Ultraviolet
C. Infrared D. Both (A) and (B)

49. The sitting of Lok Sabha can be terminated through
A. adjournment B. prorogation
C. dissolution D. All of the above

50. Cancer is caused by activation of genes
A. Regulatory genes B. Structural genes
C. Oncogenes D. Jumping genes

51. Fundamental Rights of the Indian citizens are contained in .... of the 'Indian Constitution'.
A. Part I B. Part II
C. Part III D. Part IV

52. Of which fundamental right is a foreigner in India deprived of?
A. To seek justice in court
B. To seek security of life
C. To criticise policies of government
D. To vote at the time of Parliamentary election

53. Freedom of the Press as such:
A. has been guaranteed by the Constitution
B. has not been expressly guaranteed by the Constitution
C. has been given only to selected institutions
D. None of the above

54. The Rajya Sabha is:
A. dissolved once in two years
B. dissolved after every four years
C. adjourned every six months
D. not subject to dissolution

55. Administrative Law means:
A. law passed by the Union
B. law or rules made by the executive
C. laws relating to administration of non-Governmental institutions
D. all the above

56. Printers
A. is an output device that produce text and graphics on a physical medium such as paper or transparency film.
B. are classifieds into the following categories— Impact printers and Non-Impact printers.
C. Both A and B
D. None of the above

57. A program
A. is a sequence of instructions or actions
B. must have mechanisms for carrying out processing operations (like arithmetical operations or moving information around) and for handling input and output.
C. Both A **and** B
D. None of the above

58. Output
A. The data that has been processed into a useful form and can be seen on VDU or can be taken on paper by using printer or listen to it through speakers or a headset.
B. can be saved on a floppy disk or CD for future use.
C. can be generated in the form of—text, graphics, audio, video.
D. All the above

59. Office Automation System
A. Automate routine office tasks.
B. are classifieds into the following categories- Impact and Non-Impact
C. Both A and B
D. None of the above

60. The Information System (IS) department-
A. Supports organization's information systems and also support organization's overall mission .
B. The IS department provide technical support for hardware and software, but may be involved in the design and implementation of an organization's entire information system.
C. IS professionals also ensure that systems generate all the appropriate types of information and reports required by the organization's manager and workers.
D. All the above

ANSWERS

1	2	3	4	5	6	7	8	9	10
C	C	D	D	C	D	D	D	D	D
11	12	13	14	15	16	17	18	19	20
A	D	D	C	B	B	B	B	A	D
21	22	23	24	25	26	27	28	29	30
B	C	C	A	C	D	C	D	D	B
31	32	33	34	35	36	37	38	39	40
B	C	C	D	B	C	A	D	B	C
41	42	43	44	45	46	47	48	49	50
B	A	A	B	B	D	D	A	D	C
51	52	53	54	55	56	57	58	59	60
C	D	B	D	B	C	C	D	A	D

SOME SELECTED EXPLANATORY ANSWERS

21. All except house are the places of residence of different animals.

22. The letters are alternatively moved one and two steps backward to obtain the successive terms.

23. $2 \times 1 + 1 = 3$, $3 \times 2 + 2 = 8$, $8 \times 3 + 3 = 27$, $27 \times 4 + 4 = 112$, $112 \times 5 + 5 = 565$, $565 \times 6 + 6 = 3396$
So the right number is 565.

24. The word is divided in two groups of 6 letters each and then the first six letters and then the last six letters are written in reverse order to obtain the code.

25. Cape is a land projected into water and bay is the portion of water body projected into land.

27. Carbohydrates are source of energy in the body. However obesity is caused by the excessive intake of fats.

31. In the income section, number of degrees representing
Income tax = 33% of 360°.

$$= \frac{33}{100} \times 360° = 118.8° \approx 120°$$

32. Income in excise and custom = 4% = 10 Lakh

$\therefore$ Total state income = Rs. $\frac{10 \times 100}{4}$ Lakhs
= Rs. 250 Lakhs.

33. Total expenditure of state = Rs. 20 crore.
$\therefore$ amount spent on international = 3% of Rs. 20 crore

$$\frac{3}{100} \times 20 = \text{Rs. } 0.6 \text{ crore.}$$

34. $\frac{\text{Total income from sales tax}}{\text{Total income from miscellaneous}}$

$$= \frac{35}{[100-(35+35+33+4)]} = \frac{35}{28} = \frac{5}{4}$$

$\therefore$ Required ratio = 5 : 4.

UGC-NET / JRF Exam

TEST PAPER-V

1. If majority of students in your class is weak you should
   A. not care about intelligent students.
   B. keep your speed of teaching fast so that students comprehension level may increase.
   C. keep your teaching slow which can also be helpful to bright students.
   D. keep your teaching slow along with some extra guidance to bright people

2. On which of the following statements there is consensus among educators?
   A. Disciplinary cases should be sent to the principal only when other means have failed.
   B. Disciplinary cases should never be sent to principal's office.
   C. Disciplinary cases should be totally neglected in the class.
   D. None of these.

3. The introduction of career courses in schools and colleges aims at
   A. developing the ability to make the intelligent choice of jobs.
   B. providing professional knowledge to students.
   C. increasing G.K. in students.
   D. All of the above.

4. All of the following statements about a teacher are correct except that he/she is
   A. a friend guide and philosopher.
   B. teacher that the students do not know.
   C. the leader in the class.
   D. changes his attitudes and behaviour according to the need of the society.

5. A child may have hearing impairment if
   A. he speaks loudly unusually.
   B. he comes nearer to the speaker during conversation.
   C. he generally says 'please repeat' to the teacher.
   D. All of the above.

6. The word research is derived from
   A. French word B. Spanish word
   C. Latin word D. Greek word

7. Which of the following methods implies the collection of information by way of investigators own examination without interviewing the respondents?
   A. Observation
   B. Posting questionnaire
   C. Schedule method
   D. Random probability sampling.

8. The quality of research is judged by the
   A. experience of researcher.
   B. depth of the research.
   C. methodology followed in conducting the research.
   D. relevance of research.

9. Which of the following are true about the concepts?
   I. Concepts are the blocks from which theories are built.
   II. Concepts are ideas, abstractions, that do not have meaning in themselves.
   III. Concepts have different meanings in different contents.
   A. Only I B. Only II and III
   C. Only I and III D. All of these.

10. Which of the following is/are characteristics of hypothesis?
    I. It must consists of known facts.
    II. It must be objective and specific.
    III. It can be tested.
    A. Only II and III B. Only I and III
    C. Only III D. All of these.

Directions (Qs. 11-15): *Study the following passage and give answer to the questions based on passage.*

PASSAGE

The Nobel committee, in fact, a notoriously conservative body which among other things had a marked antipathy to pure science, especially to mathematical physics. Restrained by a clause in Alfred Nobel's will that the prize should go to the person whose discovery or invention shall have conferred the greatest benefit to mankind, the committee initially ignored the great theoretical advances in Physics. Wrecked, no doubt, by guilty that he had become a merchant of death through his invention of dynamite and smokeless powder and plagued by sadistic fantasy of destruction, the Swedish chemist, engineer and aspiring poet, Alfred Nobel, who has been described as Europe's richest vagabond, left his colossal fortune to the cause of progress in human knowledge. Five prizes were installed one each for literature ('to the person who shall have produced in the field of literature, the most outstanding work in idealistic tendency') Physics, Chemistry, Medicine and Peace (to the person who shall have done the most or the best work for fraternity among nations for abolition or reduction of armies, and for holding or promotion of peace).

11. The Nobel committee has been called a conservating body because
- A. its members are old fashioned.
- B. it awards prizes only to those people who adopt a conservative approach.
- C. it is conservative in choice of subjects.
- D. its members believe in a conservative ideology.

12. In the beginning, the Nobel committee ignored the great advances in theoretical physics because
- A. the committee felt that the discovery and invention in the field did not contribute to the benefit of mankind.
- B. they proved to be merchants of death and dangerous to mankind.
- C. they were different from other branches of physics.
- D. they were concerned with theories and did not suggest its application.

13. Nobel Prize would not be given to
- A. an author who wrote a novel.
- B. a leader who have done good for peace in his territory.
- C. a doctor who invents a new method for surgery.
- D. a composer who composes a symphony.

14. Alfred Nobel left his colossal fortune to the cause of progress in human knowledge because, he
- A. felt guilty for having invented highly destructive things
- B. felt guilty for having earned so much money.
- C. was Europe's richest vagabond.
- D. was a chemist, engineer and an aspiring poet.

15. Which of the following were invented by Alfred Nobel?

A. Dynamite B. Smokeless powder
C. Both A. and B. D. All of these.

16. When Education TV was first introduced in India?

A. 1959 B. 1970
C. 1984 D. 1979

17. Which of the following is an ambitious computerisation programme aimed at connecting 60,000 government schools through internet?

A. Gyan Vahini B. Vidya Vahini
C. Vidya Vani D. Kalpana project

18. Which of the following is not a successful communicator?
- A. One who sometimes becomes informal before the receiver and developes rapport.
- B. One who knows a lot but is somewhat reserve in his attitude.
- C. One who is able to adapt himself according to the language of communication.
- D. One who presents material in a precise clear way.

19. If a receiver replying on 'hmm-mm' or 'Isee'. This type of reply is known as

A. ambiguous feed back
B. negative feed back
C. positive feed back
D. none of these.

20. In business communication, the major obstacles arise because of the .... .

A. physical barriers
B. organizational barriers
C. mechanical barriers
D. psychological barriers

21. Chlorophyll is related to chloroplast in the same way as vulture is related to

A. flesh
B. birds
C. wings
D. air

22. In this question four words are given, out of which three are alike and fourth one is different. Choose the odd one out.

A. Pageant
B. View
C. Display
D. Spectacle

23. 3, 12, 27, 48, 75, (?) 147.

A. 110
B. 108
C. 118
D. 120

24. A — B A C — D — B C D C
— 3 — 2 — 1 — 4 ? ? ? ?
d c — — b a c b — — — —

Which of the following will come at the vacant places marked by ? ? ? ?

A. 1, 3, 4, 3
B. 1, 4, 3, 4
C. 2, 3, 4, 3
D. 3, 4, 1, 4

25. If in a certain code.
'nso prt kli chn' means sharma gets marriage gift.
prt lnm wop chn means wife gives marriage gift.
tti wop nhi means he gives nothing.
What would mean gives.

A. chn
B. prt
C. wop
D. nhi

26. **Statements:** A man must be wise to be a good wrangler. Good wrangler's are all talkative and boring.

Conclusions :

I. All the wise persons are boring.
II. All the wise persons are good wranglers.

A. Only conclusion I follows.
B. Only conclusion II follows.
C. Both I and II follow.
D. None of these.

27. **Statements :**

I. During volcanic eruptions molten lava oozes out in a stream.
II. The lava comes from under the crust of the earth

Conclusion: The inside of earth must be very hot.

The conclusion drawn is

A. definitely true
B. probably true
C. definitely false
D. probably false.

28. **Statement :** Let us increase the taxes to cover the deficit.

Conclusions:

I. The present taxes are very low
II. Deficit in the budget are not desirable.
III. If the taxes are not increased, the deficit can not be met.

A. Only I and II are implicit
B. Only II and III are implicit
C. Only I and III are implicit
D. All are implicit

29. Should education in India be made free?

Arguments:

I. Yes, this is the only way to improve the level of literacy.
II. No, this would add already heavy burden on the exchequer.

A. Only argument I is strong
B. Only argument II is strong
C. Both the arguments are strong
D. None of these.

30. Study the figure and find the region which represents the students who study X and Y but not Z.

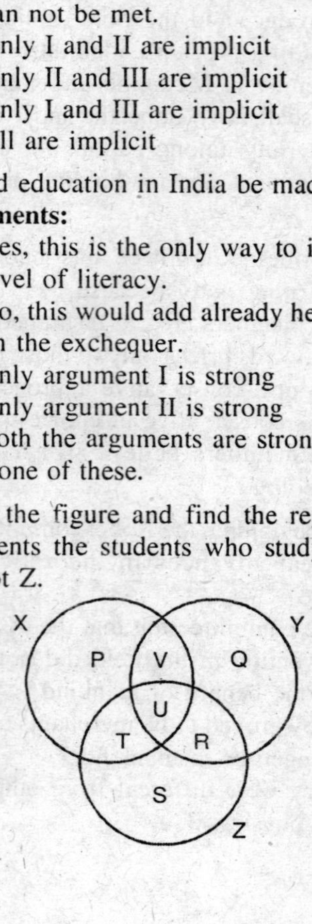

A. T
B. P + T + S
C. V
D. P + T + S + R + U + V

Directions (Qs. 31-35): *Answer the questions based on following table.*

Machines X and Y can independently produce either product P or product Q. The time taken by machines X and Y (in minutes) to produce one unit of product P and Q are given in the table below. (Each machine works 8 hours per day.)

Product	X	Y
P	10	8
Q	6	6

31. What is the maximum number of units that can be manufactured in one day?
A. 140 B. 160
C. 150 D. 180

32. If X works at half its normal efficiency, what is the maximum number of units produced, if at least one unit of each must be produced?
A. 129 B. 139
C. 109 D. 119

33. What is the least number of machine hours required to produce 30 pieces of P and 25 pieces of Q respectively?
A. 6 hr 30 min. B. 8 hr 20 min.
C. 5 hr 10 min. D. 4 hr. 30 min.

34. If the number of units of P is to be three times that of Q, what is the maximum idle time to maximize total units manufactured?
A. 2 minutes B. 0 minutes
C. 10 minutes D. None of these.

35. If equal quantities of both are to be produced, then out of four choice given below the least efficient way would be
A. 53 of each with 10 min idle.
B. 71 of each with 9 min idle.
C. 66 of each with 11 min idle.
D. 48 of each with 4 min idle.

36. DLL is
A. Data Deriving Language
B. Data Definition Language
C. Data Design Language
D. None of these.

37. LAN should ensure
A. Effective security for organisation.
B. Effective security system for data file.
C. Availability of information to all.
D. All of these.

38. The VIRUS is a
A. Software program
B. Hardware
C. Device
D. None of these.

39. Electronic Data-Ex-change is
A. Alternative name of e-mail
B. Cann't actually exchange data between two machines.
C. Provides strategic and operational business opportunity.
D. All of these.

40. C-band transponder in satellites uses the frequency range
A. 4 GHz to 6 GHz
B. 2 GHz to 4 GHz
C. 12 GHz to 14 GHz
D. None of these.

41. Which of the following are biodegradable pollutants?
I. Domestic waste
II. Agricultural waste
III. Lead
IV. Sewage
A. I, II and III B. I, II and IV
C. I, III and IV D. II, III and IV

42. Which of the following can be the effect of depletion of ozone layer?
I. Damage to our immune system.
II. Damage to our eyes.
III. Skin cancer.
A. Only II B. Only I and III
C. Only II and III D. All of the above.

43. Green mufler is used against which type of pollution?
A. Air B. Water
C. Soil D. Noise

44. Photocopying and other electrical equipments produce

A. ozone B methane
C. hydrogen D. nitrogen dioxide

45. The Minimata disease of Japan in 1953 was caused by eating fish contaminated by

A. Cadmium B. Lead
C. Mercury D. Nickel

46. IGNOU has a three tier system that doesn't consists of

A. district centres B. study centres
C. regional centres D. headquarters

47. Which of the following was created for the co-ordination and maintenance of standards in higher education?

A. UGC
B. NCERT
C. SCERT
D. Higher Education Information System Project

48. Which of the following is not created by the Act of Parliament?

A. Atomic Energy Commission
B. Backward Class Commission
C. University Grants Commission
D. Railway Board

49. How many types of political units existed in India at the time of independence?

A. 2 B. 3
C. 4 D. Only one

50. How many times has the preamble of Indian constitution been amended so far?

A. once B. twice
C. thrice D. Never

51. The Legislative Council of a State is a:

A. temporary body
B. permanent body
C. semi-permanent body
D. chamber of the nominated members

52. The Lok Sabha and the Rajya Sabha sit jointly when:

A. they like
B. there is a disagreement between the two (Houses).
C. the President summons both the Houses
D. they must meet when two years have lapsed after the last meeting
E. they must meet every 5 years

53. Ministers in the Union Cabinet are appointed by the:

A. Prime Minister
B. President
C. President of India on the advice of the Prime Minister
D. Prime Minister on the advice of the Chief Justice of the Supreme Court of India

54. Who administers the Union Territories?

A. The President through the Administrators appointed by him
B. The Prime Minister of India
C. The Law Minister, Government of India
D. The Attorney-General of India

55. Which of the following is not the federal feature of the Indian Constitution?

A. There is distribution of Powers in accordance with 2 lists
B. Written and rigid constitution
C. Independent Judiciary
D. All of these

56. Programming language

A. is a higher level language than machine code for writing programs.
B. use a variety of basic English.
C. Both A and B
D. None of the above

57. Low level languages

A. are machine dependent, i.e they are designed to run on a particular computer and in the form of 0's and 1's.
B. are also easier to learn and are not dependent on a particular type of computer.
C. need interpreter or compiler to convert into low level language so that computer can understand.
D. All the above

58. High level languages
A. are English type languages where a single statement may correspond to several instructions in machine language and human being can understand easily.
B. are also easier to learn and are not dependent on a particular type of computer.
C. need interpreter or compiler to convert into low level language so that computer can understand.
D. All the above

59. Pipelining
A. is a technique that enable a processor to execute more instructions in a given time.
B. the control unit begins executing a new instruction before the current instruction is completed.
C. Both A and B
D. None of the above

60. Ports:
A. External devices such as a keyboard, monitor, printer, mouse and microphone often are attached by a cable to the system unit the interface
B. point of attachment to the system unit is called a port. Most of the time ports are located on the back of the system unit, but they also can be placed on the front.
C. A or B
D. None of the above

ANSWERS

1	2	3	4	5	6	7	8	9	10
D	A	B	B	D	C	A	D	D	D
11	**12**	**13**	**14**	**15**	**16**	**17**	**18**	**19**	**20**
C	A	D	A	C	A	B	B	A	B
21	**22**	**23**	**24**	**25**	**26**	**27**	**28**	**29**	**30**
B	B	B	B	C	D	A	B	B	C
31	**32**	**33**	**34**	**35**	**36**	**37**	**38**	**39**	**40**
B	D	A	B	A	B	D	A	C	A
41	**42**	**43**	**44**	**45**	**46**	**47**	**48**	**49**	**50**
B	D	D	D	C	D	A	D	A	A
51	**52**	**53**	**54**	**55**	**56**	**57**	**58**	**59**	**60**
B	B	C	A	D	C	A	D	C	C

SOME SELECTED EXPLANATORY ANSWERS

23. The numbers follow the following pattern
$3 = 3 \times 1^2$, $12 = 3 \times 2^2$, $27 = 3 \times 3^2$
$48 = 3 \times 4^2$, $75 = 3 \times 5^2$, $? = 3 \times 6^2 = 108$
$147 = 3 \times 7^2$
Hence, the missing number is 108.

24. Clearly 2 corresponds to A.
Now b corresponds to C and 4 corresponds to b. So 4 corresponds to C.
C corresponds to D and 3 corresponds to C.
So 3 corresponds to D.
So, the remaining number *i.e.*, 1 corresponds to B. Thus BCDC correspond to 1, 4, 3, 4.

25. In the second and third statements the common word is gives and the common code word is wop. So wop means gives.

31. Both the machines work for 8 hours per day. Hence maximum number of units can be produced if both the machines produce product Q. Hence number of units produced

$$= \frac{8 \times 60}{6} + \frac{8 \times 60}{6} = 160.$$

32. Since efficiency of machines X is reduced to half, therefore the given table changes as follows.

Product	X	Y
P	20	8
Q	12	6

Now, in order to produce maximum number of units Q has to be produced on Y as it takes 6 minutes per piece. Since at least one unit of each has to be produced then it should be produced on machine Y as it takes 8 min. In the remaining time i.e., (480 – 8) = 472 minutes. Number of Q units produced = $\frac{472}{6} = 78$. It takes less time to produce Q and X, hence number of units produced on X = $\frac{8 \times 60}{12} = 40$. Hence, maximum number of units manufactured = 1 + 78 + 40 = 119 units.

33. Time required to manufacture 30 units of P on Y
= 30 × 8 = 240 minutes = 4 hrs.
Time required to produce 25 units of Q on X.
= 25 × 6 = 150 minutes= 2 hr 30 minutes.
Hence, total time taken = 4 + 2.5 = 6.5 or 6 hr 30 minutes.

34. Since, P has to produce in more number than Q and since time taken to produce P is least on Y, to maximise the output, the entire time on Y has to be utilized for producing P. Number of units of P produced in this time

$$= \frac{8 \times 60}{8} = 60 \text{ units.}$$

It is given, that number of units of Q should be one-third that of P, 20 units of Q should be manufactured and time taken in doing so on X = 120 minutes. Time left on X = (480 – 120) = 360.
Hence, to maximise the output it is possible to have no idle time on any of the machines.

35. Option A. gives the least production hence it is the least efficient way.

UGC-NET / JRF Exam

TEST PAPER-VI

1. Why should you prefer teaching to other professions?
   A. For the service of humanity.
   B. For love of teaching.
   C. For love to young (youth).
   D. For mastery over the subject of teaching.

2. The students who keep asking questions in the class
   A. should be advised to meet the teacher after the class.
   B. should be encouraged to participate in classroom discussion.
   C. should be encouraged to find answer independently
   D. should be encouraged to continue questioning.

3. A teacher can get important place in society if he
   A. performs the role of an active member of the political party in power
   B. is scholar and original thinker
   C. participates actively in social activities
   D. performs his responsibility honestly

4. During lecture in classroom, some students hesitate to say that they are unable to understand your lecture. What may be the reason for this happening?
   A. You are unable to communicate effectively.
   B. Your educational methodology is inadequate.
   C. Students fear you.
   D. There is a cordial relation between you and your pupil.

5. Which one of the following most suitably explains the mental growth?
   A. A growth pattern runs parallel to physical growth.
   B. A uniform rise to the middle teens and gradual levelling off during middle twenties.
   C. We can't say anything about it.
   D. A growth pattern inverse of physical growth.

6. A small proportion of a population selected for observation and analysis is known as
   A. parameter
   B. statistics
   C. sample
   D. None of these

7. What is meant by cognition in Personal Interview?
   A. The respondents accurate answers to the interviewer.
   B. The information required be such that the respondent be able to convey it to interviewer.
   C. The understanding on the part of the respondent of what is required of him, and what type of informations are required.
   D. None of the above

8. An individual when faced with the problem tries to
   A. avoid the situation.
   B. understand the exact nature of problem.
   C. seek help from others to cope up with the problem.
   D. None of these

9. If you are doing experiments on a large group of samples which method of controlling will you adopt?
   A. Elimination
   B. Elimination and matching
   C. Randomization
   D. Matching

10. The part of a thesis or research paper which summarizes the key information from every major section of the thesis or report is known as

A. Scientific Abstract
B. Descriptive Abstract
C. Educational Abstract
D. Informational Abstract

Directions (Qs. 11-15) : *Study the following passage and give answer to the questions based on it.*

PASSAGE

The superior would have to change his attitude towards people first. The staff under him must be perceived as human being with feeling and needs. They are not automation within a complex work machinery. One of the greatest needs of today's worker is to have a feeling that he is in control of his work place and not vice-versa. The best way is to satisfy this need as far as possible. He must feel, firstly, that his work is meaningful. To do this the supervisor must delegate responsibility and limited authority for the man to execute his job well. The subordinate must be properly trained to assume responsibility and authority. Once he is ready to assume these, he can be made accountable for his job. Very often supervisors assume all responsibility and accountability gives the worker a purpose in life and the need to do a job well. Most important is to sit with each worker and chalk out common objectives and agreed norms to achieve them. This gives workers a security as to what is expected of them. When he has met his objectives he certainly has feeling of achievement. This feeling of achievements is the greatest motivator.

11. Responsibility and accountability make a worker

A. tense and frightened
B. shirk his duties
C. vulnerable before his supervisors
D. do his job properly

12. Supervisors do not delegate responsibility and authority to their subordinates because

A. final responsibility is their .
B. subordinates are not capable enough.
C. they cannot trust their subordinates.
D. they are apprehensive of losing their hold on the place of work.

13. Orientation of subordinates to common objectives and how to achieve them is

A. a must
B. not very important
C. not at all necessary
D. optional

14. The greatest motivator is

A. fulfilment of purpose
B. a sense of security
C. a good supervisor
D. a good environment

15. A human attitude on the part of the supervisor towards his staff is necessary to

A. keep them happy.
B. get them to work.
C. get the best out of them.
D. have a congenial atmosphere at work place.

16. Which group of communication aspects does not distort the communication process in the class?

A. Reversing—evaluating-focussing
B. Evaluating—focussing—illustrating
C. Evaluating—focussing—exaggerating
D. Focussing—illustrating—exaggerating

17. Any effective communication system employs a feedback system in order to

A. make the necessary modifications in the process.
B. understand more about the content.
C. find faults with the sender (teacher).
D. find faults with the receiver (the students).

18. "Mass media are primarily moulders of society as well as reflectors of it."—This was stated by

A. Dennis McQuail
B. Roy Emmmersion
C. Ray Lindwall
D. Dennis Quaid

19. Which of the following is an example of one way communication?

A. Formal talk between two unknown people.
B. Street play.
C. Seminar or symposium.
D. None of these

20. Who invented the television?
A. J.L. Baird
B. Alexander Graham Bell
C. J.C. Bose
D. None of these

21. Which of the following numbers will complete the sequence?
12, 23, 44, 85, ?, 327.
A. 167 B. 166
C. 168 D. 170

22. Find the missing term in the following series :
Q1F, ?, U6D, W21C, Y88B
A. R3B B. S2E
C. R2E D. T3D

23. In this question, four words have been given, out of which three are alike in some manner and the fourth one is different. Choose the odd one out.
A. Niger
B. Mississippi
C. Colorado
D. Suez

24. Bull is related to Drought in the same way as cow is related to ......
A. Livestock
B. Milch
C. Farm
D. Fodder

25. In a certain code language SMILE is written as 36492, RUN is written as 058 then LEMUR can be coded as
A. 92658
B. 92650
C. 32658
D. 32650

26. In the following figure the Δ represents girls, the □ represents sports persons and the circle represents coaches. The portion which represents girls who are sports persons but not coaches is the one labelled as

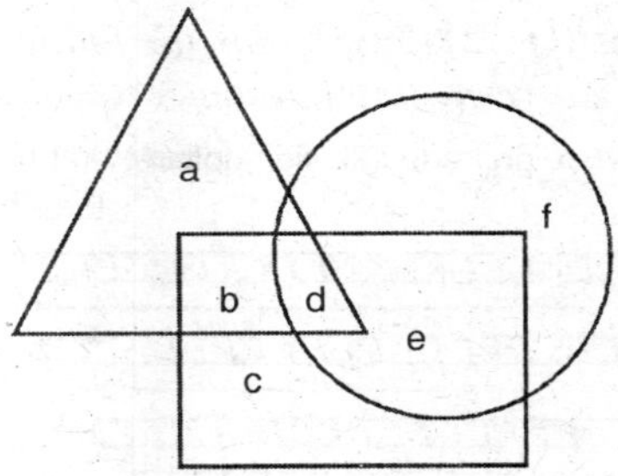

A. a B. b
C. d D. e

27. **Assertion (X) :** Legumes revive the soil fertility.
Reason (Y) : Microbes in the root nodule of legumes fix the atmosphere's nitrogen.
A. Both X and Y are true and Y is correct explanation of X.
B. Both X and Y are true but Y is not correct explanation of X.
C. X is true but Y is false.
D. X is false but Y is true.

28. You are in a bus. The bus reaches your stop but still you have not purchased the ticket because of heavy rush. What will you do?
A. Jump out quickly to avoid embarrassment.
B. Call the conductor, give him money and get the ticket.
C. Hand the money to someone sitting nearby to give it to the conductor.
D. Give the money to the driver.

29. Choose the correct alternative as the answer.
What is always in worry?
A. Difficulty B. Unrest
C. Non-cooperation D. Poignancy

30. **Statements :** All birds are dogs.
Some dogs are cats.
Conclusions :
I. Some cats are not dogs.
II. All dogs are not birds.
A. Only conclusion I follows
B. Only conclusion II follows
C. Either I or II follows
D. Neither I nor II follows

Directions (Qs. 31-35) : *Study the following graph and give answer to the questions based on it.*

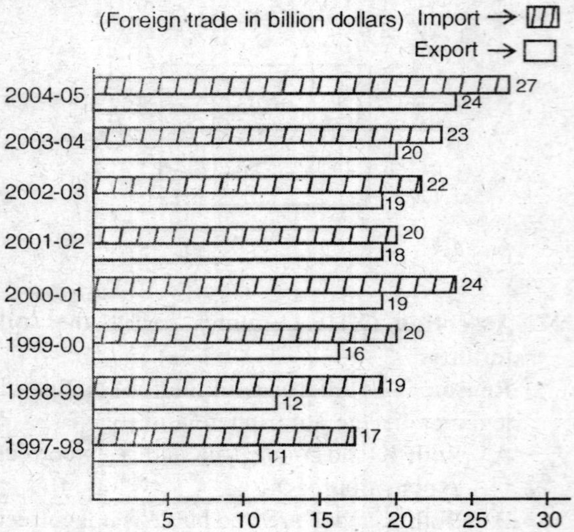

31. In which of the following years was the trade deficit highest?

A. 1997-98 B. 1998-99
C. 1999-00 D. 2000-01

32. In how many years was the trade deficit less than the trade deficit in the succeeding year?

A. 1 B. 2
C. 3 D. 4

33. Export earning in 2000-01 is how many per cent of imports in 2001-02?

A. 82% B. 85%
C. 90% D. 15%

34. In the last three years, the total export earnings have accounted for how many % of value of imports?

A. 80% B. 83%
C. 95% D. 88%

35. Which of the following statements can be inferred from the graph?

I. In all the years shown in the graph, the trade deficit is less than the export earning.
II. Export earning increased in every year between 1999-00 and 2001-02.
III. In all the years shown in the graph, the earning by exports is less than the expenditure on imports in the preceding year.

A. Only I B. Only II
C. Only III D. I and III only

36. Match List-I with List-II and select the correct answer using the code given below the lists

List-I *(Company)*	**List-II** *(Major Area/Product)*
(a) Chevron	1. Wind energy
(b) AT & T	2. Oil
(c) AMD	3. Telephone, internet
(d) Enercon GmbH	4. Micro-processor

Codes:

	(a)	(b)	(c)	(d)
A.	2	1	4	3
B.	4	3	2	1
C.	2	3	4	1
D.	4	1	2	3

37. The purpose of using computers in an organisation is ....

A. to produce reports, text, images, *etc.*
B. to be able to get an internet.
C. to process data into information.
D. All of the above

38. MICR devices can read

A. letter B. numbers
C. Both A. and B. D. None of these

39. How many rollers are responsible for movement of the cursor in mouse?

A. 1
B. 2
C. 3
D. Varies from mouse to mouse.

40. Which of the following is not an operating system?

A. LINUX B. WINDOWS
C. DOS D. C

41. What is the correct descending order of countries in terms of installed capacity of Hydro Power?

A. USA—China—Canada—Brazil—India
B. Canada—China—Brazil—USA—India
C. USA—Canada—China—Brazil—Norway
D. China—Canada—USA—Brazil—India

42. Pitchblende is the ore of

A. rubidium B. francium
C. radium D. uranium

43. Which of the following are true about Mistral?
I. It is a cold wind.
II. Originates over snow covered mountains of Alps.
III. It blows towards Mediterranean sea.
A. Only I B. Only II and III
C. Only III D. All I, II and III

44. Which of the following is not a Wet land?
A. Kabar B. Sukhna
C. Ujni D. Ketti

45. Thalghat connects
A. Pune to Mumbai
B. Nasik to Mumbai
C. Khandwa to Mumbai
D. Kolvam to Chennai

46. The members of the Council of Ministers can be dismissed by President
A. on his own.
B. on the recommendation of the Prime Minister.
C. on the recommendation of the Lok Sabha.
D. on the recommendation of the Speaker of Lok Sabha.

47. Disputes regarding the election of Vice President are decided by
A. the Speaker
B. the President
C. the Parliament
D. the Supreme Court

48. The Lok Sabha Secretariat works under the direct Supervision of
A. the Speaker
B. the Ministry of Parliamentary Affairs
C. the President of India
D. None of these

49. Which of the following bodies is presided over by non-member?
A. Rajya Sabha B. Lok Sabha
C. State Assembly D. None of these

50. Which of the following is wrongly matched?
A. Central Sanskrit Institute—Tirupati
B. Fast Breader Test Reactor—Kalpakkam
C. Indian Institute of Petroleum—Bombay High
D. Central Arid Zone Research Institute—Jodhpur

51. Directive Principles of State Policy aim at:
A. ensuring individual liberty
B. ensuring and strengthening the country's independence
C. protecting the depressed classes
D. providing social and economic base for genuine democracy in the country

52. The Council of Ministers. headed by the Prime Minister is responsible to:
A. Prime Minister B. President
C. Parliament D. Speaker

53. Usually a Gram Panchayat is not responsible for:
A. construction of village roads and tanks
B. sanitation, maternity and child welfare
C. financing of agriculturists
D. agricultural production

54. Which one of the following provides constitutional guarantee of personal freedom?
A. Quo Warranto B. Mandamus
C. Certiorari D. Habeas Corpus

55. What does the Panchayati Raj System signify?
A. single-tier structure of local Government
B. Double-tier system of self Government
C. Three-tier structure of local Govt. at the village, block and district level
D. None of these

56. Application software
A. any computer program used to create or process data such as text documents, spreadsheets, graphics etc.
B. programs to operate only mouse functions
C. a type of program designed to handle very small instruction sets.
D. None of the above

57. Desktop Publishing programs
A. belongs to Application software
B. used to literate individuals in computing
C. a type of program designed to handle very small instruction sets.
D. None of the above

58. ASCII

A. is 7 bit binary code

B. developed by American National Standards Institute (ANSI)

C. represent symbolic, numeric and alphanumeric characters

D. All the above

59. Assembler

A. is a computer program that converts assembly language instructions into machine language.

B. developed by American National Standards Institute (ANSI)

C. represent symbolic, numeric and alphanumeric characters, voice

D. All the above

60. ATM

A. stands for Asynchronous Transfer Mode

B. is a network protocol designed to send voice, video and data transmission over a single network

C. provides different kinds of connections and bandwidth on demand, depending on the type of data being transmitted

D. All the above

ANSWERS

1	2	3	4	5	6	7	8	9	10
A	D	D	A	B	C	C	B	C	A
11	**12**	**13**	**14**	**15**	**16**	**17**	**18**	**19**	**20**
D	D	A	A	C	D	A	A	B	A
21	**22**	**23**	**24**	**25**	**26**	**27**	**28**	**29**	**30**
B	B	D	B	B	B	A	B	B	D
31	**32**	**33**	**34**	**35**	**36**	**37**	**38**	**39**	**40**
B	D	C	D	A	C	D	B	B	D
41	**42**	**43**	**44**	**45**	**46**	**47**	**48**	**49**	**50**
C	D	D	D	B	B	D	A	A	C
51	**52**	**53**	**54**	**55**	**56**	**57**	**58**	**59**	**60**
D	C	C	D	C	A	A	D	A	D

SOME SELECTED EXPLANATORY ANSWERS

21. The sequence follows the following pattern

*n*th term = (*n* – 1)th term × 2 – (*n* – 1)

1st term = 12

2nd term = 12 × 2 – 1 = 23

3rd term = 23 × 2 – 2 = 44

4th term = 44 × 2 – 3 = 85

5th term = 85 × 2 – 4 = 166

6th term = 166 × 2 – 5 = 327

Hence the required term is 166.

22. The first letter of each term is moved two steps forward and the last letter is moved one step backward to obtain the corresponding letters of the next term. The number sequence runs as follows :

1 × 1 + 1 = 2, 2 × 2 + 2 = 6, 6 × 3 + 3 = 21, 21 × 4 + 4 = 81.

Hence the required term is S2E.

31. Trade deficit = (Import – Export) is highest in 1998-99.

= (19 – 12) = 7 billion dollars.

35. Statement II is not correct as export earning has remained constant for three years between 2000 and 2003. Statement III is not correct as the export in 2004-05 is more than the imports in 2003-04. Statement I is true because the trade deficit in each year is less than the export earning.

UGC-NET / JRF Exam

TEST PAPER-VII

1. As a teacher you should not demand your pupils which is beyond their stage of growth. If you do so, it only causes
   A. frustrations
   B. frustrations, heighten tension and nervousness
   C. encouragement for more learning
   D. both B. and C.

2. Which is the source of primary data
   A. Books
   B. Newspapers
   C. Respondent
   D. Reports

3. Which of the following can be termed as most import task in teaching among the given?
   A. Directing students in development of experiences.
   B. Making monthly reports and maintaining records.
   C. Making assignments and checking worksheets.
   D. All of the above

4. Which of the following is last step of teaching?
   A. Presentation
   B. Application
   C. Comparison
   D. Generalisation

5. Which of the following bodies are not responsible for curriculum making at different level?
   A. University Grants Commission
   B. State Council for Educational Research and Training
   C. National Council for Educational Research and Training
   D. Central Board of Secondary Education

6. In Research Papers (Thesis), the conclusion can be put in
   A. Result in discussion section or after it.
   B. Abstract
   C. Materials and Methods
   D. Both A. and B.

7. Which of the following persons has developed the idea of T-test?
   A. John Gloster
   B. Sir William S. Gosset
   C. A.B. Subbaiyah
   D. Ricardo L. Murphy

8. The research reports should not be reviewed in the light of
   A. Researcher's bias
   B. Cultural content
   C. Methodological factors
   D. None of these

9. Which of the following is the main problem in our higher education level?
   A. Uneven spread of research efforts and research scholars.
   B. Lack of fund.
   C. Lack of appropriate linkage.
   D. All of these

10. Who among the following considered hypothesis as an assumption or preposition?
    A. George H. Lundenberg
    B. Gorgy G. Moore
    C. Stephan Hawkins
    D. Alber D. Nero

Directions (Qs. 11-15) : *Study the following passage and give answer to the questions based on it.*

PASSAGE

I have never had much patience with the writers who claim from their reader an effort to understand their meaning. You have only to go to the great philosophers to see that it is possible to express with lucidity the most subtle reflections. You may find it difficult to understand the thought and if you have no philosophical training its implications will doubtlessly escape you, but no one with any education at all can fail to understand exactly what the meaning of each sentence is. Few people have written with more grace than Berkely.

There are two sorts of obscurity that you find in writers. One is due to negligence and other to wilfulness. People often write obscurely because they have never taken the trouble to learn to write clearly. This sort of obscurity you find often in modern philosophers, in men of science, and even in literary critics. You would have thought that men who passed their lives in the study of the greater masters of literature would be sufficiently, at least with perspicuity. Yet you will find in their works sentence after sentence that you must read twice in order to discover the sense. Often you can only guess at it, for the writers have evidently not said what they intended.

11. The author's opinion is that
- A. lucidity is the very essence of imparting instruction.
- B. lucidity may co-exist harmoniously with profundity of thought.
- C. a superficial knowledge of philosophy is required to understand the meaning of great philosophical works.
- D. the surface into depths of its thought.

12. The author's preference is for
- A. work of profound thought.
- B. works which combine lucidity and depth.
- C. works which are clear in expression.
- D. works reveal the inner philosophy of the writer.

13. A knowledge of philosophy is required to
- A. comprehend philosophical thought.
- B. realise the implications of philosophical works.
- C. understand the meaning of each sentence in an isolated fashion.
- D. Only A. and B.

14. Writers are often obscure
- A. they wish to exist in an ivory tower.
- B. their training in writing has been of such a nature.
- C. gravity of expression leads to obscurity.
- D. the layman does not have access to their exalted thoughts.

15. A statement which receives no support from the passage is this
- A. lapsing into obscurity is characteristic of all great literary critics.
- B. great philosophers have often clothed propound thoughts in simple language.
- C. clarity of expression is not an inherent trait and can be cultivated.
- D. literary critics often do not profit from their association with great writers.

16. Sharavati Hydro-electric Project is located in
- A. Orissa
- B. Tamil Nadu
- C. Andhra Pradesh
- D. Karnataka

17. Which of the following are key characteristics of communication?
- I. It is a process
- II. Communication is repeatable
- III. It is reciprocal
- IV. It begins with communicator.
- A. I, II and IV
- B. I, III and IV
- C. I, IV
- D. All of the above

18. Listening of a lecture is a type of
- A. Informational Listening
- B. Evaluating Listening
- C. Descriptive Listening
- D. Conversational Listening

19. Which one of the following is the best way to communicate with the masses?
- A. Rally
- B. Cinema
- C. Radio
- D. Posters

20. Feedback system is weakest in which of the following?

A. Interpersonal Communication
B. Intrapersonal Communication
C. Group Communication
D. Mass Communication

21. Which of the following numbers will complete the sequence:

3, 7, 16, 35, 74, ... ?

A. 155 B. 148
C. 153 D. 163

22. Which of the following combinations will complete the sequence?

MTJ, NPN, OLR, PHV

A. LUE B. LXF
C. LXE D. LWF

23. LASER is related to Acronym in the same way as DDT is related to .....

A. Antibiotic B. Abbreviation
C. Epigram D. Epithet

24. Which one of the following is different from the other three?

A. Venus B. Jupiter
C. Uranus D. Neptune

25. If in a certain code MORALE is coded as 296137 and CHARCOAL is coded as 45164913, then how will you code COLORE

A. 379758 B. 493967
C. 493917 D. 439316

26. The following fig. does not represents one of the given four relations find out the relation

A. Science, Physics, Zoology
B. Biology, Botany, Zoology
C. Wheat, Grains, Maize
D. Dog, Animals, Pet

27. **Assertion (X) :** The body of fish is stream lined.

Reason (Y) : The streamlined body helps the fish to cut its way through the water.

A. Both X and Y are true and Y is correct explanation of X.
B. Both X and Y are true and Y is not correct explanation of X.
C. X is true but Y is false.
D. X is false but Y is true.

28. **Statements :** All leaves are papers.
Some papers are pictures.

Conclusions :

I. All pictures are papers.
II. All pictures are leaves.
III. Some leaves are pictures.
IV. No leaf is a picture.

A. Only I, III and IV follow
B. Only II and III follow
C. Only III and IV follow
D. None of these

29. **Statement :** Should English be medium of instruction for higher education in India.

Arguments :

I. Yes, even in advanced countries like England and U.S.A. the medium of instruction is English for higher education.
II. Yes, English is a much widely spoken language in the world.

A. Only argument I is strong
B. Only argument II is strong
C. Either I or II is strong
D. Neither I nor II are strong

30. **Statement :** The General Manager asked four managers to either submit their resignations by the next day or face termination order from service. Three of them submitted their resignation by that evening.

Conclusions :

I. The next day, the remaining manager will also resign.
II. The General Manager will terminate his service the next day.

A. Only conclusion I follows
B. Only conclusion II follows
C. Either I or II follows
D. Both follow

Directions (Qs. 31-35) : *Study the following table carefully and answer the questions based on it.*

Number of six different products manufactured by a company over the years.

	Number of Products (in thousand)						
Year	**A**	**B**	**C**	**D**	**E**	**F**	**Total**
1997	85	106	72	47	69	94	473
1998	74	112	108	82	85	112	573
1999	63	84	132	105	102	109	595
2000	115	98	104	114	96	134	661
2001	95	101	85	92	108	115	596
2002	106	86	116	86	98	102	594
2003	88	108	118	102	108	86	610

31. The production of D-type of products in which of the following years was close to the average production of the given years?
A. 2002 B. 2003
C. 2001 D. None of these

32. The production of A-type of products in 1997 was approximately what per cent of the production of A-type products in 2000 and 2001 together?
A. 35% B. 40%
C. 60% D. 80%

33. What is the total difference between the total production of D and E-type together in 2000 and total production of C and D type in 2003?
A. 1000 B. 10,000
C. 20,000 D. 10,00,000

34. The % of production of F-type products to the total production of all types together was minimum in which of the following years among the given years?
A. 2003 B. 2000
C. 1999 D. 1998

35. What was approximate percentage decrease in the production of C-type toys from 1999 to 2000?
A. 35% B. 30%
C. 21% D. 15%

36. Which of the following is/are not true about wind energy farm?
A. The wind energy farms can be established only at those places where wind blows for most part of the year.
B. The minimum wind speed necessary for satisfactory working of a wind generator is 10 km/hr.
C. The wind energy farm requires a large land area.
D. The setting of wind energy farm is very expensive.

37. What is the full form of IUCN?
A. Indian Universal Centre of Nature
B. International Union for Conservation of Nature and Natural Resources
C. Indian Union for Conservation of Nature
D. Interaction Union for Consumption of Natural Resources

38. Which of the following National parks is famous for the Great Indian Bustard?
A. Gir National Park
B. Corbett National Park
C. Desert National Park
D. Simplipal Biosphere Reserve

39. Which of the following diseases is not caused by polluted water?
A. Typhoid B. Cholera
C. Flu D. Hepatitis

40. Chukha Hydro Electric Project is situated in
A. Sikkim B. Asom
C. Arunachal Pradesh D. Bhopal

41. Which of the following is a problem in transmission of the data signals?
A. Attenuation B. Noise
C. Delay distortion D. Cross talk

42. .... are self replicating malicious code independent of the action of the user but slow down the processes on entering a network.
A. Viruses B. Worm
C. Trojan Horse D. None of these

43. FAQ is on Website means
A. questions that are generally asked and put up by the developer himself.
B. questions that user frequently asked.

C. an urgent message.
D. none of these

44. Physical component of computer is called
A. software B. hardware
C. CPU D. program

45. Vortal is
A. an introductory webpage on a website.
B. a collection of websites on the same topic.
C. a collection of websites on different topics.
D. none of these

46. India's first Defence University is set up in
A. Haryana B. Delhi
C. Punjab D. Uttar Pradesh

47. Golden revolution refers to the development of
A. Oil-seeds B. Horticulture
C. Pulses D. Cereals

48. The Fundamental Duties were incorporated in the Constitution on the Recommendation of
A. Santhanam Committee
B. Ashok Mehta Committee
C. Swarna Singh Committee
D. None of these

49. Apart from Jammu and Kashmir, which of the following states have been provided special protection by the constitution?
A. Nagaland B. Meghalaya
C. Kerala D. Punjab

50. Which of the following Institutes is situated in Karikudi (Tamil Nadu)?
A. Central Electro Chemical Research Institute
B. Central Marine Fish Research Institute
C. Central Plantation Crop Research Institute
D. None of these

51. Out of the following, in which lesson, a geneal rule is explained first and then, knowledge is accumulated on the basis of that rule?
A. Deductive lesson
B. Inductive lesson
C. Developing lesson
D. Knowledge lesson

52. For knowledge lessons
A. Glover's Scheme is used
B. Herbart's five-stage system is used
C. Garry's scheme is used
D. none of these

53. The project education method of teaching is associated with
A. Rousseau B. Frobel
C. Dewey D. Armstrong

54. "This methodology trains the child to search for facts, rules and principles by his own efforts, organise the set of knowledge gained and delineate general rules." The aforementioned statement is about the following methodology of teaching
A. Montessory B. Kindergarten
C. Heuristic D. Play-way

55. In the project education technique, the work load on the teacher is
A. very high
B. comparatively low
C. low
D. nil

56. Backup means
A. To create a duplicate set of program or data files in case the originals become damaged.
B. Provides differtent kinds of connections and bandwidth in computers
C. the type of data transmission
D. None of the above

57. Computers are now used in
A. restaurants, automobile companies
B. offices and homes
C. research areas
D. All the above

58. Information
A. is the summarization of data
B. implies data that is organized and is meaningful to the person who is receiving it

C. should be meaningful, brief, accurate and help us to our knowledge and decision making

D. All the above

59. Data

A. can be defined as fact, observation, assumption or occurrence and is a plural of "datum"

B. in general refers to raw facts gathered from different sources.

C. denotes any or all facts, numbers, letters, symbols etc that can be processed or manipulated by a computer

D. All the above

60. Data and Information is

A. often used interchangeably

B. not used interchangeably

C. not used by people to make decisions

D. None of the above

ANSWERS

1	**2**	**3**	**4**	**5**	**6**	**7**	**8**	**9**	**10**
B	C	A	B	D	D	B	D	D	B
11	**12**	**13**	**14**	**15**	**16**	**17**	**18**	**19**	**20**
B	C	D	B	A	D	B	A	B	D
21	**22**	**23**	**24**	**25**	**26**	**27**	**28**	**29**	**30**
C	B	B	A	B	D	A	D	B	C
31	**32**	**33**	**34**	**35**	**36**	**37**	**38**	**39**	**40**
D	B	B	A	C	B	B	C	C	D
41	**42**	**43**	**44**	**45**	**46**	**47**	**48**	**49**	**50**
A	A	A	B	B	A	B	C	A	A
51	**52**	**53**	**54**	**55**	**56**	**57**	**58**	**59**	**60**
A	B	C	C	A	A	D	D	D	A

SOME SELECTED EXPLANATORY ANSWERS

21. Each number in the series is the preceding number multiplied by 2 and then increased by 1, 2, 3, ... and so on respectively.
$3 \times 2 + 1 = 7$, $7 \times 2 + 2 = 16$, $16 \times 2 + 3 = 35$, $35 \times 2 + 4 = 74$, $74 \times 2 + 5 = 153$.

23. LASER is acronym in the same way DDT is an abbreviation.

25. From the given codes :

M O R A L E
2 9 6 1 3 7

and C H A R C O A L
4 5 1 6 4 9 1 3

Hence C O L O R E
4 9 3 9 6 7.

26. Dog animal, Pet this relationship can be shown by the figure

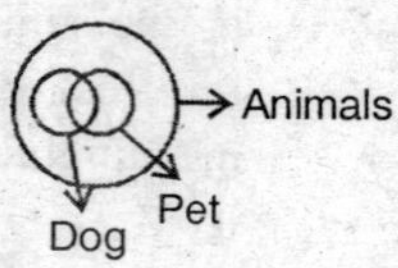

As day and pet both comes in the category of animals but some dogs can be pet also.

32. Total production of A-type in 2000 and 2001 $= 115 + 95 = 210$ thousand

$$\therefore \text{Required } \% = \frac{85}{210} \times 100 = 40.47\% \approx 40\%.$$

34. $\%$ of F-type in 2003 $= \frac{86}{210} \times 100 = 14.09\%$

$\%$ of F-type in 2000 $= \frac{134}{661} \times 100 = 20.27\%$

$\%$ of F-type in 1999 $= \frac{109}{595} \times 100 = 18.31\%$

$\%$ of F-type in 1998 $= \frac{112}{573} \times 100 = 19.54\%$

Hence it was minimum in 2003.

UGC-NET / JRF Exam

TEST PAPER-VIII

1. A teacher is successful only if he
- A. knows his subject thoroughly well
- B. produces cent precent result
- C. is approachable
- D. publishes papers in journals of repute

2. Teaching in higher education implies
- A. presenting the information given in the text book
- B. asking questions in the class and conducting examinations
- C. helping students prepare for and pass the examination
- D. helping students how to learn

3. Which is most favourable for eduction?
- A. Social Class
- B. Social Mobility
- C. Social Stratification
- D. Caste

4. In comparing the lecture and developmental lessons which one of the following is false?
- A. There is more public activity in the developmental lesson
- B. It is more difficult to ascertain public learning in a lecture lesson
- C. The lecture method is more conducive to largest class
- D. Slow children derive more benefits from a lecture than brighter children do

5. If a student becomes unconscious in the class what will you do first?
- A. Rushing to the principal's office and convassing for help immediately
- B. Telephoning (informing) student's parents and wait for them
- C. Giving first aid to him and trying to contact any nearby doctor
- D. Making arrangement to send him to his house or nearby hospital

6. In higher education, research and teaching are two different activities that
- A. cannot go together
- B. can go together
- C. can go, if at all, only in sequential order
- D. can go together at the expense of each other

7. In every field research pursuits promote systematic and gradual advancement of knowledge but discoveries are rare because
- A. research is a continuous critical investigation
- B. it is not common to be able to think beyond a groved channel
- C. sustained experimental work needed for discoveries is not easily forthcoming
- D. most people lack depth of knowledge needed for it.

8. D. Slesinger and M. Stephenson define research as

I. manipulation of things
II. concepts or symbols for the purpose of generalising to extend
III. correct or verify knowledge

- A. Only II
- B. I and III
- C. I and II
- D. All of these

9. Among the following which one is most important characteristic of research process?
- A. Communicability
- B. Generalisation
- C. Repetition
- D. Objectivity

10. Who among the following used the term "variance" for the first time?
- A. J. L. Bayerd
- B. J. L. Murphy
- C. R. A. Fisher
- D. Rudi Shawn

Directions (Qs. 11-15): *Study the following passage carefully and answer the questions based on it.*

PASSAGE

The artificial intelligence quotient should seek to replace the time tested I-Q. as a measure of mental ability is prefectly in consonance with the present day standards in a plastic society. However, the batter over grey cells whether in human or in mechanical minds whose latest round has found Uncle Sam shedding crocodile tears over Japan's failure to deliver on its promise to produce a fifth generation computer, may find the Asian Tiger Cub—the under 35 Japanese researchers having the last laugh. For, though all the boastful Tokyo talk a decade ago to build 1,000 processor compare to process knowledge - and not merely numbers which is all the silicon valley chips supposed by do-has remained just talk, the 180 young scientists in the 10-year venture has nevertheless made the big brains at silicon valley look rather silly with their products which has a yen for logical programming. The jubilation in the valley may turn to depression when the inexorable logic of this development pulls down Washington from its pedestral of super computer supremacy.

11. Asian Tiger Cubs are
- A. the big brain at silicon valley
- B. fifth generation computers
- C. young Japanese researchers
- D. mechanical minds

12. Uncle Sam reacts to the failure of Japanese with
- A. insincere sorrow
- B. jubilation
- C. sorrow
- D. depression

13. What have the cubs failed to produce?
- A. Artificial Intelligence
- B. Grey Cell
- C. Fifth generation computers
- D. Mechanical minds

14. What have they suceeded in producing?
- A. A knowledge processing computer
- B. A product which has a yen for logical programming
- C. Grey Cells
- D. A fifth generation computer

15. How is their success likely to affect Washington supremacy in the field of super computer?
- A. It is likely to have the last laugh
- B. It is likely to produce jubilation in the valley
- C. It is likely to dislodge it
- D. It is likely to make it look silly

16. An effective communication does not require
- A. change in speech pattern
- B. appropriate gesture
- C. mastery of content
- D. handsome personality

17. Which of the following will make communication more effective?
- A. Cutting jokes in between
- B. Using multi-sensory appeal
- C. Speaking with high authority
- D. Telling what is useful to the listner

18. A teacher will become an effective communicator if -
- A. he uses instructional aids
- B. he helps students get meaning out of what he teaches
- C. he helps students get correct answer to the questions on the topic
- D. he asks questions in between teaching

19. Which of the following can be termed as feed back in terms of newpaper's communication?
- A. Letters to editor
- B. Editorial
- C. News
- D. Articles

20. DTH (Direct to Home) service is related to
- A. TV communication
- B. Cinema
- C. Radio
- D. None of these

21. The following statement "English is an invaluable asset in International communication" is a/an
- A. fact
- B. advice
- C. opinion
- D. prejudice

22. ELEGANCE is related to VULGARITY in the same way as GRACEFUL is related to

A. AWKWARD B. COMELY
C. ASPERITY D. DIRTY

23. Choose the odd pair/group in this question
A. 7 - 84 B. 6 - 108
C. 5 - 75 D. 3 - 99

24. Find the next number in the following series
24, 60, 120, 210--------?
A. 300 B. 336
C. 420 D. 525

25. In a certain code language, 419 means fruit is sweet, 248 means very sweet voice and 637 means eat fruit daily then 9 stands for
A. eat B. is
C. daily D. fruit

Directions (Qs.26-27): *The following figure represents a set of persons. The triangle represents educated people, the rectangle represents policemen, the ellipse represents road tax payers and the circle represents shopkeepers.*

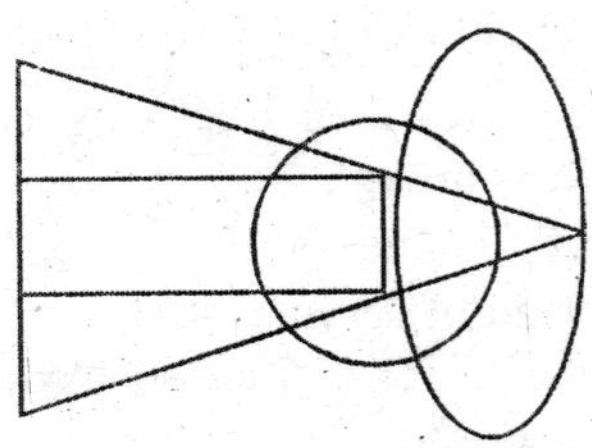

26. According to the figure, it follows that
A. policemen do not pay road tax
B. shopkeepers do not pay road tax
C. all shopkeepers are educated
D. some policemen are uneducated

27. From the above figure it can be concluded
A. Some shopkeepers are educated and some pay road tax
B. All educated policemen pay road tax
C. All road tax paying policemen are educated
D. Some road tax payers are uneducated

28. Statements :
Some players are singers.
All singles are tall.
Conclusion :
I. Some players are tall.
II. All players are tall.
A. Only conclusion I follows
B. Only conclusion II follows
C. Both I and II follow
D. Neither I nor II follows

29. Statement : Should we scrap 'Public Distribution System' (PDS) in India?
Arguments :
I. Yes, Protectivism is over, everyone must get the bread on his own.
II. Yes, the poor do not get any benefit because of corruption.
A. Only argument I is strong
B. Only argument II is strong
C. Both are strong
D. Neither of two is strong

30. Statement : During pre-harvest of *Kharif* season, the government has decided to release vast quantity of foodgrains from FCI.
Assumptions :
I. There may be shortage of foodgrains in the market during this season.
II. The *kharif* crop may be able to replenish the stock of FCI.
III. There may be a demand from the farmers to procure *kharif* crop immediately after harvest.
A. All are implicit
B. Only II and III are implicit
C. Only I and II are implicit
D. None is implicit

Study the following pie chart and give answers to the questions based on it.

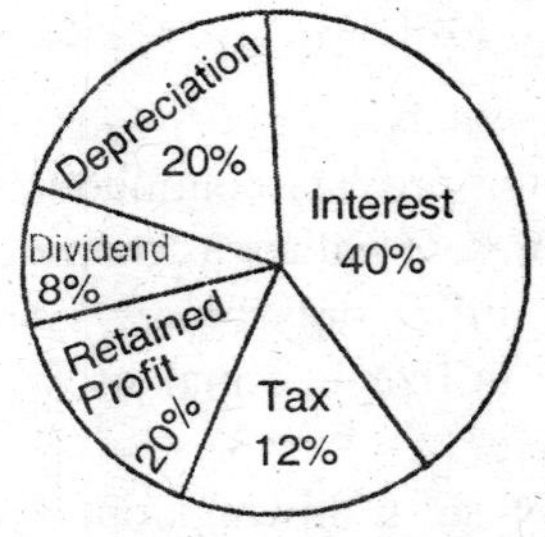

Operating profit Rs 160 Lakh
(2001-02)

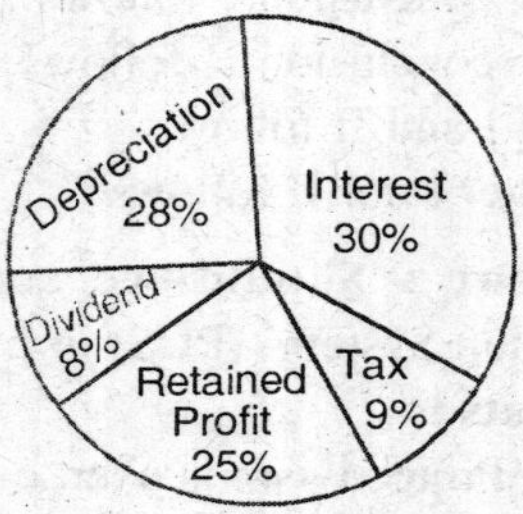

Operating profit Rs 130 Lakh
(2000-01)

31. The operating profit in 2001-02 registered an increase over 2000-01 by

A. 23% B. 22%
C. 25 % D. 24 %

32. Interest burden in 2001-02 was higher than that in 2000-01 is

A. 50 Lakh B. 25 Lakh
C. 90 Lakh D. 41 Lakh

33. If on an average, 20% rate of interest was charged on borrowed fund, then the total borrowed funds used by this company in the given two years amounted to

A. Rs. 221 Lakh B. Rs. 195 Lakh
C. Rs. 368 Lakh D. Rs. 515 Lakh

34. The retained profit in 2001-02 as compared to 2000-01 was

A. higher by 2.5 % B. higher by 1.5 %
C. lower by 2.5 % D. lower by 1.5 %

35. The equity base of these companies remained unchanged. Then the total dividend earning by the share holders in 2001-02 is

A. Rs. 10.4 Lakh B. Rs. 9 Lakh
C. Rs. 12.8 Lakh D. Rs. 15.6 Lakh

36. Digital signals

I. do not provide continuous set of values
II. Represent values as discrete steps
III. can utilize only binary system
IV. can utilize decimal as well as binary system

Which of the followings options is true?

A. Only (I) and (II)
B. Only II and III
C. Only I, II and III but not IV
D. All of these, I, II, III and IV

37. Which of the following are true about MIME?

A. It is a compressor that packages different formats into SMTP compatible type
B. It is a transport agent for e-mailing
C. It is an interface between mail client and web server
D. None of these

38. Digital Subscriber Line Access Multiplener (DSLAM) is used for

A. high speed data transfer
B. developing efficient digital network over existing one
C. accessing remote computer
D. synchronising protocols of diferent network

39. Which virus attaches itself to command.com file?

A. Trojan B. System infector
C. Boot infector D. Stealth

40. Hackers cover their tracks by masking their IP address through

A. Proxy chaining
B. Denian of service
C. Secure Sockets Layer Hacking
D. IP spoofing

41. In the interior of earth –

A. the temperature falls with increasing depth
B. the pressure falls with increasing depth
C. the temperature rises with increasing depth
D. pressure remains constant with varying depth

42. In case of distant earth quake, which waves are the last to reach the observer?

A. P - waves
B. S - waves
C. L - waves
D. All of them reach simultaneously

43. What is meant by Van Allen's radiation bets?

A. Layers of concentration of ozone in stratosphere
B. Belts in atmosphere containing most of water vapour

C. Atmospheric belts of concentration of charge particles
D. The belts on the earth receiveing maximum insolation

44. What are the characteristics of cyclones?
I. Tropical cyclones have a circular shape.
II. Tropical cyclones develop only over seas.
III. Temperate cyclones result from air mass convergence.
IV. Temperate cyclones generally develops over land.
A. Only II and III
B. Only I and IV
C. Only II and IV
D. All of these (I, II, III and IV)

45. Montreal protocol is related to
A. Ozone depletion B. Nuclear weapons
C. Sea-bed D. Landmines

46. In the context of Panchayati Raj, which one of the following is true about aram sabha?
A. This is topmost tier of Panchayati Raj
B. It consists of all the voters residing in the juridiction of a village panchayat
C. It is executive body consisting of selected representative from village panchayat
D. It consists of all the adult males of village panchayat

47. In case of absence of both the President and the Vice President who acts as the president of the country?
A. Speaker of Lok Sabha
B. The Prime Minister
C. Chief Justice of Supreme Court
D. Minister of Home Affairs

48. Who is legally competent under the Indian constitution to declare war or conclude peace?
A. The President B. The PM
C. Council of Ministers
D. None of these

49. NASA is the name of space agency of
A. USA B. USSR
C. China D. France

50. Central Forensic Science Laboratory is situated in
A. Chandigarh B. Patna
C. Patiala D. Ludhiana

51. In Garry's Plan
A. work is important
B. play is important
C. learning is important
D. all these three have equal importance

52. Under the Wennetka Plan
A. the diversity of interests of the students is recognised
B. the diversities of abilities are accepted
C. the diversities of needs are accepted
D. all of these are recognised

53. The Dalton Scheme of education is useful for which ones of the following?
A. For infants
B. For little children
C. For older children
D. For all of these

54. Why do you not support the five-stage method of Herbart?
A. In this, there is no scope for the individual diversity of students
B. Under this, it is difficult to make coordination between various subjects
C. Under this, generalisation is not required to be done while teaching subjects like language, history, geography etc.
D. all of these

55. "In the school, provisions must be made for free and natural expressions of a child." Who give this statement?
A. T. Remont B. Ryeburn
C. Montessori D. Lyndon

56. Logical data refers
A. to the way in which the data are recorded on the storage medium
B. in general refers to processed facts gathered from different sources
C. can be defined as fact, observation, assumption or occurrence and is a plural of "datum"
D. None of the above

57. Data item
A. is a basic or individual element of data
B. is identified by a name and is assigned a value
C. is something referred to as a field
D. All the above

58. Smallest addressable unit in computer
A. Byte—an arbitrary set of eight bits that represents a character
B. FM
C. TPM
D. None of the above

59. File
A. is a collection of related records
B. is a automated processing system
C. TDM
D. None of the above

60. In electronic form, data refers to
A. data fields, records, files and databases
B. word processing documents, graphics, images
C. digitally coded voice and video
D. All the above

ANSWERS

1	2	3	4	5	6	7	8	9	10
A	D	C	D	C	C	A	D	D	A
11	**12**	**13**	**14**	**15**	**16**	**17**	**18**	**19**	**20**
C	A	C	B	C	D	D	B	A	A
21	**22**	**23**	**24**	**25**	**26**	**27**	**28**	**29**	**30**
A	A	A	B	B	A	D	A	D	A
31	**32**	**33**	**34**	**35**	**36**	**37**	**38**	**39**	**40**
A	B	D	D	C	C	A	A	B	A
41	**42**	**43**	**44**	**45**	**46**	**47**	**48**	**49**	**50**
C	C	C	D	A	B	C	A	A	A
51	**52**	**53**	**54**	**55**	**56**	**57**	**58**	**59**	**60**
D	D	C	D	C	A	D	A	A	D

SOME SELECTED EXPLANATORY ANSWERS

22. The words in each pair are antonyms to each other.

23. In all other pairs, the second number is obtained by multiplying the square of the first number by a prime number.
Thus, $108 = 6^2 \times 3$, $75 = 5^2 \times 3$, $99 = 3^2 \times 11$.

24. The pattern is +36, +60, +90, --------------
i.e., $+[6 \times (6 + 0)]$, $+[6 \times (6 + 4)]$, $+[6 \times (6 + 9)]$
$\therefore$ Missing number $= 210 + [6 \times (6 + 15)] = 210 + 126 = 336$

25. In the first and second statements, the common code digit is 4 and the common word is sweet, so 4 means sweet. In the first and third statements, the common code digit is 7 and the common word is fruit, so, 7 means fruit. Thus in the first sentence 9 means is.

28. Since one premise is particular, so the conclusion must be particular. Hence only conclusion I follows.

29. The PDS system is indeed necessary to provide basic amenities to the economically backward section of population. So, argument I is vague. Also, if the objective of a system is not fulfilled due to corruption then getting rid of system in no solution. Instead efforts should be made to end corruption and extend its benefits to the people for which it is meant. So argument II is not valid.

31. Required % increase in operating profit

$$= \frac{160 - 130}{130} \times 100 = 23\%.$$

32. Interest in 2000-01 = 30% of 130

= Rs. 39 Lakh.

Interest in 2001-02 = 40% of 160

= Rs. 64 Lakh

∴ Difference (64 – 39) = Rs. 25 Lakh

33. Total interest = 39 + 64 = Rs. 103 Lakh

Given Interest is calculated on 20% of borrowed fund.

Hence borrowed funds = $\frac{103 \times 100}{20}$

= Rs. 515 Lakh.

34. Retained profit in 2000 - 01 = 25% of 130 = Rs. 32.5 Lakh

Retained profit in 2001 - 02 = 20% of 160 Rs. 32 Lakh

% change = $\frac{32.5 - 32}{32.5} \times 100 = 1.5$ %. decrease.

35. Total divided earned by share holders in 2001-02

= 8 % of 160 = 12.8 Lakh.

38. Digital signals represented by 0 and 1 do not provide continuous set of values, they represent values in discrete steps, utilize only binary system, and cannot utilize decimal system.

UGC-NET / JRF Exam

TEST PAPER-IX

1. Which of the following is true about Modern Annual Examination System?
- A. It encourages attaining knowledge by cramming.
- B. It doesn't encourage the habit of regular study.
- C. It doesn't encourage students to attain their classes regularly.
- D. All of these

2. To gain popularity among students, teacher should :
- A. personally help them in their study
- B. frequently organize tours
- C. dictate notes while teaching
- D. maintain good social relationship

3. Which of the following is a disadvantage of teaching machine?
- A. The insurance of attention
- B. Their universal use for different kinds of programmes
- C. The tracking of errors
- D. All of these

4. Of the following, the educator who is not an advocate of radical educational reform is :
- A. Postman
- B. Illich
- C. Bestor
- D. Kozol

5. A culturally disadvantaged child is best served by the school system that :
- A. places him/her in a class with other culturally disadvantaged children.
- B. gives him/her annual intelligence test
- C. trains teacher to understand his/her impoverished home background
- D. assesses his/her strengths and needs and provide for an individualized learning plan.

6. With regard to standardised testing, which of the following statements is correct?
- A. The testing of intelligence began in Germany
- B. The Weschsler Intelligence Scale for Children (WISC) is a group test
- C. The Rorschach test uses ink bot
- D. The Thematic Apperception Test (TAT) is easy to interpret

7. The research which tests the hypothesis developed through exploratory research and suggests a new idea or a new opportunity is known as :
- A. Applied Research
- B. Conclusive Research
- C. Descriptive Research
- D. Action Research

8. Which of the following is not a characteristic of hypothesis?
- A. It must consist of known facts.
- B. It can be tested.
- C. It must be clear in concept.
- D. All of these are characteristics of hypothesis.

9. A researcher wanted to know the future of Congress (I). Which one of the following steps, is most appropriate for him?
- A. Personal Interview
- B. Mail Questionnaire
- C. Rating scale
- D. None of these

10. If a social researcher wants to find some fact abut society without using any verbal or written methods like interview and questionnaire respectively, what will he do for it?
- A. Observation
- B. Implications
- C. Work scheduling
- D. None of these

Directions (Qs. 11-15) : *Study the following passage carefully and give answer to the questions based on it.*

PASSAGE

Mountaineering is now looked upon as the king of sports. But men have lived amongst the mountains since prehistoric times and in some parts of the world, as in the Andes and Himalaya, difficult mountain journeys have inevitably been part of their life. However, some of the peaks were easily accessible from most of the cities of Europe. It is quite interesting that while modern mountaineers prefer difficult routes for the greater enjoyment of sports, the early climbers looked for the easiest ones, for the summit was the prize they all set their eyes on. Popular interest in mountaineering increased considerably after the ascent of the Alpine peak of Matterhorn in 1865 and Edward Whymper's dramatic account of climb and fatal accident which occurred during the desceut.

In the risky sport of mountaineering the element of competition between either individual or teams is totally absent. Rather one can say that the competition is between the team and the peaks themselves. The individuals making up a party must climb together as a team, for they depend upon one another for their safety. Mountaineering can be dangerous unless reasonable precautions are taken. However, the majority of fatal accidents happen to parties which are inexperienced or not properly equipped. Since many accidents are caused by bad weather, the safe climber is the man who knows when it is fine to turn back, however tempting it may be to press on and try to reach the summit.

11. Mountaineering is different from the other sports because :
A. there is no competition between individuals.
B. it is thrilling and exciting.
C. it can be fatal.
D. it is risky and dangerous.

12. People living in the Andes and the Himalayas made mountain journeys because :
A. it was a kind of sport.
B. they had to undertake them in their day-to-day life.
C. they lived in pre-historic times.
D. of the challenge offered by the difficult journey.

13. Mountaineers climb as a team because :
A. the height is too much for an individual.
B. they have to rely on each other for safety.
C. there is no competition among them.
D. the competition is between peak and individuals.

14. ".... the summit was the prize they all set their eyes on. In the context of passage this means.
A. they choose a route from which they can easily see the peak.
B. reaching on top is their exclusive concern.
C. they cared for nothing except the prize of reaching the summit.
D. none of these

15. "To press on" the phrase means :
A. to continue in a determined manner.
B. to work fearlessly.
C. to force upon other.
D. to struggle in a forceful manner.

16. In which year, the first printing press was established in India?
A. 1774 B. 1556
C. 1674 D. 1574

17. Which of the following is/are a prerequisite for effective mass communication like a lag rally?
(*i*) Audience involvement and their feedback.
(*ii*) Appropriate gestures of the communicator.
(*iii*) Voice modulation.
(*iv*) Good communication ability.
A. Only (*i*), (*ii*) and (*iv*)
B. Only (*ii*), (*iii*) and (*iv*)
C. Only (*i*), (*iii*) and (*iv*)
D. Only (*i*), (*ii*) and (*iii*)

18. Which of the following channels provides coaching on TV for different classes of secondary and higher secondary level?
A. Jagaran B. Shakti
C. Zee Network D. None of these

19. Match the following:

List-I (Type of Communication)	**List-II (Use)**
(a) Intra personal communication	1. An interview
(b) Interpersonal communication	2. A big rally
(c) Group communication	3. Talking to oneself
(d) Mass communication	4. Communication in a class

Codes :

	(a)	(b)	(c)	(d)
A.	1	2	3	4
B.	3	1	2	4
C.	2	4	1	3
C.	4	3	2	1

20. SMS is a :

A. audio-visual way of communication.
B. written communication.
C. audio-communication.
D. visual communication.

21. Find the next number in the following sequence :

1, –8, 9, –64, 25, –216, ?, ?

A. 49, –512
B. 36, – 343
C. 64, –343
D. None of these

22. Complete the following series by choosing the best alternatives given below

RAP, MAP, HOT, FUN ?

A. HNE B. CAT
C. TEA D. GHK

23. What is the missing number × in the following series?

9, 15, 23, 33, ☒

A. 42 B. 38
C. 40 D. 45

24. Two words are given which are related in some manner. You have to pick out from the given option which has the same relationship as the original pair.

Zoology : Biology

A. Communication : Computer
B. Door : House
C. Astronomy : Physics
D. Geography : History

25. If in a different language Air is called water, water is called dust, dust is called green, green is called blue, blue is called sky, sky is called yellow, yellow is called red. Then what will be the colour of oceans?

A. Green B. Sky
C. Blue D. White

26. Which one of the following figures will represent the relationship between vehicles from Mahindra Scorpio, Bolero?

A. 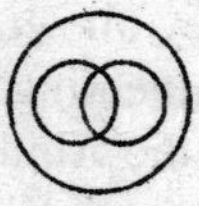

B. 

C. 

D. 

27. In this question there are two statements followed by four conclusions. Choose the best one after applying logical reasoning :

Statements : Gold is ductile.
This substance is not ductile.

Conclusions :

A. This substance is not gold.
B. All ductile things are gold.
C. This substance is gold.
D. None of these

28. **Statement :** Should military training be made incumbent on all school and college going students:

Arguments :

(*i*) Yes, it will inculcate discipline among them.

(*ii*) No, it will bring regimentation in education.

A. Only argument (*i*) is strong
B. Only arguments (*ii*) is strong
C. Both arguments (*i*) and (*ii*) are strong
D. Neither (*i*) nor (*ii*) is strong

29. Statement: Indian scientists working abroad do not come back and serve their mother land.

Assumptions:

(i) India lacks such highly sophisticated labs, instruments and other amenities as they have there

(ii) India cannot afford to pay them as much as they are getting there.

A. Only assumption (i) is implicit
B. Only assumption (ii) is implicit
C. Both assumptions (i) and (ii) are implicit
D. Neither (i) nor (ii) is implicit

30. On the basis of logic, find the answer of this questions.

Statements :

(*i*) There is dampness in the climate of Congo.

(*ii*) Too much dampness in the climate is harmful to the health of its inhabitants.

Conclusion : Dampness in Congo forest is harmful to the health of its inhabitants.

A. Only first statement supports the conclusion
B. Only second statement supports the conclusion
C. Both the statements together support the conclusion
D. Neither of them supports the conclusion

Directions (Qs. 31 - 35) : *Study the following table and give answer to the questions given below.*

A Company was started in 1999 with certain initial strengths in different units as shown in table. In the beginning subsequent years some of the workers left and new workers joined.

Year / 1999 initial strength	A (156)		B (132)		C (98)		D (76)		E (125)	
	Joined	Left	Joined	Left	Joined	Left	Joined	Left	Joined	Left
2000	15	12	32	23	36	12	26	06	13	11
2001	18	17	14	16	19	08	28	17	15	11
2002	20	09	12	12	14	17	16	09	16	19
2003	40	32	17	14	35	23	23	12	14	23
2004	35	22	15	11	25	18	24	14	38	32
2005	32	26	21	17	18	13	19	11	36	21

31. What was the strength of unit B in 2003?

A. 142 B. 207
C. 165 D. 132

32. What was the strength of all the five in 2001?

A. 647 B. 670
C. 697 D. 703

33. Which unit had the highest number of workers in 2004?

A. A B. B
C. C D. D

34. Strength of unit C in 2001 is approximately what % of strength of unit 'E' in 2002?

A. 94 B. 104
C. 84 D. 114

35. Initial strength of unit 'D' increased/decreased by approximately what % in 2003?

A. 64.47% increase B. 67.47% decrease
C. 47.67% increase D. 47.67% decrease

36. A fire-wall does not block :

A. inbound traffic from an authenticated source.
B. inbound traffic from a non authenticated source.
C. inbound traffic without any source address.
D. none of these

37. The activity of sending commands to other computers and receiving the output, is known as :

A. File Transfer Protocol (FTP)
B. Gopher
C. Telnet
D. None of these

38. ... is the agency that interacts with hardware to process via ... in UNIX.
A. Kernal, shell commands
B. Shell, Kernal commands
C. Kernal, Data
D. Shell, Data

39. Which of the virus overtakes computer system when it books and destroy information?
A. Trojan
B. System infectors
C. Boot infectors
D. Stleath virus

40. 8087 is :
A. Integrated circuit
B. Mathematical Processor
C. Peripheral
D. All of these

41. Which of the following states receives maximum cyclones in India?
A. Andhra Pradesh B. Gujarat
C. Maharashtra D. Goa

42. Great channel separates India from :
A. Sri Lanka B. Myanmar
C. Bangladesh D. Indonesia

43. Renukoot is famous for :
A. Penicillin factory
B. Ispat Industry
C. Aluminium
D. Fertilisers

44. Earthquakes are most frequent in the areas of :
A. Volcanoes
B. Plate Boundaries
C. Active fault
D. None of these

45. Which among the following states/union territories has no identified tribal community?
A. Uttar Pradesh B. Uttarakhand
C. Delhi D. Chhattisgarh

46. Which of the following energy is most utilized in biomass?
A. Solar energy
B. Tidal energy
C. Geothermal energy
D. Atomic energy

47. The state government does not enjoy any control over local bodies.
A. in financial matters
B. with regard to legislation
C. with regard to personnel matter
D. with regard to grievances of citizen

48. Match the following :

List-I	List-II
(a) Control of wind erosion of soil	1. Desertification
(b) Effect of soil erosion	2. Agricultural base
(c) Biodegradable waste	3. Acid rain
(d) Sulpher dioxide	4. Aforestation

Codes :

	(a)	(b)	(c)	(d)
A.	4	1	2	3
B.	1	2	3	4
C.	3	4	1	2
D.	2	3	4	1

49. Who of the following enjoys the distinction of being first Chief Justice of India (CJI)?
A. Mehar Chand Mahajan
B. Patanjali Shashtri
C. Hiralal J. Kania
D. B. K. Mukherjee

50. Match the following :

Central University	Year of Establishment
(a) University of Hyderabad	1. 1922
(b) University of Delhi	2. 1985
(c) Pondicherry University	3. 1974
(d) Banaras Hindu University	4. 1916

Codes :

	(a)	(b)	(c)	(d)
A.	3	1	2	4
B.	4	2	1	3
C.	1	4	3	2
D.	2	3	4	1

51. According to Dewry, education is a

A. Social need
B. Personal need
C. Psychological need
D. theoretical need

52. In the context of education, some views of Gandhiji have been appended below. Which one of them is incorrect?

A. In education, experimentation, work and research must be given due places
B. Education must be self-dependent
C. Literacy is education
D. Education must be such as to develop all the powers and inherent qualities of children

53. Who is known as the father of educational psychology?

A. Pestology B. Devy
C. Herbart D. Spencer

54. "There should be no difference between the words and deeds of a teacher." who gave this statement?

A. Meckennan B. John Locke
C. Rousseau D. Aristotle

55. Who gave the principle of "pupil activity?"

A. Rousseau B. Handezrson
C. Comenius D. Binet

56. Data processing is the

A. process of converting data from physical format to logical format
B. digitally coded voice and video
C. Both A and B
D. None of the above

57. Electronic mail is the

A. transmission of letters, messages and memos over a communications network
B. Distribution of all information functions in the office
C. Both A. and B.
D. None of the above

58. The back bone of an E-mail system is a communication network that connects remote terminals to a

A. central system or local area network that interconnect personal computers
B. digitally coded voice and video
C. Both A and B
D. None of the above

59. FAX or Facsimile

A. is the communication of a printed page between remote locations
B. terminals scan a paper form and converts its image into analog code for transmission over private lines/public dial-up telephone system
C. receiving terminal reconverts the codes into images and prints a "facsimile" of the original page
D. All the above

60. Data processing cycle consists of

A. three basic steps—Input cycle, Processing cycle, Output cycle
B. terminals which scan a paper form and converts its image into analog code for transmission
C. receiving terminal reconverts the codes into images and prints a "facsimile " of the original page
D. All the above

ANSWERS

1	2	3	4	5	6	7	8	9	10
D	A	A	C	D	C	B	D	B	A
11	12	13	14	15	16	17	18	19	20
C	B	B	B	A	C	B	B	B	B
21	22	23	24	25	26	27	28	29	30
A	B	D	C	B	B	A	B	C	C

31	32	33	34	35	36	37	38	39	40
A	B	A	B	A	A	C	A	D	D
41	**42**	**43**	**44**	**45**	**46**	**47**	**48**	**49**	**50**
A	B	C	C	C	A	C	A	C	A
51	**52**	**53**	**54**	**55**	**56**	**57**	**58**	**59**	**60**
A	C	C	A	D	A	A	A	D	A

Some Selected Explanatory Answers

21. This sequence contains two series together :

I. 1, 9, 25, ... It is an odd sequence which is increasing with the pattern of n^2.

II. –8, – 64, –216, ... It is even sequence increasing with the pattern of $(-n)^3$.

It means the sequence is going with an alternative pattern of n^2, $(-n)^3$

1st number $= n^2 = 1^2 = 1$
2nd number $= (-n)^3 = (-2)^3 = -8$
3rd number $= 3^2 = 9$
4th number $= -4^3 = -64$
5th number $= 5^2 = 25$
6th number $= (-6)^3 = -216$
7th number $= 7^2 = 49$
8th number $= (-8)^3 = -512$

so the required numbers are 49, –512.

22. Here, in the given sequence one vowel is between two consonants.

The same pattern is in CAT. In TEA, there are two vowels.

24. Zoology is a branch of Biology in the same manner Astronomy is a branch of Physics.

31. Strength of unit B in 1999 =132

Number of workers who left till 2003=
23 + 16 + 12 + 14 = 65

Number of workers who joined till 2003
= 32 + 14 + 12 + 17 = 75

Hence strength of unit B in 2003
= 132 + 75 – 65 = 142.

32. Strength of unit A in 2001 = 156 + (15 – 12 + 18 – 17) = 160

Strength of unit B in 2001 = 132 + (32 – 23 + 14 – 16) = 139)

Strength of unit C in 2001 = 98 + (36 – 12 + 19 – 8) = 133

Strength of unit D in 2001 = 76 + (26 – 6 + 28 –17) = 107

Strength of unit E in 2001 = 125 + (13 – 11 + 15 – 11) = 131

Hence total strength of company in 2001 = 160 + 139 + 133 + 107 + 131 = 670.

33. Strength of unit A in 2003 = 156 + (15 – 12 + 18 – 17 + 20 – 9 + 40 – 32 + 35 – 22) = 192

Strength of unit B in 2003 = 132 + (32 – 23 + 14 – 16 + 12 – 12 + 17 – 14 + 15 – 11) = 146

Strength of unit C in 2003 = 98 + (36 – 12 + 19 – 8 + 14 – 17 + 35 – 23 + 25 – 18) = 144

Strength of unit D in 2003 = 76 + (26 – 6 + 28 – 17 + 16 – 9 + 23 – 12 + 24 – 14) = 135

Hence, in 2003 the strength was highest of Company A.

34. Strength of workers in unit C in 2001
= 98 + (36 – 12 + 19 – 8) = 133

Strength of workers in unit E in 2002
= 125 + (13 – 11 + 15 – 11 + 16 – 19) = 128

Hence required % = $\frac{133}{128} \times 100 = 103.9\% \approx$ 104%.

35. Strength of workers in unit D in 1999
= 76

Increase in strength of workers in 2003
= 26 – 6 + 28 – 17 + 16 – 9 + 23 – 12 = 49

Hence % increase $= \frac{49}{76} \times 100 = 64.47\%$.

UGC-NET / JRF Exam

TEST PAPER-X

1. Teacher's professionalism means :
   A. the extent to which a teacher subscribes to a professional code
   B. a teacher has to teach for the sake of getting salaries
   C. a teacher must have completed professional teachers training course before his appointment
   D. All of these

2. Which of the following is not a quality of teacher?
   A. Teacher should be keen in his work and should be enthusiastic and anxious to keep his knowledge fresh and update.
   B. He should have feelings of love and sympathy.
   C. His language should be understandable to students.
   D. He may not know child psychology.

3. A serious minded teacher as a rule :
   A. allows the mistakes to be committed and explains how to minimise those mistakes
   B. never allows mistakes on the part of his students
   C. takes all precaution so that students never commit mistakes
   D. should mildly punish students who commit mistakes

4. When one of your best friends seeks your assistance to get his ward's admission in the institution. How would you extend your co-operation to him?
   A. You would extend all type of support as have special relationship.
   B. You would not help him.
   C. You would put forward some lame excuses.
   D. None of these

5. The major duty entrusted to the teacher community is :
   A. to change human nature to conform to social expectation
   B. to adjust his/her pupils to conform to the demands of society
   C. to teach students how to adjust themselves to the social demand
   D. to harmonise the needs of the child and the demands of society for the benefit of both

6. On matter of academics (knowledge) a researcher should consider himself as :
   A. entirely dependent on the teacher
   B. open minded and radical
   C. a status quo maintainer
   D. fairly knowledgeable

7. A farmer considered age old method of ploughing better than the latest methods available to him. In arriving at this conclusion he is being influenced by :
   A. tradition B. experience
   C. reasoning D. experiment

8. The systematic and objective analysis and recording of controlled observations that may lead to the development of generalisation principles or theories, resulting in prediction and possibly ultimate control of event is known as :
   A. research B. hypothesis
   C. variables D. none of these

9. The research which tests the hypotheses developed through exploratory research and may suggest a new idea or new opportunity is known as :
   A. conclusive research
   B. descriptive research
   C. fundamental or pure or basic research
   D. none of these

10. What is the full form of TAT?

A. Technologically Approved Thesis
B. Thematic Appreciation Test
C. Thesis Approval Test
D. Technology Approval Test

Directions (Qs. 11-16) : *Study the following passage and give answer to the questions based on it.*

PASSAGE

For much of Africa and most of its people, the twentieth century is ending almost as it began, it in a state of utter despair and anomie. Some Africanists have started to draw parallels between the current malaise and the Africa of the mid-19th century 'after the end of the slave trade and before the imposition of direct colonial domination' when, paradoxically, the continent was marginalized from the world economy and yet 'highly dependent on it.' By the end of that century, however, African societies found themselves at the receiving end of socio-economic forces of contraction and expansion, which resulted in the establishment of colonial rule by European powers. Who would have anticipated that, barely halfway into the twentieth century, the enfeebled, conquered, and colonized peoples of Africa would orchestrate one of the most spectacular victories of our time: the largely peaceful overthrow of European rule. And who would have guessed that by the end of the twentieth century some Africanists and Africans would be advocating a return to colonial domination.

As we approach the turn of the century, three competing perspectives and prevalent images dominate the theoretical and disciplinary discourses on Africa. The first- which we shall call neo-Malthusian Afro-pessimism- is characteristically hyper-sensational but also simple and sufficiently objective in its description of the facts to command the widespread attention of diplomats, policy-makers, and scholars. Aside from its descriptive ease, the popularity of this school, derives from two interrelated factors: its origins in iconoclastic academic sources which are ipso facto unfettered by 'the established styles of scholarly research'; and its timings in that unique moment in history 'when considerable power over African agendas, and their study, lies with the international financial bodies and large bilateral aid agencies; and when the political and economic situation itself is chilling in many places.'

The second major perspective, apparently the official view of international financial institutions and donors and which we shall call Afro-realism or doxological optimism, gratefully accepts the seriousness of the African condition with an enfeebled hope for a brighter future based primarily on the pathological realization that the continental woes could have been much worse than those described by the pessimists. The basis of optimism derives less from contemporary evidence of social progress than from faith and hope. Finally, there is the minority yet growing recolonization school which shares the dire predictions of the pessimists but describes various mechanisms of recolonization as the surest hope of saving Africa from the scourge of anarchy. We shall examine each school below.

Afro- pessimism has long been a formidable intellectual current in African discourse. After all, resistance to decolonization was based on the pessimistic assumption that since Africans were incapable of self- governance, colonialism was the surest way of civilizing Africans and ensuring their protection from self- inflicted savagery and from the depredations of a competitive global political economy. Such thinking was easily overshadowed by the progress of the early post-colonial African states and, for reasons of 'political correctness,' could regain currency even as things began to fall apart in one African country after another from the mid- 1960s on. However, the silence of Afro-pessimism was irretrievably broken in 1981 when a major study by the World Bank drew attention to the impending collapse of successive African economies. Since, then, many writers and essayists have seized the initiative. Robert Kaplan's 'The Coming Anarchy.' Which graphically portrays for the rest of the world life in anarchic West Africa, remains the bluntest study yet on the potential domino effect of institutional and societal decay in much of Africa. Aided by macabre pictures of the human victims of war and disease juxtaposed with that of an unperturbed modern-day vampire guarding an outpost to one of several 'killing zones' in Sierra Leone, Kaplan argues that 'tyranny...is not part and parcel of an increasing lawlessness' on a continental scale and that 'it is Thomas Malthus, the philosopher of demographic doomsday, who is now the prophet of West Africa's future...and that of most of the rest of the world.

11. Africa in the middle of the 19th century was not characterised by :
A. end of slave trade
B. high dependence on world market
C. marginalisation of African economy
D. industrial revolution

12. The parallels between the present and past situation is drawn because of :
A. similar geo-political situation
B. similar economic situation
C. similar political structure
D. All of the above

13. Which of the following is incorrectly matched in reference to the source of the idea?
A. Doxological optimism — International Financial Institution.
B. Afro-Pessimism — Diplomats, policy makers and scholars.
C. Afro-Realism — African leaders.
D. Recolonisation — Pessimists.

14. One of the following is matched incorrectly in reference to the source of the idea?
A. Pessimistic thinkers call for recolonisation of Africa.
B. Pessimistic thinkers call for decolonisation of Africa.
C. Pessimists opine that liberation of Africa resulted in anarchy.
D. Pessimists want the liberties of African's curtailed.

15. The tone of the passage can be described as :
A. narrative
B. critical
C. descriptive
D. cynical

16. The author is most probably :
A. Foreign Policy Expert
B. Social Scientist
C. Political Commentator
D. Journalist

17. Communication is classified as :
A. Front Back
B. Right Left
C. Up, Down, Across
D. None of these

18. Which of the following groups of communication aspect can distort the communication process in the class?
A. Reversing – Evaluating – Focussing
B. Evaluating – Focussing – Illustrating
C. Evaluating – Focussing – Exaggerating
D. All of the above

19. There are various media for communication like oral, written, audio, visual and audio-visual. The use of medium with which receivers/decoders are not familiar would turn the medium itself into a barrier. This type of barrier is known as :
A. psychological barrier
B. linguistic and cultural barrier
C. ignorance of medium
D. mechanical barrier

20. 'Big Digital TV DTH' is a subsidiary unit of
A. Dish T.V.
B. Tata sky
C. Bharti Airtel
D. Reliance Communications

21. In this question, there is a certain relationship between two given words. Choose the given alternatives which one pair has the same relation as the previous.
HERPETOLOGY : AMPHIBIANS
A. Occultism : Supernatural
B. Oology : Eggs
C. Virology : Viruses
D. All of these

22. In this question four words are given, out these three are similar in some manner and one is different. Find the odd one out.

A. Intimacy B. Enmity
C. Attachment D. Friendship

23. What should come next in the series 19, 2, 38, 4, 114, 8, (. . .), (. . .)?

A. 228, 16 B. 256, 12
C. 352, 10 D. 456, 16

24. If pen is table, table is fan, fan is chair and chair is roof, on which of the following a person sit?

A. Fan B. Chair
C. Roof D. Pen

25. A, B, C, D, E and F are six members of a family. One couple has parents and their children in the family. A is the son of C and E is the daughter of A. D is the daughter of F. Who is mother of E?

Who are the male members of the family?

A. A and C
B. C and F
C. A, B and D
D. Cannot be determined

26. On the basis of the information given in question 25, answer this question :

Which of the following pairs is the parent of the couple?

A. AB B. AF
C. BC D. CF

27. Which of the following will represent the right relation between, Professional, Doctors, Lawyers and Females?

A. 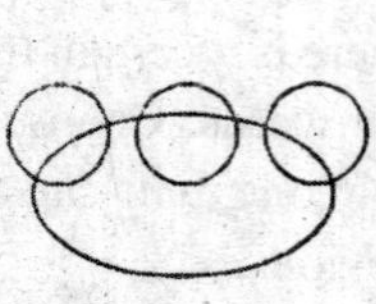 B. 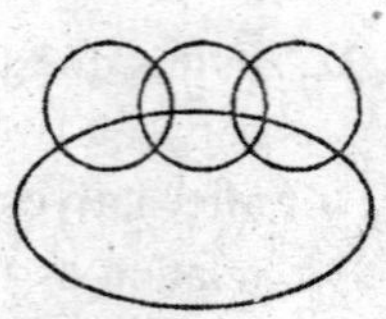

C. 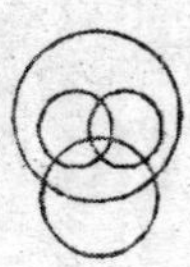 D. 

28. Assertion (X) ; India imports jute from Bangladesh.

Reason (Y) : India has most of the jute mills, whereas Bangladesh has maximum jute production area.

A. Both X and Y are true and Y is correct explanation of X
B. Both X and Y are true but Y is not correct explanation of X
C. X is true but Y is false
D. X is false but Y is true

29. Statements : All cars are tables.
Some children are tables.

Conclusions :

(*i*) Some cars are children.
(*ii*) Some children are cars.

A. Only conclusion (*i*) follows
B. Only conclusion (*ii*) follows
C. Both (*i*) and (*ii*) follow
D. Neither (*i*) nor (*ii*) follows

30. Statement : The NDMC and MCD (Civic authorities of Delhi) appealed to the people for reduction in usage of water as there may be an acute shortage during the coming weeks.

Assumptions :

(*i*) There will be no rain in recent future.
(*ii*) People are ready to follow the advice of the civic authority.

A. Only assumption (*i*) is implicit
B. Only (*ii*) is implicit
C. Both (*i*) and (*ii*) are implicit
D. Neither (*i*) and nor (*ii*) is implicit

31. Statements :

1. I watch TV only if I am bored.
2. I am never bored when I have my brother's company.
3. Whenever I go to theatre I take my brother along.

Conclusions :

A. If am bored, I seek my brother's company.
B. If I am not bored, I do not watch TV.
C. If I am bored, I watch TV.
D. If I am not with my brother then I watch TV.

Directions (Qs. 32-35) : *Study the following diagram and answer the question 32 - 35.*

The diagram represents the rate of onion in two cities (Nagpur and Delhi):

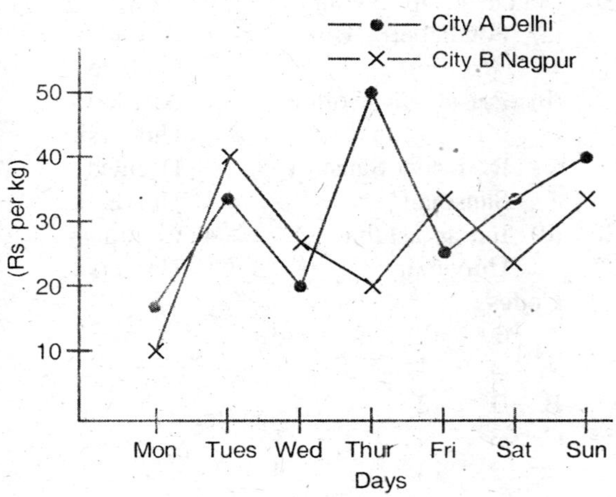

32. On which day the rate in city B is equal to the Friday's rate of city A?

A. Saturday B. Friday
C. Wednesday D. Tuesday

33. Between which two days the difference in rate is highest in city A?

A. Friday and Saturday
B. Wednesday and Thursday
C. Monday and Tuesday
D. Saturday and Sunday

34. Between which two days the difference in rate is lowest in city B?

A. Thursday and Friday
B. Friday and Saturday
C. Wednesday and Thursday
D. Sunday and Monday

35. In which town the fluctuation in rate of onions is the highest and between which days?

A. Monday and Tuesday
B. Thursday and Friday
C. Wednesday and Thursday
D. Thursday and Friday

36. Back up means :

A. to create a duplicate set of programme or data files in case the original is damaged.
B. provide different kinds of connections and band width in computers.
C. the type of data transmission.
D. all of the above

37. The IS (Information System) department :

A. supports organisation information system and also support organisation's overall mission.
B. the IS department provides technical support for hardware and software, but may be involved in design and implementation of an organisation's entire information system.
C. the IS professionals also ensure that system generate all the appropriate types of information and reports required by the organisation's manager and workers.
D. all the above

38. What is the full form of AWiFS?

A. Advanced Wide Field Sensor
B. Automated Wide Field Sensor
C. Automated Wide Field Scanner
D. Advanced Wide Field Scanner

39. Which of the following countries used India's satellite launching capabilities to launch their own satellites?

A. Belgium B. Germany
C. Korea D. All of these

40. Which of the following is/are steps of software developments?

A. Specify the problem
B. Analyse the problem
C. Test the program
D. All of these

41. Emission of Radon gas can give prior information abut which of the following geological activities?

A. Volcanic eruption
B. Earthquake
C. Mass Wasting
D. Cyclones

42. Which of the following is/are sources of soil pollution?

A. Mining and Quarrying
B. Sewage sludge
C. Demolition and Construction
D. All of these

43. Which of the following is responsible for Acid rain?
A. Carbon monoxide
B. Nitrogen dioxide
C. Volatile organic compounds
D. Particulate matter

44. Which one of the following is responsible for blue baby syndrome?
A. Nitrate B. Lead
C. Fluoride D. Arsenic

45. What is the present (Apr. 2006) operating capacity of India's Wind Power generation?
A. 900 MW
B. 4500 MW
C. 5400 MW
D. 2200 MW

46. Fundamental duties of citizen are mentioned in which of the following articles of constitution?
A. Article 51A
B. Article 19(1)
C. Article 352A
D. Article 42

47. Which of the following is a salient feature of our constitution?
A. Establishment of Union Public Service Commission.
B. Provision for Amendments in Constitution.
C. Adult tranchise.
D. All of these

48. Who administers the Union territories?
A. The President through the Administrator appointed by him.
B. Prime Minister of India through Lt. Governor.
C. The Law Ministry of Govt. of India.
D. None of these

49. The President of India is
A. the head of the state.
B. the head of the Government.
C. the head of state as well as government.
D. none of these

50. Match the following :

(a) Pondicherry University	1. Autonomous College
(b) Presidency College	2. Affiliating University
(c) Rashtriya Sanskrit Sansthan	3. Deemed University
(d) Indraprashtha University	4. Central University

Codes :

	(a)	(b)	(c)	(d)
A.	4	1	3	2
B.	1	2	4	3
C.	3	4	2	1
D.	2	3	1	4

51. Personalised System of education
A. does not inculcate a feeling of socialisation in students
B. does not inculcate a feeling of competition in students
C. leads to wastage of time and energy
D. all of these are true

52. The educational system of today promotes "educated unemployment". The reason is that
A. education gives theoretical knowledge only
B. professional education is not a part of education
C. the objective of education is not vivid
D. all of these

53. The teacher ought to know about the problems prevalent in the field of education. The reason is that
A. only a teacher can do something about solving them
B. he can tell about the same to another teacher
C. teachers can tell the government about it
D. with this knowledge, the teacher can have information about education

54. In the wake of serious shortages of resources and rising population of our nation, you have the following views about the programmes for improving the standards of education (under the aegis of national policy of education).

A. They are impractical
B. They are courageous and laudable efforts
C. They are new forms of traditional programmes
D. They increase the workload of teachers

55. In your view, arrangement for "education on environment" in the school
A. is important for creating an awareness among students about the environment
B. is likely to put more burden on students
C. is a mode of entertainment for students
D. is like giving work to teachers

56. An Input operation performs two functions, they are
A. It causes an input device to physically read data, and transmits the data from the Input device to an Input area of CPU
B. It causes an input device to transmits the data, convert into image form
C. It causes an input device to physical read data, transmits the data to printer
D. None of the above

57. During processing cycle, a computer performs operations of
A. data transfer, ALU operations that operate on Input data
B. sends data to an output area lies within the CPU (which is setup by each program)
C. Both A and B
D. None of the above

58. An output operation causes
A. information to be transmitted from the output area lies within the CPU to an output device such as printer
B. CPU to record/display information on some medium
C. Both A and B
D. None of the above

59. Computers
A. help you with your banking by using automatic teller machines (ATM) used to deposit or withdraw money
B. are present in every aspect of daily living-in workplace, home and in the class room
C. an electronic machine operating under the control of instructions stored in its own memory that can accept data (Input), manipulate the data according to specified rules (process), produce results(output) and store this result for future use
D. All the above

60. A person that communicates with a computer or uses the information it generates is called
A. user B. processor
C. commentator D. None of these

ANSWERS

1	2	3	4	5	6	7	8	9	10
A	D	A	A	D	B	A	A	A	B
11	**12**	**13**	**14**	**15**	**16**	**17**	**18**	**19**	**20**
D	B	C	B	A	A	C	D	C	D
21	**22**	**23**	**24**	**25**	**26**	**27**	**28**	**29**	**30**
D	B	D	C	D	C	D	A	D	B
31	**32**	**33**	**34**	**35**	**36**	**37**	**38**	**39**	**40**
B	C	B	C	A	A	D	A	D	D
41	**42**	**43**	**44**	**45**	**46**	**47**	**48**	**49**	**50**
B	D	B	A	C	A	D	A	C	A
51	**52**	**53**	**54**	**55**	**56**	**57**	**58**	**59**	**60**
D	B	A	B	A	A	A	A	D	A

SOME SELECTED EXPLANATORY ANSWERS

21. Herpetology is the study of amphibians. Similarly occultism is study of supernatural; Oology is study of eggs and virology is study of viruses.

22. All other except enmity are synonymous.

23. The sequence is a combination of two series :
I. 19, 38, 114, (. . .) and
II. 2, 4, 8, (. . .)
The pattern followed in I is × 2, × 3, × 4
so first missing number is 114 × 4 = 456.
The pattern followed in II is 2^1, 2^2, 2^3, 2^4
so second missing number is 2^4 = 16.
Hence the numbers are **456, 16.**

24. A person sits on chair and chair is called roof. Hence a person sits on roof.

For Q. (25, and 26) : E is daughter of A and F is mother of E, so A is the father of E and husband of F. Now D is daughter of F, so, D, and E are daughters of A and F. Also A is son of C. Now only B remains. Thus B and C are parents of A.

25. The sex of B and C cannot be determined from the given information.

26. Clearly B & C are parent of couple.

27. Both Doctors and Lawyers are Professionals. Some females are professionals, some of them are Doctors and some are lawyers.

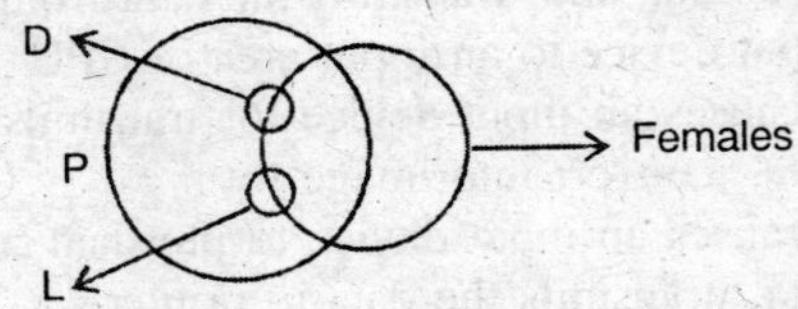